RIVALS

Jennifer Lane

PSYCHED
PUBLISHING

Published by Psyched Publishing

First published, March 2021

The characters and events in this book are fictitious. Any similarity to real persons, living or dead, is coincidental and not intended by the author.

ISBN: 978-0-9979970-3-3

10 9 8 7 6 5 4 3 2 1

Cover design by Dan Irons

Book Design by L. Diane Wolfe

Printed in the United States of America

Dedication

*To coaches who bring out the best in us, especially Jim Steen
from Kenyon College Swimming.*

"A good coach can change a game. A great coach can change a life."
~John Wooden

Table of Contents

Smoking
Lauren

I am so *getting fired*.

As those big, brown eyes blink at me, waiting for an answer, I sneak a glance at the cabinet in the family's living room. But there's no welcoming ice bucket or liquor bottle. Why does the country's best club volleyball setter have to come from a family of teetotalers?

"Coach?" Mr. Watkins prompts. Sitting next to my prized recruit, Emma Watkins, he wraps his arm around his daughter's shoulders. "Will you answer Emma's question?"

"Absolutely." I swallow. "The reason we didn't have a good season last year was simply bad luck. Too many injuries."

Emma straightens her spine. Because she's six-foot-three, I have to look up to meet her shiny eyes as she speaks. "Ohio State hasn't been great for the past *three* years. Are you saying you had lots of injuries then, too?"

Shit. I tick through the typical excuses in my mind. *The Big Ten's the toughest volleyball conference in the country.* Can't use that one, especially with Emma's scholarship offer from another school in the conference—Michigan, our rival, nonetheless—just waiting to be claimed. She'll want to play for the best team in the conference, which hasn't been The Ohio State University for some time. *We're just one great recruit away from reclaiming the national championship, and that recruit is* you. For some reason, I can't bring myself to say that to yet another prospective student-athlete. Emma's expression is too earnest, or maybe it's her father's protectiveness that makes me hesitate.

I let out a breath. "I know I'm a good coach, but something's felt off the past few years. I'm not really sure what it is. I've been fighting and fighting to recapture what we've had, but I've come up short. I'm sorry."

Emma and her father stare at me, seeming surprised by my honesty. I'm surprised as well. No way she'll become a Buckeye now, and I have only myself to blame.

The front door slams, and all three of us jump.

"Evan!" hollers a voice from the kitchen—probably Emma's mother, who disappeared into the house after I met her ten minutes ago.

"Sorry, Mom," says the door-slammer.

His head is mere inches from the ceiling as he turns the corner into the living room. Those recognizable brown eyes look more indifferent than contrite, despite his apology. Emma's fraternal twin sizes me up. His flinch conveys the exact moment he notices the Block O on my jacket.

Evan's eyes narrow, an expected reaction from the quarterback recruited to save Michigan football. Wolverine fans have pinned their hopes on this rising star, praying his arrival on campus this fall will signal an end to recent domination by their rival three hours south: Ohio State, the school I represent.

But instead of aiming his vitriol at me, he glares at his twin. "*Really,* Emma? Why is she here? When'll you stop messing around and sign the damn UM scholarship?"

"Watch your language," Mr. Watkins barks, earning an eye roll from his son.

I tilt my head. The 18 year old isn't allowed to use the word *damn*? I see the cross on the wall, reminding me of their faith. I think back over what I've said to the family so far, hoping I've reined in my potty mouth.

"We all know you're going to Michigan, so stop the stupid drama," Evan rails at his sister. "Why don't you just sign?"

"Maybe I don't want to go to the same school as *you*," Emma replies.

Interesting. I'd thought her twin's full-ride to Michigan would lock Emma in to accepting hers, creating a superstar athlete twin vortex, but maybe Evan's fame is more of a deterrent. Maybe that's why she still hasn't signed, despite the start of college looming four months from now.

What's even more intriguing is Evan's reaction to Emma's insult. He's gone from cocky to wounded in no time at all. His lower lip trembles, and he inches back a step. *What a wuss.* He'll fit right in at Michigan.

Emma's eyebrows scrunch. "Oh, Evvy…"

"Don't call me that!" He puts a hand on his hip and pouts, reminding me of a toddler. An overgrown, he-man toddler.

I look at Mr. Watkins, but he avoids my gaze. He must know how ridiculous his son is.

At this point, I curse my fate. Why did I choose a career that relies on the whims of 18-year-old children? If I don't cajole Emma into choosing OSU, we will suck for yet another season. And my boss has assured me that a losing record will mean goodbye to my career as a Buckeye, despite the national championship I have under my belt.

"I'll sign soon," Emma says. "I just have to make sure it's right."

"The only right place for you is Michigan," Evan responds. "I have to learn all these new plays, and you're the best at helping me. I *need* you, Emmy."

She sighs. "I know, I know."

What the fuck is their deal? "What about *your* needs, Emma?" I blurt.

All three Watkins turn their attention to me, and I read anger in the tense set of their jaws, like I've violated some family rule. I wish my filter worked better.

"I mean…" I shift on the floral sofa, which is about as comfortable as a dilapidated sports arena seat. "Evan's obviously meant for greatness. But Emma, you're even more talented."

Evan's mouth drops, but his father speaks before he gets the chance.

"We treat our kids the same," says Mr. Watkins. "We don't favor one over the other."

Ugh, favoritism. I get accused of this all the time by my players, but how can I treat them equally? They're unique individuals, and I click with some of them better than others—it's just human nature. I gravitate toward the gritty athletes who work their butts off, the dysfunctional girls with something to prove to the world. They're my people.

"That's a nice theory, Mr. Watkins." I pause as his face darkens. "But how are you treating them the same if Emma's school choice is about supporting her brother instead of focusing on her own career?"

Her father scowls at me, and I realize I've violated recruiting rule #1: woo the parents.

I avoid Evan's glower and turn to Emma, who's biting her lip. "Emma, this is an important choice for you, and I know you're feeling a time crunch here. We are, too, and we deeply want you to play for the scarlet and gray. We've talked about what an immediate impact you'll have as our starting setter."

Evan harrumphs, deciphering my dig at his school's All-American sophomore setter. Emma might not get much playing time at Michigan, especially as a freshman.

I continue, "Truth is, you're looking at some solid universities. You can't go wrong with any of these choices." I pat her fidgeting hand and smile. "Just go with your gut. You got this."

* * *

Back outside and inhaling soothing nicotine, I grip my phone as I lean back against my car door. "Why don't the fuckers just fire me now and get it over with?"

"No, Lauren!" Samantha says through the line. "How will I survive without you?"

I blow out a stream of cigarette smoke. Sam's my best friend and the head women's swim coach at Ohio State. If they fire me, I don't know how I'll survive without her, either. We're part of a small group of female head coaches on staff. A cold breeze stirs the trees on the side of the Watkins' house, making me shiver. April in the fabulous metropolis of Toledo, Ohio—it doesn't get much better than this. I had been about to drive away from my recruiting fail when Sam called. Though it's cold out here, at least I can grab a smoke without stinking up my car on the drive back to Columbus.

"So, you got bad vibes from this Emma girl?" Sam asks.

"No, I like her. She asks tough questions, and she's kind of sweet to her tool of a brother. But I did get awful vibes from all the Michigan crap in their house." I recall the garish navy pillow with a huge gold M that clashed with their floral sofa.

"Gag," Sam scoffs. "Are the twins legacies or something?"

"Mr. Watkins played football at Michigan, but he got injured early in his career. I think Emma's mom played basketball somewhere else."

"Doesn't sound good. Hold on a sec." I hear Sam yelling at her team, something about sprinting. I'm not surprised she called me from the pool deck, her second home. Her team practices two or three times a day, even in April, the off-season. "Okay, I'm back. So you'll offer the scholarship to that Italian recruit, then?"

I close my eyes. The Italian setter looks good on video, but she's shorter and slower than Emma. And international student-athletes often need time to transition to a new culture. How can I expect the Italian to lead my team from the get-go? My throat tightens. I have to decide soon—an unused scholarship will all but sign my name to a forced resignation letter.

"I'll probably have to get the Italian." As I say those words, though, I know I'll wait a little longer on Emma. My instincts tell me she's worth it.

A black SUV pulls up behind my car as I take another drag from the cigarette. Since I'm parked a little ways down from the Watkins' house, I'm guessing the car belongs to one of their neighbors. A slab of muscle wearing a navy-blue jacket and jeans climbs out. He stares at me through sport sunglasses that have no purpose on this cloudy day other than to intimidate and impress. And those glasses have the desired effect as he closes the car door, distracting me from whatever Sam is saying.

Holy shit, he's approaching me. My chest blooms with heat, and I hear only one word rattling in my brain: *Hot. Hot.* I tense as he comes nearer. *Smoking hot.* I didn't know they grew them so strong and magnetic in Toledo. Maybe I'll move here after my athletic director fires me. As I listen to my lustful thoughts, I wonder what the hell my problem is. I usually couldn't care less about guys. I'm too busy with coaching.

When I unzip my jacket to try to cool down, I realize the disgusting cigarette is still lodged between my fingers. I throw the butt to the pavement and grind it under my Nike gym shoe.

The man's face lights up with a grin as he arrives at my car. He runs a hand through his thick, brown hair—a little on the longish side—and gazes down at me from his impressive height. Though I'm five-foot-ten, I'm used to my players towering over me. I wonder if he's a former athlete, too.

"I doubt Mr. and Mrs. Watkins would view a smoker as a positive role model," he says.

I recoil. "What?" *Who is this guy?* Then he shifts to slide his hand into his pocket, and I notice the gaudy M on his jacket. My gasp widens his grin.

"You're here to recruit Emma." He lowers his shades and peers down at me over the top, revealing green eyes crinkled with amusement. "Too late. She's a Wolverine through and through."

"Lauren?" Sam's voice cuts in. I'd completely forgotten I'm still clutching my phone. "Are you there? Who're you talking to?"

I stroke my neck, wishing I had a cigarette or something to hold on to. "Hey, hon, I gotta deal with a nasty-ass situation. See you tonight?"

"Sure." I hear Sam start shouting at her swimmers again before she hangs up. I'll have to fill her in about this Michigan turd over drinks later.

"I'm a nasty-ass situation?" he asks, still grinning. He's removed his sunglasses, offering me a full view of those gorgeous eyes. He's clean-shaven, and the scent of his aftershave is subtle but yummy. I hope I don't smell like an ashtray.

I pocket my phone and try to match his smile. "Being near any Michigan coach is, uh, unfortunate. I suppose you're here to check up on your star recruit?"

"And you as well, Coach Chase."

He knows my name? I've worked out that he must be an assistant football coach for the school up north, but beyond that, I'm drawing blanks.

"I know Jim Dawson," he adds.

"Ah." Jim Dawson is the UM volleyball coach. "You're the… quarterbacks' coach, then?"

He sticks out his hand. "Jeremy Trent."

During the week before OSU-Michigan football games, students skulk around the Columbus campus with red tape, marking an X over every M in every sign. The electronic scroll on buses reads, "Beat ichigan"; suicide prevention signs in parking garages change from "You matter" to "You atter." So, I take my time in deciding whether to shake the hand of my enemy. When I finally give in, his hand is big, warm, and soft. Not threatening at all.

Still holding on to my hand, he tugs me closer. "The Watkins family is strait-laced. Too bad I'll have to narc on you about your smoking."

I yank my hand away. *Bastard*. "Too bad your friend Dawson will lose the nation's best setter to the Buckeyes."

"We'll see about that." His shitty grin is back.

"Yes, we will."

He dips his head in a mini bow. "It's been a pleasure, Lauren."

I fake a curtsy. "As nasty as expected, Jeremy."

"Don't get a speeding ticket on your drive home." He turns and takes long strides toward the house.

How in the holy hell does he know about my speeding tickets? Yet another reason the Watkins clan would disapprove of me. Refusing to let him get the last word in, I shout, "Not that your players know anything about speed!"

He swivels to face me, the sunglasses back on. He opens his mouth, but instead of speaking, he gives me slow shakes of his head. His non-response is more effective than my childish barb.

When he turns and continues up the driveway, I zone in on the muscular curve of his butt, hugged by his jeans. *Damn*. Why am I still focused on his assets? He's a dickwad about to slash the gossamer threads holding my career together.

I am *so* getting fired.

Drooling
Jeremy

The squeal of Lauren's tires turns my head as I arrive at the Watkins' porch. I watch her car disappear, heading south, at a speed more appropriate for a Tesla than the gray Ford sedan she drives. I bet the Athletic Department pays for her car as a perk of being a head coach. I'm only an assistant, but I get a free car, too. Because, football. Football pays the bills—everyone knows which sport is king.

Before I knock, the door opens. I'm pleased to see that the lanky boy in the doorway looks stronger than he did at my visit three weeks ago. When Evan's mother refused to let him graduate early from high school and join us in January, I implored Mrs. Watkins to shove food into her son at any opportunity. Skinny quarterbacks mean injured quarterbacks, and we can't afford any damage to the nation's number-one recruit.

"What up, Coach Trent?" Evan asks.

I bump his offered fist and pull him in for a back-slapping hug. After recruiting him for three years, I view Evan more like a son than a player—a pain-in-the-butt teenage son. "Doing okay." A cold wind ruffles my hair and blows through my unlined windbreaker. "You?"

He wrinkles his nose. "Trying to get rid of the smell in here."

"Smell?" I cock my head.

"The Buckeye smell." He shudders. "Did you see that stupid coach who was just here?"

I chuckle. *Sure did.* I recall her mouthing off as she tossed her long hair over her shoulder. The flare of her blue eyes fills my mind, curving my mouth into a smile. I bet she never backs down to anyone or anything, and I love her sass. She would definitely be fun to play with again, if I ever cross her path.

But I hope it won't be through the Watkins twins. "Emma won't buy what she's selling, right?"

Evan shakes his head. "No way."

"Evan!"

He opens the door wider to reveal his mother entering the foyer.

"Where are your manners?" she demands. "Invite Coach Trent in—it's freezing out there."

"Sorry," he mumbles and steps back to allow me in. "Didn't want to expose him to the stink."

Mrs. Watkins gestures to the living room. "Please come in, Coach." She looks at her son. "I don't know what you're talking about. My house smells wonderful."

"It does," I agree. A floral scent with an undertone of roasted coffee beans greets me as I head toward the sofa.

"I guess it smells okay," Evan says, "now that the Buckeye scum has left."

Mrs. Watkins points at the pocket of Evan's khakis. "Do you want to lose your phone again?"

"Mom!" he whines. "Scum's not a swear word."

She shakes her head. "It's disrespectful. We taught you better than that—you need to respect your elders. Speaking of respect, go pour a cup of coffee for Coach."

"No need," Mr. Watkins says. He enters from the other side of the living room, carrying a steaming cup of joe with what looks like the perfect amount of soy milk. After he sets it on the coffee table, he pumps my hand with vigor. "I heard my favorite coach arrive and had to quench his thirst right away."

"Thank you, sir." I'm relieved when he finally releases my hand. There's another full coffee cup sitting on a UM coaster next to mine. *Lauren's coffee?*

Mr. Watkins beckons his son closer. "Evan, did you tell Coach?"

"Tell him what?"

Mr. Watkins elbows his son as he grins at me. "He benched

two-ten yesterday."

When both father and son beam, I don't have the heart to tell them that's a marginal number for a college quarterback.

Evan's gifts are his height and accuracy, not his power. He proved as much at the Elite Eleven, a high-school quarterback competition. But we'll amp up his strength once he arrives at our state-of-the-art weight room. "Great improvement," I manage.

"How's spring practice going?" Mr. Watkins motions to the uncomfortable sofa, and I lower myself onto it. Evan circles around the coffee table to sit next to me, and his father settles onto an adjacent love seat.

I consider the obscene number of interceptions my starting quarterback threw in our most recent practice. "The defense is looking tough."

Mr. Watkins scoots forward. "But the offense needs help, right?"

I take a sip of strong java and glance at Evan's mother, who still stands by the stairs, eyeing her husband. "You make the best coffee, Mrs. Watkins."

Her gaze travels to me. "Thanks, Coach. It's Peruvian."

I nod, remembering that their family traveled to Peru on a church mission trip over the winter holidays.

"Bet you can't wait to get Evan in there at QB," Mr. Watkins pushes.

I feel Evan tense next to me and try to figure out a way to temper his father's excitement. The boy already has a brick-load of pressure on his back, and he hasn't taken one snap in college.

But before I get the chance to reply, Mr. Watkins looks up at his wife, perhaps noticing her stare. "What is it?" he asks.

Her slanted eyebrows and half-smile create a look of pity. "You're drooling again, honey."

He sits back against the cushion with a frown.

"He's not drooling," Evan says.

Mr. Watkins grunts. "Your mother's telling me to get some perspective and stop fawning all over Michigan football."

She nods, seeming satisfied that her message hit the target.

I smother a laugh. During every visit here, Evan's mother

has been polite, treating me probably the same way she treats any other guest. His father, on the other hand, has been a total sycophant. Mr. Watkins' incessant phone calls and questions about the offense have overloaded me, especially during the season. I relax back into the sofa now that his wife has zinged him on his snowplow parenting. Self-awareness is rare among the parents of prospects.

"And?" she adds.

Mr. Watkins' brows furrow.

She gives him a hint by tilting her head in the direction of their son.

"And…" Mr. Watkins looks at Evan. "I need to stop putting so much pressure on you."

Bingo. Damn, she's good. I notice the tender smile she shares with her husband. What would it be like to be married? To have a woman call me on my crap like that? She's older than me, and quite attractive. It's obvious where the twins got their shiny hair and eyes, both in shades of chocolate brown. And, she's got presence. With her height and lean musculature, no wonder she had so much success in college ball and the WNBA.

Evan presses his lips together. "I can handle the pressure."

"Really?" Mrs. Watkins asks. "What about your insomnia?"

Evan's eyes widen. "Mom!" He gives me a quick glance, then looks down, like he's embarrassed she shared that with me.

What he doesn't know is that insomnia is rampant in college student-athletes. We've been tracking the sleep patterns of our players, and they're pathetic. The sport science guys need to figure out a way to help our players get more zzzs before the season starts this fall.

Mrs. Watkins now aims her tender smile at her son. "God loves you, no matter how many touchdowns you throw."

"I know." Evan's forceful tone sounds like they've had this conversation a thousand times. He keeps watching his feet.

But he *doesn't* know. The kid will need a foundation—God's love or whatever grounding force he can lean on—to survive. Cruel fans on Twitter will tell him he's the worst quarterback they've ever seen. UM students will sidle up to him, trying to befriend him or seduce him, not because their interest is genuine but because they want a piece of his status. The media will prop him up, then tear him down after one mistake. And all of that will only happen if he's able to snag a starting role, which won't be easy, no matter what ESPN has predicted. Nothing's guaranteed in this bloodthirsty world of Bowl Championship Series football. If Evan lands on the bench, nobody will think twice about him. He's a boy about to play against men. It might get ugly.

"Is Emma up in her room?" Mrs. Watkins asks.

Mr. Watkins' eyes roll up to the ceiling. "Think so."

"Good. I want to talk to her." She climbs the stairs two at a time.

After another sip of coffee, I pat Evan on the back. "Coach Froth asked about you."

Evan's eyes light up at the mention of the head coach, my boss. "What'd he say?"

"We have some players going on a service trip to Puerto Rico in May." I glance at the crucifix hanging on a side wall. "Coach wanted to make sure you know about all the opportunities we have for student-athletes like yourself."

"Cool." Evan shrugs, his excitement seeming to fade. "Will you tell him about my bench press?"

No. "Of course."

"It means a lot to us that you and Coach Froth value faith in your lives," says Mr. Watkins.

I lift my cup and take a sip to hide my consternation. Early on, I made it a point to tell Mr. Watkins I'd attended Catholic school as a child. But who has time to make it to mass as a Division I coach? Likewise, the only spirituality Coach Froth values is faith in his play-calling. He hasn't seen the inside of a church in about twenty years. However, I won't correct the family's misperception. After the disappointment of last year's game against Ohio State, we still need an aggressive pass rush on Evan. I can't imagine him attending another school with the shrine to Michigan evident in throw pillows, coasters, and framed photos all around me. But I can never be too careful. I've lost recruits before at the last minute, and I won't let it happen this time.

"It's hard to think about our twins off on their own, without our guidance," Mr. Watkins continues. "We want Evan and Emma to learn from good examples."

It's the perfect time to tell them about the OSU coach's smoking. I set down my coffee cup. "Yeah, about that…"

Evan and his father wait for me to finish my sentence. I picture Lauren sliding her hand down her long neck as she ended her phone call. Her fingers lingered at the top of her cleavage, and I wished she'd unzipped her jacket farther. A sour taste fills my mouth as I remember she called the person *hon*. A boyfriend, maybe? She wasn't wearing a wedding ring.

When Jim Dawson stopped me outside of a coaches' meeting a year ago, he pumped me for information about Emma. He knew I'd signed Evan, and he was frustrated that Emma hadn't accepted her own full-ride scholarship to Michigan. He asked what other schools were his competition besides Ohio State. When I expressed surprise that Evan's sister would even think about OSU, Jim gave me a strange look. Of course Emma would consider a program that had won the national championship a while back, he explained. But he seemed equally confident that Emma wouldn't become a Buckeye now that they no longer dominated the conference. "*Lauren Chase is a mess*," he told me. "*It was a fluke that she had so much success. They'll probably hire another head coach soon.*"

Intrigued, I'd looked up her profile after our conversation, finding a photo of her pretty smile and intense blue eyes framed by wavy blond hair. She'd played volleyball at Ohio State—a home-grown Buckeye. Her year of graduation made her current age 36, three years older than me. Sure enough, she'd become one of the youngest head coaches to win the NCAA Final Four in volleyball. She'd achieved my very dream: to lead a team to a national championship. How had she done it? I'd wanted to pick her brain.

But after that early success, her team had barely finished in the top five in the conference, often exiting the NCAA tournament in the first round. While part of me reveled in the downward slide of any OSU team, I also wondered what had changed for

Lauren.

"Coach Trent?" Mr. Watkins prompts.

I tap my thigh. "Where was I?"

"Talking about setting an example," he hints.

"Yes." *Should I tell them about Lauren's smoking?* My college coach, Chris Hanlon, had taught me to avoid negative recruiting. *Don't badmouth other schools—it reflects badly on you.* Even if that other school is Ohio State. But that's not my only hesitation in spilling the beans. For some reason, I'm intrigued by the woman I just met. She experienced the pinnacle of success, then lost it. Michigan football has been a bit lackluster recently, but we're building an astounding program, especially with the arrival of Evan. Will either of us find the victory we so deeply crave? If so, who will get there first?

"Our coaches *and* players set a fine example," I say. "I'm about to meet my players at the children's hospital. We're visiting cancer patients, trying to inspire them."

"What an honor," Mr. Watkins marvels.

We actually visited the hospital two weeks ago—my true pressing task today is to chew out my backup quarterback for missing a class last week. And then I need to plan a trip to Texas for a home visit with a high-school quarterback. But Mr. Watkins doesn't need to know those details.

I stand and look at Evan as he rises. "You're eating more protein?"

"Yeah."

Mr. Watkins frowns at his son. "That's *Yes, Coach*, or *Yes, sir.*"

Evan mumbles, "Yes, Coach."

I clap his back, shake his father's hand, and walk to my car. A surprising glimpse of the sun has brightened the atmosphere. Still, I'm eager to leave dumpy Ohio and return to campus. We've got some games to win, especially the November one in Columbus. I'll show Lauren that Michigan will prevail.

3

Recruiting
Lauren

A week after my visit to Emma's house, I'm back on the road. I just scouted a ninth grader playing in a club tournament in Louisville, and I'm driving back to Columbus to meet Sam for drinks. My Kentucky recruit is a middle blocker who's only fifteen but already six-foot-two. She's an uncoordinated beanpole who can't pass or set worth a damn. However, when she missed an easy block, she stomped her foot, and I could see the fire in her eyes. Then she stuffed the next three hits right back at the opponent, pumping her fist each time.

I've been feeling that same fire in practice this past week. Typically, I'm out of town recruiting most of April, letting my assistants run practices, but I decided to stay in Columbus last week when a California tournament got cancelled. Maybe the missed jet lag has infused more pep in my step, or it could be that I'm looking forward to a break in May. Whatever the reason, I welcome the increased enthusiasm. It's been too long since I've felt excited about the game.

Remembering I haven't heard from Emma Watkins squelches my fervor. She probably accepted the Michigan scholarship once that asshole coach ratted me out to her family. As if *he's* some paragon of virtue. Football coaches are famous for swearing like truckers. When I notice an ache in my hands from gripping the steering wheel, I light up a cigarette to relax. If I'm going to lose a recruit because of the repulsive habit, I might as well make use of it.

Over drinks at Woody's last week, Sam and I checked out Jeremy Trent's coaching profile on the UM Athletics website.

We learned that he'd played ball at the University of Oklahoma. Knowing nothing about football, Sam giggled about him playing tight end, without realizing how apt the position was for the man. Since Jeremy graduated, he's moved all over the country—not unusual for young coaches—from Central Washington to Northern Illinois to Arizona State, finally landing at Michigan three years ago.

In Ann Arbor, his career will probably die, especially if we beat them again in November. When a head coach gets fired, the whole damn staff gets the boot as well. Despite the flow of nicotine in my bloodstream, my jaw clenches. What will my assistants, Patrick and Dana, do after I get fired? Patrick just told me his wife is pregnant, due in November, right as our season ends. How will he support his family if he's unemployed, thanks to me?

"Move it, fuckwit!" I growl at the hybrid car in front of me. The stupid-ass driver doesn't understand the rules of the passing lane. Tailgating him, I'm about to flash my lights when I see a stealthy police cruiser in a cross-median coming up on my left. "Shit." I tap my brake and check my speedometer. I'm going far below seventy thanks to Shitty Slowpoke ahead of me.

Before I pass the po-po, I lower my cigarette. Why do I feel like smoking is a crime? Probably because I encourage my players to take care of their bodies, and I don't want to be a hypocrite. I stub out the cigarette in my ashtray, lower the window a crack, and pull up a coaching podcast on my phone. Two swigs of Mountain Dew help maintain my caffeination.

Just as I'm passing through the I-71 North tunnel in Cincinnati, an incoming phone call interrupts my podcast. When I see who's calling, I groan, but I accept the call. "Hi, Mom."

"Hi, sweetie! Where are you?"

I press my lips together. My parents live in Cincinnati, but I don't want to visit them. "Uh, driving back to Columbus after a recruiting trip."

"You're driving?" Her voice picks up an edge. "Maybe I should call you later."

"I'm fine, Mom. I talk and drive all the time."

She pauses. "I don't want you to get in an accident."

I glance over at my coaching briefcase, a black, leather, over-the-shoulder bag with a block O on the flap, on the passenger seat. Did I throw in some Swedish Fish before I left Columbus?

"Does your hip hurt after a long drive?" asks Mom.

Evidently, she's decided my safety is adequate enough for her to continue the conversation. But she doesn't let me answer.

"*My* hip's been killing me. I spent the whole day in the yard yesterday."

Noticing my speed has crept up to eighty, I take my foot off the gas and scan for cops. "Have you been doing those hip-flexor stretches I taught you?"

"They don't work."

Of course not. I bet she didn't try them. "Your hip's been hurting for a while, right? Maybe you should see a surgeon."

"I still can't believe you got surgery," she says. "I'd never trust a surgeon to cut on me like that."

"He didn't cut. It was a scope." I roll my head back and tap the crown of my head against the headrest a few times before returning my eyes to the road. When the doctors diagnosed the torn labrum in my hip a few years ago, my mom was against the recommended arthroscopy. Despite her disagreement, it was kind of her to come up to Columbus and nurse me through the post-operative recovery. It was almost two years before I totally healed, but I'm glad I had the surgery because now I can coach without chronic pain.

"Maybe my hip would feel better if I got a little help around here," she continues. "Do you know who sat on his butt all day and watched the Reds while I cut the lawn and weeded?"

Ah. We've arrived at the real purpose for her call: bitching about my dad. I offer up the name of their cat. "Furlock Holmes?"

She ignores my little joke. "Your father thinks he can just sit around while I take care of the entire house..."

I rummage through my briefcase and hear the satisfying crinkle of a full bag of candy as she harangues my dad's laziness. Taking my hands off the wheel, I rip open the bag and stuff three red gummy fish into my mouth.

"And do you know what he said when I marched upstairs and turned off his TV?"

Does she want me to answer? My mouth is too gummed up to speak.

"Well, he didn't say one word." Her throaty exhale indicates disgust. "He just went downstairs and read the paper."

I keep chewing, accustomed to these one-way conversations. My dad won't listen to her—I don't blame him—and she won't let friends into her life due to her trust issues. She had a bad childhood, and I should cut her some slack. Fueled by guilt, I vacuum up more candy.

I pass a sign that tells me I have eighty miles left before I hit Columbus. I wait for a gap in the monologue, which takes a few miles. "Mom, I'm almost home, so I better go."

"Okay. Hey, ask your surgeon for a referral in Cincinnati."

I squint. "Thought you said you'd never get surgery."

"I want to look into it."

"I don't see my surgeon anymore." I frown. "Why don't you ask your doctor for a referral?"

"Hmm… She referred me to a physical therapist, but he got a bad review when I looked him up online. Lauren, what's wrong? You sound down."

WTF? I haven't said two words the entire phone call. "Nothing's wrong." My tone sounds caustic, though.

"You can tell me," she prods. "I'm a good listener."

Wow. Almost half the bag of candy has disappeared, and I need to end this frustrating conversation. "Mom, I gotta go."

"Wait—what's the name of that cat litter you liked so much?"

Cat litter? My cat died over a year ago. "Mom, I have to go."

"Be careful." I know what she's about to say next, and I mouth the familiar refrain along with her as she tells me, "Don't get mugged."

"Gotta go, bye!" I hang up the phone and relax into the seat, exhausted. The coaching podcast resumes, but I'm not really listening. I replay the phone call in my head, wishing I could have more patience with my mother. My parents paid for expensive private schools and club volleyball for me to pursue my dream, but their relationship is so sad that I find myself avoiding them now.

I wonder if I have time for a nap before I meet Sam for Saturday-night drinks.

***

"So then the guy said, 'How 'bout a hotel day?'" Sam sips her whiskey sour.

I lean over our high-top table. "A *hotel day*? What's that?"

"Exactly my question." She shakes her head. "For our second date, he evidently wanted to get a hotel room, swim in the hotel pool—because he knows I love swimming—and watch movies."

I sit back in my chair as I suck vodka tonic through a straw. "Basically, a sex fest."

"Right? How dumb does he think I am? He probably wants to hook up at a hotel so I don't meet his wife at home."

Unlike me, Sam still wades into the dating pool. God bless her. I gave up on men years ago, but she continues to post online profiles and attend speed-dating events. Every time she tells me about another loser she's met, I feel validated for staying out of the freaky fray. Our lives are like a romantic comedy, except there's no romance, and it's only us laughing at our jokes.

"Not that I'm opposed to getting laid," she clarifies. "Just not with him and his skeezy ideas about romance." She wrinkles her nose.

We're at our favorite bar, Woody's. It's close enough to our houses that we can walk home, if needed, but far enough from campus that we won't run into our student-athletes.

"Any word from the wonder twin?" she asks.

My shoulders slump as I shake my head.

She pats my hand. "Sorry."

I notice her sparkly nails in a design of turquoise and purple. "Ooh, I love your nails. They look like shiny fish scales."

"Thanks." She waggles her fingers. "This design's called Mermaid Brigade."

My team's athletic trainer, Courtney, hosted a party where she sold us nail polish strips we can apply ourselves, and we've been hooked on trying different designs and colors ever since. I'm not a girly-girl, but painted nails make me feel more feminine. My current color is scarlet—not that wearing my school color is helping me any with the recruiting.

I sigh. "Emma doesn't even have the decency to call and tell me she's going to Michigan."

Sam sets down her glass. "You know that for sure?"

"Well, no, but after that fuckhead coach badmouthed me to her parents, there's no way they'll let Emma go to school here."

"I can't believe he did that." She glowers. "I *hate* the school up north."

"At least you beat them at Big Tens this year."

She blows a breath out the side of her mouth. "Barely. And I hear they signed this amazing Georgia sprinter." Her gaze flickers to the bar behind me.

I remove the straw and knock back the remnants of my drink. "What's the latest with the backstroker from Holland?" With my fingers, I sort through the lime wedges to scoop an ice cube out of the glass and into my mouth.

She perks up. "I'm flying over there next month."

"You're *excited* about the trip?" Work travel sounds glamorous to everyone except work travelers. Living out of a suitcase gets old fast.

She looks over my shoulder at the bar again. Then her eyes return to me. "I've never been there before. Maybe I'll meet a Dutch hottie." She inhales. "You should go with me!"

I pull up my calendar, but we determine the dates of her travel coincide with my rescheduled California trip. When her gaze floats behind me again, I demand, "Okay. What're you looking at?"

"This guy at the bar." She licks her lip. "He keeps staring at you."

My teeth stop crunching ice mid-chew. "Who is he?"

"How the hell do I know?" Her eyes dart over my shoulder, then back at me. "He's not bad looking, that's for sure. Kind of a big dude."

My curiosity piqued, I turn to unzip my purse, which is hung over the back of the chair. After I dig out my lipstick, I casually look up. Staring back at me from across the bar are two green eyes.

"Son of a bitch." I swivel back to the table, all attempts at surreptitiousness gone.

Sam squints at me. "You know him?"

"The fuckhead," I whisper. When she still appears confused, I hiss, "Jeremy!"

Her lips part. "What's he doing in Ohio?"

"Probably stealing our best football players. Is he coming over here?"

She watches for a moment, then shakes her head. "He's sitting next to a hot brunette."

I let out a breath. "Don't tell me his girlfriend lives in Columbus." I look at the tube of lipstick in my hand. I'd planned to apply it, but I don't want him to think I'm dolling myself up for *his* benefit. After he messed with my career, he doesn't deserve my time. And I don't give a damn what the bastard thinks of me, anyway. I scowl. If his opinion doesn't matter, why am I sitting here debating whether to put on fucking lipstick?

"Want me to go over there and tell him off?" asks Sam. She's only five-foot-two, and her fierce sneer makes my mouth tremble—with laughter.

To hide my smile, I apply red lipstick. "What would you say to him?"

"Ann Arbor is a *whore*!"

The venom in her expression lingers for a moment, but then we both start giggling. T-shirts with that slogan sold out before the last rivalry game.

"Yeah, you should definitely tell him that," I say, wondering why her eyes are growing big. I reach out to squeeze her hand. "I love you, hon."

"Oh," says a man's voice as a shadow falls over our table.

I yank my hand away from Sam's and close my eyes. *Fucknuts.* I know that voice. Looking up, I find Jeremy holding a glass with clear liquid and about seven lime wedges. Just the way I like it.

He sets the drink down in front of me. "If I'd known you two were together, I'd have bought you both a drink."

Together? My head angles to one side as I stare up at him. Instead of that hideous navy jacket, he's wearing a long-sleeve, army-green polo shirt that complements his eyes and broad shoulders.

"Coaches at Michigan aren't too smart, are they?" Sam says as she slides out of her chair. When she stands, the top of her head is the same level as his armpit. "Just because we're single and into sports doesn't mean we're gay." She grabs her empty glass. "I'll get my own refill."

I want to beg her to stay—I have no idea how to deal with this man—but she scoots away. After she leaves, he grins at me. Why is he smiling after she just insulted him?

"Got enough limes there?" he asks.

I look down at the yummy green wedges floating in the bubbles. "I like limes." I stir the drink with the straw, and I'm about to take a sip when I hesitate. He wouldn't poison an OSU coach, right? "Aaron made this drink?"

He glances at my favorite bartender and back at me, frowning. "Of course. How else would I know you like limeapalooza in your vodka tonics?"

His response earns him a small smile. I look toward the bar, hoping to catch Sam's eye, but she's laughing at something Aaron said. Then I see the brunette gawking at us, and I wheel back around in my chair. I suppose I should ask Jeremy if he wants to sit after he bought me a drink and all, but I don't want to be an asshole and intrude on his date. Wait a minute—*he* bought *me* a drink. While he's on a date. Who's the asshole now?

"Do you always treat women this poorly?" I ask.

He bristles. As he keeps staring at me, a storm seems to rage in his eyes. "I treat women with the utmost respect."

"I see. You're respecting your girlfriend by buying another woman a drink?"

"My girlfriend?" His laugh is a deep rumble that shoots heat through my core.

Moving
Jeremy

I've gone from relieved, to ticked, to amused in less than one minute. Relieved that Lauren's not dating the shorty who just left the table. Pissed off that she accused me of treating women with disrespect. But now, I laugh at her cluelessness.

"What's so funny?" Lauren asks. When my chest keeps shaking, her eyes narrow further. "You think your ho-bag girlfriend finds this amusing?"

My laugh stops on a dime. "Watch what you call my sister."

"Your *sister*?"

When she covers her mouth, I notice her nail polish is the same shade of red as her lips. She stares up at me with big eyes. *Good*—she should be contrite. Her hand darts from her mouth to her glass, lifting it to suck up her drink through the straw, drawing attention to her lips. They're plump and pouty, and the way they caress that straw makes me jealous of a piece of plastic—even though none of us should be using straws since they harm the environment. Still, I want to be that straw. As I imagine that sensual mouth on mine, I inch closer to the table.

She lowers her glass. "Sorry about that." Her chin sinks as her shoulders rise in a shrug. "I have zero filter."

Her cute apology, spoken through those sexy lips, further dissipates my anger. I notice no lingering smell of cigarettes tonight, only a waft of tropical coconut.

"Thanks for the drink." She peers into the glass. "I don't *taste* any poison..."

Unbelievable. I shake my head.

"I suppose I should invite you to sit. Unless Sam's coming

29

back…" She looks over her shoulder toward the bar, and I follow her gaze. Lauren's friend, Sam—probably another OSU coach since she's into sports and clearly not a fan of Michigan—has taken my former seat next to Taryn.

"Oh!" Lauren licks her lips as she looks up at me. "Looks like Sam won't be back right away. She's talking to your, uh, *sister*…" A smile spreads over her mouth.

"Taryn," I supply as I slide into the seat across from her. Why is Lauren smiling? Could she be pleased that I'm not with a "ho-bag girlfriend," just like I can breathe easier knowing she's not into women? "Taryn's never met a stranger. Your friend might not be able to escape for hours."

"Then I guess you're stuck with me." Once the words leave her mouth, she freezes like she can't believe what she said. She squirms for a second before gulping down another sip. Her head inclines to one side. "You're not drinking?"

"Had a couple of beers already. Don't want to drink more and let my guard down in Buckeye country. It might be dangerous if someone recognizes me."

She smirks. "Don't worry. No one will recognize an *assistant* coach."

Damn. The girl's filter did indeed leave town a long time ago. But she's not remorseful this time. Her blue eyes blaze, and I try to think of a comeback. "More people will recognize a football assistant than the head coach of an inconsequential sport like volleyball."

Color rises to her cheeks.

I sweep my arm across the bar. "I don't see fans clamoring for your signature, Coach."

"That's because we're not on campus, *Coach*." She leans in. "And what're you doing here, by the way?"

I sit back and enjoy the furious blink of her eyes. "Visiting my sister. Taryn lives here."

Lauren plays with her silver necklace as she considers my response. "She lives near Woody's?"

It's ridiculous how this town cherishes Woody Hayes. The former football coach may have won some national championships, but his career ended when he *punched* a player. Interesting choice of a hero. Bo Schembechler, Woody's Michigan rival, was obviously the better coach.

"She does as of today," I say. I watch Lauren stroke her necklace and use it as an excuse to eye the creamy skin of her chest, exposed by the scoop neck of her black, long-sleeve shirt. The form-fitting top hugs her curves just right. I swallow. "We just moved Taryn from her apartment to a house down the street, owned by one of her professors. She's going to house-sit while her prof's on sabbatical."

She blanches. "Your sister goes to school here?"

"Grad school." I scramble for a way to redirect the conversation.

"Which university?"

I close my eyes for a moment. "I tried to convince her to apply to Michigan, but she said they're too research-focused. Taryn's brilliant. The programs she applied to only accept one percent of applicants, though, so she didn't get many offers."

A corner of Lauren's mouth ticks up. "Your sister's a Buckeye."

I look away as she laughs. The girlish lilt doesn't match her solid, athletic build, but the loud volume seems to fit. She emits a happy sigh as she ends her laugh, a downward slide in pitch that sounds like satisfaction and stirs arousal in me. I want to hear that sound again. I feel a strange desire to try to satisfy her. Could I? Would she let me?

"Do your colleagues at Michigan know where your sister goes to school?"

I rub the back of my neck. "I plan to tell them."

Lauren studies me. "How long ago did Taryn start grad school?"

"She's only in her first year."

"So, August?" Her eyebrow quirks. "As in eight months ago? What's holding you back? Afraid of some taunting?" Her grin turns evil. "Now I have a secret about *you*. Once I tell them, we'll be even."

Then it dawns on me. *She thinks I told the Watkins about her smoking.* A bolt of hot anger strikes through me. How could she think I would play dirty to sabotage her? *Oh.* Because I threatened to do so right to her face. This is probably why she's so hostile toward me tonight. *Smooth move, Trent.*

"Well, we won't be even, exactly," Lauren adds, her eyes still narrowed. "You catching shit from other coaches is nowhere near the same as me getting shit-canned."

I pull back. "You're not getting fired. Give me a break."

Her lips press together. "What do *you* know?" Her voice quavers on the last word.

"But…" I frown. "But you won a national championship."

"We both know athletics is all about 'what have you done for me lately'." Her shaky voice and rapid blinks alarm me. Jesus, she's not going to cry, is she?

She looks at her almost-empty glass, avoiding my gaze.

"Hey." She still won't look at me. "I'm one step away from getting fired myself."

After a beat, those pretty blue eyes look up, thankfully dry. "If you lose the game again this year."

Yep. The game in November, in Columbus—UM vs. OSU. "Fuckeyes," I mutter.

A hint of a smile returns on her face. "What's your sister studying at Ohio State?"

Her subject change jars me. "Uh, clinical psychology. She's going for her doctorate."

"Interesting." Lauren glances back at the bar, where Taryn and her friend are still engrossed in conversation. She sips the remaining liquid from her glass. "Is your sister psychoanalyzing my friend? I hope so. Sam needs help."

"Yeah? Why's that?"

She shrugs. "She's a head coach, like me. We're all messed in the head."

I nod and smile. "Certifiable, for sure. What sport does Sam coach?"

"Swimming."

It grows quiet between us for a moment, and I wonder when I'll get to be a head coach. The assistant thing is growing old. There aren't many female head coaches at Michigan, even for the women's sports. "Must be tough to be a head coach as a woman."

Lauren stares me with a forceful gaze, like I've intrigued her. But instead of responding to my comment, she changes the subject again. "That was kind of you to move your sister. I don't have siblings, but luckily my dad helped me move into my house."

I feel my muscles tighten, my jaw clench—the same way I felt when she questioned my respect for women. No way did my narcissistic father help with Taryn's move. No way does he ever help us. I strive to be nothing like him.

Lauren stills. "Are you all right?"

I must have a murderous expression on my face given the way she's leaning back, shifting in her chair, looking like she's about to bolt. I take a slow breath, but my words are low and tight. "Our father isn't part of our lives."

"Okay?" She scratches her head.

"He left us when we were young."

"I'm sorry." She's back to fiddling with her necklace. The hollow of her neck is smooth, and I bet the skin there is soft. What would it be like to kiss that groove? I'd rather be kissing her neck than thinking about my dad.

"I'll get you another drink." I slide her glass toward me.

"No, thank you." She steals back her glass with a smirk. "I need to see if I survive this drink first."

Christ! I should let her know I didn't say anything to Mr. and Mrs. Watkins.

"Jeremy."

I look up at my sister, who has materialized by the table. She towers over Lauren's friend, Sam, the swim coach. "Can we go?" Taryn asks. "I'm exhausted."

I get to my feet, and Lauren stands as well. "Taryn, this is Lauren Chase," I say.

Lauren's an inch or two shorter than Taryn, but they both have long hair—Lauren's straight and blond, Taryn's wavy and brown like mine.

Lauren shakes my sister's hand. "Always good to meet a

fellow Buckeye." She smiles at me while I glare.

"So, you heard Taryn's going to OSU," Sam says to Lauren.

Taryn drapes her arm across Sam's shoulders and grins at me. "Sam is so awesome. Did you know she lives a block away from Professor Stevens' house? She's been telling me all about the neighborhood and fun stuff to do in Columbus."

Lauren stiffens as she watches my sister gush over Sam. *What's that about?* I look at my sister. "Think Sam's lying to you, Ryn. There's *nothing* fun about this city."

Taryn slugs me in the chest.

"Ooh." I rub my pectoral muscle. "I'm sore from moving all your damn books."

"Sorry!" Taryn's eyes expand. "I should be *thanking* you, not hitting you."

"Just kidding, little sister." I encircle her neck with my elbow and draw her head down, where I knuckle a noogie into her hair with my free hand.

Taryn shrieks and laughs at the same time. "Let me go, you creep!"

I release her and find Lauren watching us with a faint smile.

"Hey, Jeremy," says Sam. "Lauren lives around here, too. Just down the street."

Lauren shoots Sam a look.

"Really?" I eye Lauren up and down. "Maybe I should visit this horrid town more often."

Lauren's gaze bounces from Sam to me. "As long as you leave your stupid Michigan jacket at home. You look much better without it." She steps closer and pats my chest, then retracts her chin. "Wow." Her fingers are pricks of fire as they press against my muscles, moving side to side like she's testing my strength. "You'll be just fine protecting yourself from rabid Buckeye fans."

***

I rub my chest, the same spots Lauren probed earlier, as I wait for Taryn to unlock the front door of her new home. I felt a tingle when Lauren touched me through my shirt. How would I feel with her hands on my bare skin?

"Urggh." Taryn jangles her keys. "Should've turned the front porch light on before we left."

I realize I'm fantasizing about Lauren's hands on me instead of doing my real duty—keeping my sister safe. I scan the driveway and lawn behind me, but they're empty.

Once Taryn unlocks the door, I corral her inside. I must have gotten too close and impatient because she wheels around and pushes me back, thrusting me into the closed front door. "Dang," I say. "You learn that move in college ball?" She played basketball at Loyola University in Chicago.

"We're not allowed to shove when we're boxing out."

"Then why shove me?"

"Because you're hovering!" When I frown, she adds, "You've been up in my grill all day."

I'm about to say I'm just looking out for her, but I'm too tired to argue. I make a beeline for the couch and collapse. Even with my strength-training regimen, I'm going to be sore tomorrow. Moving countless boxes of clothes and books out of a third-story apartment with no elevator was torture. At least we didn't have to move furniture—Taryn's roommate is keeping it all since Dr. Stevens' house is furnished. "I just don't like the idea of you living here alone."

"I'll be fine." She heads to the kitchen. "Want something to drink?"

"Nah. Got any food?"

She returns a minute later with a Pop-Tart in her mouth. She tosses the open box of cinnamon frosted Pop-Tarts at me.

"Seriously?" I scowl.

Her lips purse. "C'mon, I just moved! Fresh out of vegan delights."

I ignore her dig at my diet and scrounge around in the box for a sugar bomb. All of the moving has made me hungry. I suppress a moan as frosted-cinnamon crack meets my taste buds.

"Besides..." She hangs her legs over the side of the easy chair next to the couch, talking with her mouth full. "Sam and *Lauren* live by themselves."

I realize Taryn is responding to my earlier comment about her living alone. She often does this, sometimes letting hours go by before returning to a conversation and expecting me to know exactly what she's talking about.

"Lauren lives alone?"

"Sam told me everything." She chews. "Lauren hasn't dated in forever, so you're clear to move in on her."

"Who says I want to do that?"

When she cackles, a few tart crumbs spill out of her mouth. Dr. Stevens has no idea what a slob my sister can be. "I saw that look on your face when she touched your muscles. You're bewitched, brother."

"She *is* kind of witchy. Do you know she thought I poisoned her drink?"

"You must've deserved it."

Probably. I break off a clean corner from the Pop-Tart and sink my teeth into it. Do I want to 'move in' on Lauren? Several factors stand in my way. The first is rather obvious: she coaches at a school I loathe. I still can't believe Taryn will graduate from OSU. Michigan, with its superior academics, would be so much better. But the second may be even worse: Lauren seems closed off, unavailable. It's like she's already in a relationship, but instead of with a man, she's with her job. Up until she touched my chest tonight, she hadn't shown much interest in me. And if she hasn't dated in forever, maybe she's not interested in dating at all.

I don't know why I'm even thinking about her in a romantic way. Smoking is pretty gross, and the fact that the bartender knows her regular drink—and that everyone at the local watering hole knows her name—indicates she may spend too much time there. Then there's the whole long-distance thing. Both of us coach fall sports, so we won't have one minute of free time come August, much less three hours to drive north or south.

"I'm off to bed. There's a guest room upstairs for you." Taryn yawns as she stands.

I thump the leather cushions. "Thought I was sleeping here." It's definitely nicer than the thrift-store sofa in Taryn's old apartment.

"Didn't you say your back was hurting you, old man?" She raises her chin, a recurring expression of hers that begs for another noogie. She's still in her twenties, five years younger than me.

My lower back does hurt, as usual, but I won't admit it. I get to my feet, then stoop over like a nursing-home resident, one hand cradling my back. "That's true." My voice is an old-man warble. "Dagnabbit, after moving all of your books, little whippersnapper, I'll be lucky to make it up the stairs."

She shakes her head, but leans in for a quick hug. "Thanks for always being there for me, Remy."

I pat her shoulder. "Always."

When I'm cozy under the covers a few minutes later, supported by a firm yet pillowing mattress, I'm grateful for a bed, even if it's not extra-long like mine at home. I wonder how comfy Lauren's mattress is. Visions of plump, red lips and feisty, blue eyes fill my mind as I drift off to sleep.

5

Signing
Lauren

"**G**reat back-set," my assistant coach says, nodding at my computer screen as he lifts a piece of broccoli into his mouth. Patrick's expertise with chopsticks impresses me. I rely on a plastic fork to shovel in chow fun noodles.

Once I swallow a large bite of chicken, I point at the video of the Italian setter. "But she just missed that block."

"She was there for the cover, though. She has good court awareness."

I sigh. Patrick wants me to offer a scholarship to the Italian. I know he's right. It's been almost two weeks since I visited Emma Watkins, and there's still no word from her.

Patrick is particularly keen on the Italian setter because he's her lead recruiter. He elected to be the one to fly to Milan to watch her play a few weeks ago, knowing he won't be free to take many international trips once his wife gives birth in November. Not that it will matter if we don't have jobs by then.

"Time's a-tickin'." Patrick runs a hand through his black hair.

I groan. *This is all Jeremy Trent's fault.* If not for him, Emma Watkins would've signed with us by now. I set my plastic bowl from our favorite Asian bistro on my desk and close my eyes. In truth, the blame for losing Emma rests on my shoulders. I've coached my program into the ground despite maximum scholarships and countless resources. At least that's what my boss, Rhonda, tells me. *"Ohio State has the largest budget in college sports,"* she said during my evaluation last month. *"There's no excuse for your poor performance."*

Remembering that meeting, I silently hum "Help Me,

Rhonda," but switch the lyrics to *"Fuck you, Rhonda. Fuck, fuck you, Rhonda."* Our senior women's administrator is a former sports dietitian who rose to the rank of associate athletic director through her savvy awareness of politics and back-stabbing. She knows nothing about managing coaches. All she knows is vegetables and protein shakes. I lean back in my office chair as I take a sip of Mountain Dew.

On the scouting video, I watch the Italian setter serve the ball. "She doesn't have a jump serve."

"We can teach her," says Patrick, exuding confidence I don't feel.

"All right." I blow out a breath. "I'll ask Rhonda to draw up a letter of intent."

He flashes a grin, then attempts a somber look as he rises from his chair at the side of my desk. "I know the Italian's not your first choice, but we'll train her." He scoops up his bowl of stir-fry and bottled water. "I'll be in my office if you need anything."

Once he leaves, I sink farther into my chair. I do *not* want to call Rhonda today. My phone buzzes with a text—Dana, my other assistant, is checking in. As I read her message about her next planned stop on a South Carolina recruiting trip, a call lights up my phone. I see the caller ID and my heart skips. Recruits usually text me, so a phone call feels ominous. Here ends my career as OSU coach.

"Emma Watkins," I answer, striving to infuse some warmth into my shaking voice. "Great to hear from you. How's it going?"

"Hi, Coach Chase." Her tone sounds rather friendly for a player about to crush my soul. "I'm, uh, good." She pauses, and I think I hear whispering in the background. "How are you?"

Is someone there—her father, maybe?—to coach her through this phone call? Pushing his daughter to break the bad news when she'd rather just ghost me? "I'm good, too. Just watching some recruiting videos and eating Chinese food."

"Ooh, I love Chinese. What's your favorite?"

I scrunch my eyebrows. Is this really the conversation she wants to have? Seems like Avoidance 101, going off-topic to delay stabbing a chopstick through my little coach heart. "Any noodle dish is good with me. What do you like?"

"I used to eat kung-pao shrimp, chicken with mushrooms, oh, and beef with broccoli, though Evan likes that better than me, um, but now I like string beans…" She emits a little laugh, like she realizes she's babbling, then her voice adopts a serious tone. "My mom says I should stop stalling."

So, her mother, not her father, is the one whispering in the background. My shoulders tense as I wait for the destruction of my career. I wish OSU would let me smoke in my office.

"I need to tell you my plans for next year." When she hesitates, I stop breathing. "I just signed your scholarship offer. I want to be a Buckeye."

"Woo-hoooooo!" I spring to my feet to jump and gyrate, letting my shout reverberate through the office. "The best news I've heard all year!"

Emma giggles, and it sounds like her mother laughs as well in the background.

Patrick pops his head into my office, probably to make sure I'm still alive after my scream. I re-hinge my jaw, then point at my phone and mouth, "Emma Watkins." He's staring at me, not fully understanding, but after I give him an emphatic thumbs up, his eyes widen. He pumps a fist into the air.

"That is *fantastic* news." I try to catch my breath, still in shock. I've been pining for Emma to be on my team for over a year, and now I'm not sure what to say. "Patrick's here with me, and he's equally excited."

He hollers toward the phone, "Welcome to the Buckeyes, Emma!"

"Thank you!" she says.

"Dana's gonna lose her *shit* when I tell her!" I freeze as the swear word leaves my mouth. Will I set the record for the fastest scholarship decommit in history?

But Emma keeps laughing. Maybe she's enjoying our adulation, basking in the spotlight for once instead of hiding in the shadows behind her brother.

"I'll go tell Dana," Patrick whispers before he skedaddles out of the office.

"When can I start?" asks Emma. "Is, um, June okay?"

I can't stop grinning. "For sure. We already have our other three incoming freshmen signed up for summer school, getting the lay of the land before the season ramps up. Our summer bridge program is excellent—you'll meet student-athletes from other sports, learn how to cope with the demands of college, and get started on classes."

"Sounds awesome!" Her giddy voice is infectious.

Typically, Dana makes the housing arrangements with recruits, but I'm swept up in Emma's eagerness. I shuffle through the papers on my desk. "We have a dorm ready for you. You'll room with…Kaylee Stenstrom, an outside hitter from Arizona."

Emma's squeal broadens my grin. "Can I see it?" she begs. "My dorm room?"

"Absolutely!" As I feel my legs tremble, I sink into my office chair. "When can you come down?"

"Maybe this weekend." There's more whispering. "Oh, right, I leave for a tournament in Chicago on Friday. Um, next week?" She pauses. "Nope, darn. My mom says I have to study for AP exams."

Not only is Emma a talented athlete, but she's also smart, as evidenced by the three advanced-placement courses on her schedule during her last year of high school. She's the whole package. And she's *mine*.

Her next words are muffled, then she tells me, "My mom's gonna talk to you to arrange a date, okay?"

"That's fine. I hope we get to see you soon, Emma. This is a tremendous opportunity for us both." *One I better not fuck up.*

"Okay, bye!"

An older voice takes over. "Sorry about the murmuring in the background. I wanted Emma to practice speaking on the phone—a lost art for teenagers these days."

That's actually a good idea. Last year one of my sophomores almost missed registering for classes because she was too scared to call the financial aid office.

"But they *are* masters of texting." We both chuckle. "Mrs. Watkins, we're *so thrilled* Emma's choosing us. We won't let you down."

"I know you won't, and please call me Jenna."

This familiarity is good. "And I'm Lauren. Wow, I'd almost given up hope. You've definitely restored my faith! I'm curious—what made you decide on Ohio State?"

"Well, Emma's a fighter. She really wants the opportunity to be a starter and contribute right off the bat. And listen, we totally understand that she has to *earn* that spot. No divas here—if Emma ever fails to give an excellent effort, please let us know, and we'll come down there to straighten her out right away."

I love this family. I wish all of my players had such accountability from their parents. Instead, many student-athletes feel entitled, and their parents chew me out when they don't get playing time.

"But honestly, Coach?" she continues.

I frown. I invited her to call me Lauren.

"I appreciate how genuine you are. You were brutally honest about the status of your program—you really pulled us to your side. Emma wants to be there for the uprising, when you turn things around. And some coaches, like the one who recruited my son, made such a ruckus of my basketball career. They gush over me. But *I'm* not the recruit—my kids are."

Her basketball career? I'd heard she played college ball, but beyond that, I'm clueless. It sounds like she's a big fucking deal in the basketball world. How did I not know that? My cheeks warm, and I pull up a search engine on my desktop to type in her name. *Jenna Watkins* gets some hits for Facebook and LinkedIn pages, but nothing about basketball.

I realize there's silence on the phone, and I need to speak. My heartbeat kicks up—what should I say? "Your kids are quite the recruits. It's a, a wonder-twin athlete duo!"

Damn it, why aren't there any basketball references on these search results? *Duh.* Watkins is her married name. What's her maiden name? *Jenna basketball*, I type next.

As I scan the results, I say, "Other coaches fawned over you, huh?"

I bet the Michigan volleyball coach was one of them. *Ha-ha,*

Jim Dawson, you pompous prick! We get Emma, not you! Wait—Jenna mentioned her son's recruiter. Jeremy Trent must've been one of the fawners, too. *Did he tell her about my smoking?*

"Michigan coaches sure are suck-ups," I add.

When she doesn't reply, my fingers hover over the keyboard. How do I broach this? "I hope you didn't buy any smack Jeremy Trent tried to talk about me."

"I'm not sure what you're referring to."

I tense. Is it possible Jeremy didn't say anything? Or is she too classy to admit what she knows?

"Do you know Coach Trent?" she asks.

"We met outside your house a couple of weeks ago."

"Ah!" Her voice lightens. "That must've been...*interesting.*"

That's one word for it. So, it appears Jeremy didn't smoke me out like he threatened. My shoulders lower as I blow out a long breath. Recalling his smirk that day outside the twins' house, I angle my head to one side. *Why* didn't he narc on me? Surely, he wants to exploit every recruiting advantage he can get. Why show mercy on an Ohio State coach? I wouldn't do the same if the tables were turned. What's his game?

"This rivalry is intense," Jenna continues. "I hope Emma and Evan can stay friends the next four years."

Good luck. The twins will catch hell from both sides. I scroll through search results but still can't find anything about their mother's basketball career.

"You sound kind of busy, so maybe we can find a date later..."

Shit. I realize I haven't spoken for a while, and I'm being a jerk to the mother of my most important player. "I'm sorry, Jenna." She said she values honesty, so here goes. "I'm embarrassed to say I don't know about your basketball career. I was trying to google you while we were talking, but I suck at multi-tasking."

"Oh." When she pauses, I worry I made a mistake in telling her that. Me and my big mouth. After a long moment, she says, "Francis."

I run my tongue along my lower lip. "Francis?"

"My maiden name."

"Got it." My fingers fly over the keyboard, pulling up a photo of a young Jenna Francis taking a fadeaway jump shot in a USA basketball uniform. My mouth drops open. "You played in the *Olympics*?"

She doesn't answer, and I keep reading. "And you led the WNBA in scoring?"

She's quiet for a moment. "Many years ago."

"I should've known Emma's mom was such a stud. Your twins obviously got their talent from somewhere, and it's not coming from a has-been Michigan football player like their dad."

Silence greets me. *Fuck nuggets*—I went too far this time. Insulting her husband...what was I thinking? But when she starts laughing, tension drains from my body.

"I knew I liked you, Lauren." Her laughter fades into a sigh. "And so it begins. I don't know if my family is up for this insane rivalry."

"It'll be an adventure, for sure." I continue reading her USA Basketball player bio and see her college stats. "At least you didn't play for Ohio State."

She makes a scoffing sound. "Tyler Watkins would've never married a Buckeye."

I contemplate her response. A romance between a Buckeye and Wolverine is indeed implausible. My brain knows it, but my body hasn't gotten the message. Remembering the feel of Jeremy's hard chest muscles beneath my fingers makes them tingle. Now that I know he didn't interfere with my career, I don't need to shut down fond feelings for him when I replay our interactions.

"How'd you and Tyler meet?" I ask.

"Hmm, that was a long time ago. University of Connecticut—I was an undergrad, and he was working on his master's in education."

Her husband is a high-school teacher and athletic director in Toledo. And of course she played for Connecticut, the nation's top women's basketball dynasty.

"Tyler did a GA fellowship in the athletic department, and as part of that, he led UConn's Athletes in Action chapter." A smile enters her voice. "He was such a charmer. I totally fell for him."

They met in a group for Christian athletes—not surprising. I'm not religious at all. I wonder if Jeremy is.

"It was tough at UConn, but Tyler got me through it. We married right after I graduated. Then we moved to Houston when I signed with the Comets. After I got pregnant with the twins, we wanted to be near our parents, so we moved to Toledo."

"Both your parents live in Toledo?"

"Mine do, but his live in Michigan."

"Figures," I mutter.

"Ha. How'd you like your days at Ohio State?"

I think back to my volleyball career. "I loved my teammates, but I hated my coach. He was cold, cruel. I wasn't the best student, and he used to rip into me for my grades." I probably drank too much to excel in school, though I'm not telling her that. "I started as a biology major, and I bombed. But I didn't know what else to major in. Can you believe Ohio State has over two-hundred majors?"

She inhales. "Yikes. Emma doesn't know her major yet."

"That's normal. We have some great academic advisors and career counselors who can help her. Me, I was too stupid to ask for help. Luckily, my dad suggested sports industry, and it was a great fit."

"Why sports industry?" she asks.

"My dad said he was tired of hearing me complain about my coach. He said I had big ideas on how to coach, so I should become one myself." I recall that pivotal conversation. What if I'd chosen a different major—a different career? Would I be happier? The pressure to win is overwhelming sometimes. I can only hope Emma will help us earn more of those wins.

By the time we identify a date for Emma's visit and end the call, an hour has passed. I've never spoken to a recruit's parent that long, but Jenna Francis Watkins is so easy to talk to that I can't wait for her to arrive with her daughter in tow. I hope Emma and I can find that ease in our relationship. *Squee!* My hands flutter with excitement. She's mine!

If I had a bottle of champagne, I'd pop it. I suppose OSU wouldn't like alcohol in coaches' offices, though. I'm basking in the glory of landing the nation's number-one recruit, looking forward to calling bitchy Rhonda and telling her she might not get to fire me this year, when I sit up with a start. I picture green eyes crinkled with amusement, looking down at me after I ground the butt of my cigarette into the pavement.

What will he think of me now?

He didn't share my secret, but I told everyone his!

6

Revealing
Jeremy

As I stroll through the training room before practice, I hear a soft snicker. I turn to the sound, and an assistant athletic trainer ducks his head, appearing engrossed in his ultrasound on a player's lower spine. I frown when I recognize the player—it's one of my backup quarterbacks, Quentin Hill.

Hill's a rising senior on the practice squad, and the defense's repeated hits throughout his years have taken their toll on his body. Still, I bet the ultrasound treatment is more for psychic pain than back pain. My head coach freaking *fried* him last week after he fumbled the ball in practice. Hill probably never wants to play again, and chronic back pain may help him accomplish his goal.

From his position on his belly, Hill looks up at me. Once our eyes meet, his dart to the floor. *Yep, he's faking.* I walk off in disgust.

As I enter my office, I realize the reason for the snickering. In the middle of my desk are two plastic figures, miniature mascots for Michigan and Ohio State. I've had a vicious gray Wolverine dressed in a maize-and-blue football uniform on my bookshelf for years. Some jerk has moved Wolvy from my bookshelf to my desk and stuck him beneath a figurine with red pants, a jersey with red and gray stripes, and an oversized, round head in the shape of a tree nut. It's bad enough that the idiot put Brutus Buckeye in my office at all. But the lewd position of their tangled arrangement is even worse. Brutus's plump, circular head rests on the wolverine's crotch.

I shake my head, and a chortle escapes. I'm wondering

which assistant coach set up this little suck-off scenario when I hear a throat clear behind me. Rotating, I find my head coach in the doorway. He glances at the prank on my desk, but he doesn't crack a smile.

"Coach Froth." I nod. "Anything you need?"

"It's true, then," he grumbles. The etched lines around his eyes seem deeper today, chiseled into his face by sharp criticism from grumpy Michigan fans. The fans chip away with extra pressure after every loss to our rival. *Tap, tap, tap.*

I tilt my head. "What's true?"

"Your sister goes to OSU."

Well, that explains my desk—Lauren must've ratted me out. I arrange my face in a neutral expression. "Yeah. It's just grad school." *What's the big deal? Who the hell cares what school my little sister attends?*

"Your loyalty's intact, then?"

A bloom of heat flares up my chest. How *dare* he question my loyalty? Doesn't he realize the sickening frustration I swallow on the daily to demonstrate my devotion to him and this program? The humiliating way he talks to his staff? The times he makes horrible calls on offense, placing my quarterbacks in peril? The countless occasions he's attacked my QBs' character, squashing their performance?

My hand shakes as I grab Brutus Buckeye and whip him into the trash. "Absolutely." I force a smile. "Go, Blue."

"When's the next time you see the Watkins kid?"

"I just visited Evan two weeks ago."

Froth's eyes narrow. "Not what I asked."

Deep breath. "Evan's mother wants him to study for his AP exams, so she asked me to limit my visits the next couple of weeks."

"Who runs the show with this family, Trent? We're going to make that boy millions in the NFL, and you couldn't even get him to start here in January?"

My stomach ties into a knot. We've had this pointless argument several times. What was I supposed to do? Kidnap the boy from his parents so he could enroll early?

"I don't know why you refuse to talk to your friend Nichols," Froth adds. "He could've convinced the boy to start early."

I stifle a groan. Froth has long been on my case to involve Adrian Nichols, starting quarterback for the Jacksonville Jaguars, in Evan's recruiting. Like me, Adrian's from Chicago, and we roomed together at University of Oklahoma. But no way will I abuse that friendship by asking him to convince one of my recruits to go against his parents' will. "Adrian didn't start school in January, though."

"Nobody did back then," Coach Froth replies. "Now you'll have less than two months to train the kid. No way he'll have a solid grasp on the offense by the time we play Notre Dame."

"Evan's a smart boy," I say. I hope my antacid tablets are in my desk, not at home.

"Then he'll do fine on his damn AP tests. Visit him soon. You still have allowable contacts left with him, right?"

The NCAA has rules regarding how many times I can contact a recruit for this very reason—so we don't interfere with their lives before they even arrive on campus. Not that Froth cares.

"Right."

"Then get on it." He scowls as he heads for the door. "For now, we're stuck with the worst quarterbacks in the Big Ten."

Once he's gone, I sink into my office chair. Why's he busting *my* balls? My predecessor recruited most of our current quarterbacks, all of them turning into flops. *I'm* the one who landed Evan.

My stomach reminds me to hunt for an antacid. Where the hell is that bottle? I slide out the bottom drawer of my desk but come up empty. My gaze lands on the trash can a few inches away, and I tilt it toward me. I dig Brutus Buckeye out.

As I stare at his lifeless eyes and stupid grin, I think about Lauren. It had to be her who let the cat out of the bag about Taryn. I give the mascot a little shake, but his synthetic smile remains frozen. *Et tu, Brute?*

***

An hour later, the ball sails through the air in a tight spiral— not a bad throw despite Hartford's off-balance footing when he launched it—and flies straight into the waiting arms of the safety. *Dammit.* I knew that was an ill-advised pass. The defender tucks the intercepted ball into his elbow and dodges two missed tackles as he zooms back toward us.

"Tackle him!" I scream from the sideline.

I watch in horror as the safety breaks more tackles in his rush toward our end zone. The only offensive player left to stop him is our starting quarterback, Austin Hartford. But Hartford's wearing a no-contact pinny and can't tackle him in spring practice, so it's no surprise when the speedy defender blows by him. The defense cheers when the interception earns six points for their side.

"A pick *six*?" bellows Coach Froth. He glares at me before he slams his clipboard to the ground and marches toward Hartford. Silence blankets the outdoor practice field, which means the team, coaches, athletic trainers, equipment guys, and video staff are about to hear the head coach laying into my QB. "What the fuck was that, Hartford? Your dumbass decision with that pass just lost the game for us. This disaster's all on *you*."

I want to point out the poor tackling by the entire offense, not just my unit, but I keep my mouth shut.

Coach Froth spins and jabs his finger toward three of the smallest players on the sideline. "Kickers! See if you can fuck up the PAT, and you'll *complete* this shitshow!"

Strapping on his helmet, a short kicker jogs onto the field as special teams set up for the point-after-touchdown field goal.

Hartford and the offense head for the sideline, their helmets hanging low. When Hartford veers away from me, my throat burns with a hotter rage. "Austin!"

He pauses, then drifts my way in a hesitant meander. It's a warmer day on one of our last spring practices, and most of the offensive players remove their helmets, but Hartford keeps his on. When he gets closer, I can see why. The boy's close to tears.

I sigh. I want to chew him out, but I should try to pick up the crumbled pieces of his ego instead. Damn that Bill Froth. He's dismantling Hartford's remaining confidence. Coach Froth already destroyed my two backup quarterbacks earlier this spring by lambasting them in front of the whole team. How does he expect my guys to lead when he treats them like misbehaving schoolchildren? My Oklahoma coach never humiliated Adrian like that after he made a mistake.

"What were your reads?" I bark.

Hartford takes me through his visual scan of each well-defended receiver, and I'm relieved to hear that at least he remembered the correct play. "Then the linebacker was coming for me, and I thought I saw AJ get open, so I threw before the defense could touch me."

My jaw ticks. Besides the muffed tackles after the interception, the missed blocks by the offensive line are also not Hartford's responsibility. We have a veteran center returning, but we lost our All-American left tackle to the pros, and we have a true freshman taking his place this spring. That last play provides ample evidence that our newbie left tackle hasn't provided great protection to our quarterbacks.

"So, basically..." I eye him. "You panicked."

He lets out a breath as he slumps. "Yes, sir."

"We need to practice more, keep running through your reads on each play till they're automatic. How 'bout tonight?"

"Um..." He chews his lip, angering me with his indecision. "I got a final tomorrow? I kind of need to study?"

Screw your final. I manage a terse nod and walk away from him. I pass an athletic trainer who wears a T-shirt saying, *I Set My DVR to Record The Biggest Loser and It Keeps Taping OHIO STATE Games.*

After practice, I grab some celery and hummus from the fuel zone, thankful for changes in NCAA legislation that allow us to feed our players throughout the day. Since I'm at the facility for long hours and don't have time to run out for food, my fellow coaches and I often raid the spreads laid out by the sports dietitians.

As I watch video of the practice, I take notes for my next individual session with Hartford. He seems to have forgotten the changes we made to his footwork. I gnaw on a celery stalk.

When I hear the administrative assistant's voice float down

the hallway, I rise and stick my head out of my doorway. *Yes.* Froth's back is to me, and he passes by the admin without one look in her direction. He's probably leaving early for a speaking engagement at an alumni or donor dinner.

Another assistant coach across the hall, in an office closer to the head coach's suite, leans out of his doorway as well. After we watch our boss leave, the coach turns back to his office and catches a glimpse of me. We share a conspiratorial grin. *While the wolverine's away, the rabbits will play.* Or something like that—whatever the hell wolverines eat. None of the assistant coaches feel it's safe to leave the facility before Froth does. And during the season, the jerk's often here till after ten p.m.

"Want to grab some pizza and beer?" asks the other coach.

I consider his offer. My back is still hurting from moving Taryn's crap last weekend, and I want to spend some quality time in bed watching the Cubs game tonight. Plus, the linebackers' coach can't get enough pepperoni and sausage on his pizza— he'll give me shit for wanting vegetables and no cheese on my half. "Take a raincheck?"

"Yeah." He rubs his chin. "Should probably use this opportunity to get home early to the wife and kids."

He has two young children he rarely sees. "Good idea. See you tomorrow."

I'm almost to my car outside of Schembechler Hall when I halt. In the space next to my Nissan Pathfinder is a gray Ford sedan with Ohio plates. Lauren sits on the hood, watching me with careful eyes. She probably thinks I'm angry with her for spilling the Buckeye beans. But for some stupid reason, she's a welcome sight after a long day. I smile at her.

She slides off the hood. "Are you limping?" Her blue eyes peer at me, her face aglow in the waning sunlight.

I hesitate. I typically hide my aching back from my fellow football coaches, not wanting to make excuses or give them a leg up on me. "Don't think so."

"Did you get hurt in practice or something?"

Only my ego. "Just some back pain now and then."

"That's too bad. Chronic pain sucks." She lifts her hand to

the pocket of her black jacket but then returns it to her side.

There's something off about her jacket that I can't place.

I'm touched by her concern. "Sounds like you know what you're talking about."

"Ugh." Her eyes roll up to the sky. "I had a hip scope to repair a torn labrum two years ago."

"That's a big deal. One of our players didn't return to the game after a torn labrum." My gaze floats down to her hips, then back up to her face. I feel a curious twinge in my groin, and my mind travels in a mischievous direction—how flexible is she after a surgery like that? "Is your movement, ah...limited now?"

Her lips part, and a blush pinks her cheeks. It seems she understood the meaning of my question. *Not so sassy or aggressive* now, *are you, Coach Chase?*

"I'm good," she says after a beat. "Full range of mobility." There's a hint of a smile on those red lips. "I bet you've had lots of injuries as tight end."

Her crisp enunciation of my former position ignites a seizure of tightness down below. I swallow. "Torn meniscus and some other little things. But the worst were the concussions—too many to count."

"Explains a lot, all those head injuries." Her smile grows, and the high-spirited sparkle returns to her eyes. "Like why you took a job at Michigan."

I now realize she's wearing her jacket inside out, and my heartrate kicks up. She's hiding the Ohio State logo on her jacket like it's not safe for her to reveal herself here. Nor is it safe for me to talk to an OSU coach right outside my workplace. My gaze darts around the parking lot. Crap, does Froth know I'm talking to her? I exhale as I remember he left a while ago. But other coaches or staff could walk out any moment. I look at the exit near the coaching offices.

"Everything okay?" asks Lauren.

I frown at her. "Why are you here?"

She takes a step away from me, a line creasing her forehead.

Worried that I hurt her feelings, I add, "You're not stealing recruits, are you?"

"Hey, you came down to *my* state to recruit your QB." She juts out her chin.

"You really want to claim Toledo as your own?"

She lets out a girlish laugh, gratifying me. I want to make her laugh more.

"I guess Toledo's closer to you than to me." She tosses her blond hair over her shoulder, her smile fading. "I'm here because I owe you." She presses her lips together. "You didn't snitch on me like you said you were going to."

I feel a twist of disgust in my gut when I realize what she means. "Evan's twin committed to the Buckeyes."

"As of yesterday. You haven't heard?"

I shake my head. "Mrs. Watkins asked me not to bother Evan before his AP tests."

"She said the same thing about Emma. Overprotective much?"

I smirk.

"If all goes well, you may have just saved my career," she continues. "I got my star recruit thanks to you—my rival." Her head inclines to one side. "And I'm left wondering...why? Why didn't you say something about my smoking?"

I nibble on my lip as my breath quickens. Her gaze penetrates me, demands a response. I don't know if I can explain why I kept her secret, but I'm grateful she's here to talk about it. My body feels alive when she's close, despite the danger of being caught with the enemy. "I don't believe in negative recruiting."

When she keeps staring, I try to explain myself.

"Power-five athletic departments are sleaze-buckets. They pretend they're into developing students, developing good *people*, but all they care about is money." Her vigorous nods keep me going. "So, when I get a chance to be human—to prioritize people, not dollars—I take it. We're rivals, but we know what it's like to be on the chopping block if we're not making them enough money. And we both know the thrill of getting the best out of our athletes despite the obstacles they throw in our way. I guess I wanted you to have that chance."

She has edged closer during my little speech, bringing the

light scent of coconut my direction, with no hint of cigarette smoke. Looking up with her mouth slightly open, she scoffs, "Oh, great. Now I feel like a total D-bag. You do me a solid like that, and I turn around and blab about your sister?"

My eyes narrow. "Who'd you tell, by the way?"

"Did I make things hard for you?"

I remember my confrontation with Froth. "They would've found out anyway."

"Eventually." She squares her shoulders. "You want to know why I'm here." She waits a beat as she rubs her black athletic pants. "I want to make it up to you...by taking you to dinner."

Wow. This is unexpected—but appreciated. "You drove over three hours to get here? You seem pretty confident I'll accept your offer."

"I'm *hoping* you'll accept." She shrugs. "But if you don't, I'll call Emma Watkins and ask if I can visit on my way home."

"And defy overprotective Mama Watkins?" My eyebrows lift.

"Emma's getting straight As—she can take a night off studying. Evan maybe not so much. I got the smarter one."

I scowl, and then an insane idea enters my mind. "You know, my boss is on my butt to visit Evan. Maybe we drive down there together tonight."

When her eyes widen, I silently curse. Too much, too fast. She feels obligated to buy me dinner, but then she wants to get out of here, probably never see me again.

She hasn't replied yet, and I add, "We can take our recruits out for a bite to eat."

"But we can't pay—" We both say at once, then laugh together. The compliance office has engraved recruiting rules into our brains.

Lauren strokes the exposed skin of her neck and collarbone as she seems to consider my idea. "You know, recruiting *is* kind of lonely..." Her head dips. When she glances up again, wisps of blond hair have blown into her face, covering one cheek. "Maybe that is a good idea, to go down there together."

I fight the urge to brush the hair off of her cheek. "I'd like that." When she smiles at me, my chest warms. *Screw it*—I give up the fight and step closer. She inhales as I tuck the wayward strands behind her ear. Her hair is so soft.

"Whose car should we take?" she asks, her voice unusually quiet.

We're standing close, drawing my attention to her mouth. What would it be like to kiss the red velvet of her full lips? "I thought I'd follow you." When she squints at me, I add, "So you don't have to go out of your way—to backtrack up north before returning to Columbus."

"Oh. I have a friend nearby I can stay with tonight. He lives in Ypsilanti."

I step back from her as I cock one eyebrow. "*He*?"

Her face lights up, and her laugh sounds mocking. "He's gay, Coach Trent."

Thank God. "I'll drive, then."

"Great." She opens the passenger door of her car, extracts her leather OSU bag, and slings it over her shoulder. "I'll call Emma to make sure she's free."

I need to do the same with Evan. I glance at my windshield and notice my UM parking sticker. "Wait a minute. You shouldn't leave your car here, or you'll get a ticket. How 'bout you drive?"

"Sure." She opens the passenger door for me before crossing to the driver's side and tossing her briefcase in the backseat. She peels off her inside-out OSU jacket, revealing a gray collared shirt that hugs the curve of her breasts and shows off the lean musculature of her forearms. I'm glad when she pitches the jacket into the back as well.

From the corner of my eye, I see a fellow coach—the offensive coordinator—exit the building. Hustling into Lauren's car, I set my briefcase on the floor. There's a yellow rectangular paper near my feet, and I pick it up as she backs out of the space.

I look over at her, holding up the speeding ticket. "What's *this*, Coach Chase?"

7

Maturing
Lauren

"Give me that, dickweed!" I hit the brake and lunge for the ticket, but Jeremy stiff-arms my shoulder as he extends it away from me. He's trying to read the details, and his hand on my shoulder is an unyielding force. *Shit, he's strong.*

Turning to face me, his eyes expand. "They clocked you going eighty-seven—twenty-two miles over the speed limit?" He whistles through his teeth. "That's gonna cost you."

Once he relaxes his hold on the damn ticket, I steal it back and tuck it into the center console. "Thanks, math genius." I put the car into drive and head toward US-23 South, the highway where a callous cop gave me the ticket after I crossed the Michigan border. I was distracted by some yahoo's bumper sticker: O HOW I HATE OHIO STATE. "I got a late start after practice, and I wanted to make it here before you left for the night."

"That's a legitimate reason to get a speeding ticket, then." He beams at me, and his white teeth contrast with his darkening five o'clock stubble. "You were eager to see me."

I want to rub my hand along his jaw to feel the roughness. Lest he get a big head, I say, "Not really. I get tickets for all kinds of reasons."

His grin grows, like he can see through my denial. I'm unsure how to deal with the charged-up flutter of my heart. I decide to direct the conversation elsewhere.

"You said something about my speeding the first time we met," I remind him. "How'd you know?"

When I sense his eyes roving over me, my breath catches. Does he like what he sees? I've never thought much about my body—I've only cared how high I can jump or how fast I can dive for a ball—but now I'm hoping he doesn't judge the roundness of my belly or ass. Since retiring from volleyball, my muscles have shifted into curves, but I can still keep up with my players on the court when needed.

"You're a fast woman," he says.

My mouth drops open as I stare at him. "You think I'm promiscuous?"

"*What? No!*" He frowns. "Bad choice of words. I meant that you—you *move* fast. You seem like you're always on the go, running a hundred miles an hour." He points at the green plastic bottle in my cup holder next to a bag of Twizzlers. "Swigging your Mountain Dew, gobbling candy, zooming all over the country to recruit, demanding the best from yourself and your players—you're...zesty, or something. You don't take crap from anyone."

We've barely spent any time together, and his keen observations of me are unnerving. The inside of the car falls quiet as I take them in. I realize the woman he's described is the old me, back when I started coaching at Ohio State. I was full of passion and optimism then. Lately, I've just been resigned.

But I don't feel tired or jaded now. Jeremy's solid presence fills my car and tickles my skin. There's a grass stain on the knee of his khaki pants, and he smells earthy, with a trace of masculine aftershave.

I can feel him watching me. "You're intuitive about people," I say. "I can see why you're a good coach."

He blinks. "I don't have a national championship, though."

I blow a breath out through my nose. "You keep mentioning that, but it's not that big of a deal."

His eyes tighten before he looks ahead and stares out the windshield. I study his profile. His nose is prominent, but not too big for his size. There's a slight indent in the slope, and I wouldn't be surprised if he's broken it at some point. When I look back at the road, I notice we're almost out of Ann Arbor.

"I better call Emma, make sure she's free." I press a button on my steering wheel. "Call Emma Watkins."

A ring sounds on my hands-free phone, eliciting a look from

Jeremy. "Fancy," he grumbles.

"You don't have this feature in your car? No wonder we keep beating you."

Emma answering the phone cuts off his growl.

"Hi, Coach Chase!" Emma's voice is full of sunshine.

"How's my favorite six-foot-three setter? My favorite future Buckeye?"

Jeremy's glower indicates he's caught my attempt to rub it in. Well, if *he* gets a wonder-twin, then I deserve one, too.

Emma shifts into a foreign language. "Buena. Estudio para mi examen AP de español."

I squint. "Emma, I have no freaking clue what you just said."

"She's studying for her AP Spanish exam," says Jeremy.

I look sideways at him, impressed. I suffered through two years of German to fulfill Ohio State's foreign language requirement, and about the only vocabulary I remember is das Arschloch, their word for asshole. I used to mutter it under my breath in reference to my head coach. I realize a connection between Emma and my starting middle blocker, Mariana.

"That's great you speak Spanish, Emma! You can talk to—" I stop as I remember a Michigan coach sits next to me. Jeremy might tell other coaches that my setter will be able to speak with my Colombian blocker, Mariana, in her native tongue. If Jim Dawson has Latin American players, he'll play them on the front line to eavesdrop on our plays, thereby shutting down a potential advantage when we play Michigan.

"Coach?" Emma prompts. "You still there?"

"Yeah, sorry about that." I search for something to say. "I thought I saw a police car."

Jeremy chuckles as he gestures toward my speedometer. "Dang, girl. Maybe you'd worry less if you lighten that lead foot."

Why would I want to do that? I scowl at him as I snatch a piece of red licorice from the bag. Censoring myself around both Emma *and* Jeremy stresses me out. I offer Jeremy a Twizzler but he shakes his head.

"Is Patrick with you?" asks Emma.

"Actually..." I swallow a bite. "Coach Trent is with me."

There's a pause. "*Really?*"

Jeremy and I share a grin at the incredulous tone of her voice.

"Hey, Emma." His deep voice fills the car.

"Hi, Coach. Um, isn't it illegal or something for you guys to talk to each other?"

"Totally illegal," I say as I meet Jeremy's eyes. "We're breaking all the rules."

The smoldering look he gives me buzzes my body, and I clutch the steering wheel tighter. What the hell am I doing in a car with him—alone? The plan was to buy him dinner to free myself of my debt.

Okay, maybe I wanted to see him again, too. Maybe it's not so bad to get another look at his broad chest, strong jawline, and incisive green eyes. He's wearing a white collared shirt with a navy windbreaker over khaki pants, and the coach's garb makes him look powerful. Even though I'm the one driving, it seems like he's the one in charge, and I'm not sure how I feel about that. As a head coach, I'm the one who runs the show.

"Why're you driving together?" Emma asks.

It takes me a moment to remember I'm still on the call. "I know you're busy studying, Emma, but I want to stop by to talk about getting you started at Ohio State. Is that okay?"

"I have to ask my mom and dad."

I nod. "Of course."

"Is your brother around if I text him?" Jeremy asks. "We could all go out to dinner."

"He's in his room, but you can't text him," Emma says.

Jeremy rubs his jaw. "Studying hard, huh?"

"Probably not." Emma giggles. "He got in trouble, and my mom took his phone."

Jeremy's hand stops stroking his stubble. "What'd he do?" He winks at me. "Use a swear word?"

"Don't think so." Emma sighs. "He was probably disrespectful. He's been acting rude lately—his ego's all bloated and puffed up. I doubt my mom will let him go out." She pauses. "Want me to ask her if you can at least stop by?"

"That'd be great." When the phone goes quiet, I press the mute button and look at Jeremy. "You've got a handful with Evan Watkins."

His eyebrows pull together. "What do you mean?"

"You know. His parents have such a tight hold over him, he's gonna rebel like hell once he gets a taste of freedom."

His eyes cloud. "They're just as strict with Emma. Aren't you worried about her?"

"Possibly. She seems advanced for her age, though." I shrug. "I've been wrong about recruits before. But girls are way more mature than boys, especially as young adults. Evan strikes me as a little punk."

When he laughs, tension drains from his face. He shakes his head. "He's a huge punk. He and his dad have been a giant pain in my ass for three years."

"Good luck with that." I smirk.

"Want to trade?" A mischievous glint enters his eyes. "Emma undoubtedly has a better arm than the three sad-sack quarterbacks I got."

I can't believe he's confessing that to an Ohio State coach. "Hell, no. Evan would impregnate half my team the first week."

His eyes widen, then he thumps the armrest. "Thanks for that. I already worried about him failing out of school, but now I have to ward off all the jock-sniffers trying to dive into his pants, wanting his babies."

A snicker bubbles up my throat, and soon we're both laughing.

"We're such idiots, letting these kids control our livelihoods," he says. "What the hell were we thinking when we chose to become coaches?"

I've lamented the exact same thing many times. "We're dumbshits for sure. Total gluttons for punishment."

I check my speedometer—not too bad—and gobble another Twizzler as we wait for Emma.

"So, what about people in their thirties?" Jeremy asks.

I cock my head, not understanding his question.

"Are girls still more mature than boys?"

I point my licorice stick in the air. "I am *very* mature." When one corner of his mouth quirks up, I narrow my eyes. "Is that a dig at my age?"

"Not at all. I like experienced women."

Holy hell. Can he hear my heartbeat over the hum of the tires? I feel warmth in my face, and a glance in the rearview mirror confirms a red flush on my cheeks. Despite my ancient age of thirty-six, I'm *not* experienced. I hooked up a couple of times in college—more drunk lust than meaningful attachment. And the one man I've been with since graduation...well, that hardly qualifies as a relationship. My face gets hotter, and a knot twists in my belly as I remember him.

I need to calm down. My hand twitches, and I almost reach for the center console before I remember I can't smoke around Jeremy. It's such a gross habit—I shouldn't smoke at all. I've thought about vaping, but they say that's bad for you, too. And I don't want to act like a teenager.

"Coach?" Emma returns to the line. "My mom says you guys can come over for dinner."

I look at Jeremy as I unmute the phone. "We don't want to impose—"

"Thank you, Emma," Jeremy butts in. "We'll be there soon. Or maybe sooner, the way Danica Patrick over here drives."

The second after I end the call, I gape at him. "We're eating dinner with Emma's *parents*?"

"What's wrong with that?" His shoulder lifts. "They're a great couple."

"They are. It's just..." I run my hand through my hair. "I usually have to psych myself up to meet with recruits' parents. They don't like me very much. Especially Mr. Watkins—he makes me nervous. I might say the wrong thing. What if I let a *fuck* slip out?"

"News flash, Lauren." He pats my thigh. "You've already won them over. No need to impress them now."

His warm hand rests on my leg for a moment, and I feel its absence when he pulls away. He's right, of course, and the idea of eating dinner with a clan of Jesus cheerleaders somehow seems less intimidating with him by my side. Still, I'm nervous.

A little while later, we pull into the Watkins' driveway. He unbuckles his seatbelt and turns to face me. "Okay, Chase. Let's get you ready."

I scrunch my eyes. What's he up to?

"Do you need a cigarette?"

I flinch. How does he know? Can he see my hands shaking? I was hoping to sneak a smoke outside the restaurant at some point tonight.

He searches my eyes, and I wilt under his gaze. "I don't *need* one." I slump. "But I sure would like one." I shake my head. "I can't go in there smelling like smoke, though."

He nods. "Yeah, hmm..."

"Oh." I sit up and reach for my briefcase in the backseat. Opening the flap, I extract a package from the drugstore that Sam delivered when she came over last night. "*You got your star recruit!*" she told me. "*Time for a fresh start. You can do this, Lauren.*"

I glower at the package of nicotine patches. Sam wasn't being pushy when she bought them for me—I'd told her many times before about how much I wished I could quit. Still, the prospect of trying this again collapses my blackened lungs. "Yay."

"Do you *want* to quit?"

I look at him, but I don't see judgment. The relaxed set of his jaw and slight angle of his head make him seem curious, almost kind, as he watches me.

"Maybe," I confess.

"You tried to quit before?"

"Lots of times." I feel an uneasy flurry inside of me, wishing he didn't know this part of me—my addictive personality. I'm going to disappoint him like I do with everyone else. "Don't get your hopes up."

He engulfs my hand in both of his. "Hey."

My breath halts.

"I have high hopes." His thumb strokes the back of my hand.

We stay suspended in this moment, my body overwhelmed by his warmth, his energy, his misguided belief in me, until he lets go of my hand and unwraps the box of patches. "Okay, let's get this puppy on you." He peels off the backing from one patch. "Where does it go?"

I stretch for the patch. "I can do it."

"Let me."

His stern tone elicits a pout from me. *Really mature, Chase.* With a scoff, I extend my arm for him. "Slap it on my forearm. I'll wear my jacket to cover it."

"Good girl," he coos.

"Peckerhead," I counter. Despite my scorn, I have to admit that his touch on my elbow skitters electricity up my arm and into my chest.

His little smile tells me he's enjoying this interaction. "Okay, next step. Let's get all of the swear words out of your system."

"What?"

He presses the patch to the inside of my forearm. "Let 'em rip. Go for it."

"Your ears might bleed."

"Seriously? I coach football. My boss swears like a beast—I've heard them all before."

"Okay, you asked for it." I unleash a string of curse words. Just when I think I'm running out of good ones, a few more come to me. And then a few more. I'm even impressing myself.

Jeremy's shoulders are shaking but no sound is coming out of his mouth. His head slowly turns side to side. "I stand corrected. *Jizzbreath?*" He lets out a laugh. "I've never heard *shitnubbin* or *bitchtits* before, either."

"Poor you. So deprived." I inhale as I look at the suburban home. "You ready?"

His nod is decisive. "Let's do this."

Breaking
Jeremy

Mrs. Watkins answers the door with a smile. "Well, this is a surprise, coaches! C'mon in."

I gesture for Lauren to go first, then follow her inside. "Sorry to barge in on you like this, Mrs. Watkins. We didn't give you much notice."

"Yeah," Lauren agrees. "We appreciate it, but you don't need to cook us dinner, Jenna."

Jenna? My eyebrows arch at Lauren, and she smirks back at me.

"It's my pleasure." Mrs. Watkins leads us to the sitting area, and I cross over to the loveseat to avoid the hard cushions of that floral sofa. My back always hurts after a drive. But I don't sit yet because the two ladies are still standing.

"Tyler's at a lacrosse game tonight, so I could use some adult company," Mrs. Watkins explains. "Can I take your jackets?"

Lauren's eyes flash with fear, and she gives her head a quick shake. "No thank you."

"Would you like something to drink, then?"

Lauren sits on the sofa. "I'm good, thanks."

"Me, too." I nod.

Jenna leans on the stair railing. "You sure you wouldn't like some coffee, Coach Trent?"

She always makes me feel at home. "You *do* make the best coffee, Mrs. Watkins. Sure, I'll take a cup."

"Lauren?" asks Mrs. Watkins.

What's this first-name business? Before she can respond, I say, "*Lauren* doesn't drink coffee."

Mrs. Watkins eyes me with a faint smile. "Gotcha. Coming right up."

After she leaves for the kitchen, I lower myself onto the loveseat.

Lauren leans in and whispers, "Suck up."

I feign umbrage.

"How'd you know I don't like coffee?" she asks.

"I'm intuitive about people, remember?" I grin at her. "Besides, no respectable coffee drinker would down Mountain Dew like you do."

She holds up her pinky and forefinger in what looks like a skateboarder's salute. "Do the Dew."

I squint. "Yeah, you *definitely* don't seem older than me."

"Especially when you're hobbling around like a goddamn geezer. Maybe you should get that back looked at."

Damn. I thought I'd covered better than that. I'm lucky I get to make a living through football, but the sport has ravaged my body. I lower my voice. "Do you think the warden will let us see our recruits tonight?"

"Only if you keep sucking up to her."

I reach out to pat the nicotine patch beneath her jacket sleeve. When she gets my jab at her hypocrisy, she yanks her arm away to cradle it around her waist.

"How well's the patch working?" I whisper.

She frowns. "Should've worn two. What if I mess up? All I can think about is the word, *twatwaffle. Twatwaffle, twatwaffle.*"

I imagine Mrs. Watkins' shocked face if Lauren were to say that in her presence and suppress a smile.

There's a rustling behind me, and Mrs. Watkins circles around the corner of the loveseat carrying a steaming cup of coffee. As I get to my feet, I see Lauren's blue eyes expand. Did Mama W overhear us?

"You like soymilk, right?" she asks as she sets the coffee in front of me. "No sugar?"

I nod. "Perfect."

Lauren cringes. "That sounds bitterrific."

Mrs. Watkins smiles as she rounds the coffee table and sits

next to Lauren. "I agree. But Emma's been on a vegetarian kick, so she's making us all eat better. My quinoa casserole has a few more minutes in the oven. Should be right up your alley, Coach Trent."

As I retake my seat, I muse that the girl twin continues to sound more appealing than the one I'm stuck with.

Mrs. Watkins leans in. "What were you two whispering about like teenagers?"

Lauren fidgets with the sleeves of her jacket and rubs the hidden nicotine patch. I read somewhere that when smokers try to quit, they need something to do with their hands. I have a few activities in mind.

"Throw pillows," I answer. I thump the giant M on the pillow next to me. "Lauren isn't a big fan of this one."

Lauren meets my eyes with a grateful look.

"I can imagine," says Mrs. Watkins. "We need to buy a pillow with a block O on it to balance it out."

Gag. "No need for that."

Mrs. Watkins twirls her wedding ring as she studies us. "So, Coach Trent, Lauren tells me you two met in our driveway?"

"Yes, ma'am."

One side of Lauren's mouth lifts. Is she mocking me? Accustomed to my respectful address, Mrs. Watkins takes it in stride.

"And now you drove here together?" Evan's mother laces her hands together. "What made that happen?"

"I had—" A buzzer from the kitchen interrupts Lauren's explanation.

Mrs. Watkins hops to her feet. "Hold that thought—my casserole's done. Kids!" She strides toward the bottom of the stairs and hollers, "Dinner's ready!"

A few minutes later, we sit in the dining room facing plates of steaming casserole and salad. I'm in Mr. Watkins' usual place, across from Mrs. Watkins, with Evan on my left. Two thick turkey sandwiches sit on Evan's plate, in addition to the casserole. Emma pulled an extra chair from the corner and set it next to hers, placing Lauren on my right.

The quinoa enchilada dish looks mouthwatering, but the suspicious slant of Lauren's eyes as she studies the brown mixture tells me that she doesn't share my eagerness to dig in. Still, she picks up a fork and spears some black beans.

"Coach Trent." I look at Mrs. Watkins, who continues, "Would you say grace?"

Lauren jolts, seeming to echo my panic at the request, then lowers her fork to her plate. Her full lips quiver, and there's a hint of laughter in her voice as she says, "Yes, Coach Trent. Please say grace."

Twatwaffle. I'm going to get her for this. A glance at Evan shows the shine of amusement in his eyes as well. I take a deep breath as I close my eyes. "Lord, please bless this food...that Mrs. Watkins so kindly made for us." I sound like a total poseur, and my stomach gurgles. A Cub Scout grace enters my mind: *God is great, God is good, and we thank Him for this food.* Jesus, I can't say that. I need to step up my game.

I peek around the table and everyone's eyes are closed except for Lauren's, as she simpers at me. She sucks at this prayer thing.

I go on. "God, we're grateful for this opportunity to share a meal together. Breaking bread with those who differ from us is a chance to deepen our connection and caring for each other. We may root for different teams, but we all praise You. In your glory, love, and sacrifice. Amen."

The Watkins murmur, "Amen."

Lauren squirms in her chair.

"That was beautiful, Jeremy!" Mrs. Watkins beams as she places her napkin in her lap.

Yes! I've achieved first-name status.

I take a savory bite of tomatoes, corn, and quinoa, with cumin and other spices providing a punch of flavor. Evan's already halfway through his first sandwich. *Good boy.*

"This is yummy, Mom," says Emma.

After a swig of ice water, I nod. "I agree. So, Emma, you're a vegetarian now?"

She sits up. "Now and forever. It's the only way to go."

"That may be a bit strident, Em." Mrs. Watkins smiles at her. "You'll need a lot of protein with your intense practice schedule in college, and that might be difficult if you're not eating meat."

Lauren finds her voice. "You can meet with one of our sports dietitians—they'll help you figure it out. We have five of them at OSU."

Five? I frown.

"I bet Michigan has more than that," Evan speaks with his mouth full. "Right, Coach Trent?"

We only have two, but I don't want to admit that. "Football has our own dietitian. She's great."

"But how many total do you have?" he presses.

Ignoring him, I look at Evan's sister. "You can make vegetarianism work as an athlete, Emma. As you know, I've been vegan for years."

Lauren recoils, her lower lip turning down. "You *have*?"

Mrs. Watkins laughs. "I had the same reaction when Jeremy wouldn't eat my pot roast last year. Not something you expect from a football coach."

I watch Lauren. Does she think I'm weird?

She looks at Mrs. Watkins, and then her gaze flickers back toward me. "I'm sure he's just full of surprises. Can't wait to find out more."

Her hint of a smile shoots heat to my groin. I notice Evan looking back and forth at us.

"We got interrupted earlier," Mrs. Watkins says, "when I asked why you two drove here together."

Lauren sets down her fork as she glances at me. "I visited Coach Trent in Ann Arbor this afternoon." She pauses. "I needed to ask his forgiveness."

Evan stops chewing. "For what?"

I'm curious now. If she admits to snitching about my sister, her cigarette secret might go up in smoke.

"Oh…" Lauren rubs her jacket sleeve. "You know. Coach stuff. No need to get into the details." She sips her ice water.

Mrs. Watkins watches us with that little smile she wore earlier tonight. "So, did you grant her forgiveness, Jeremy?"

Lauren holds still as I consider my response. Do I forgive her for putting me in a situation in which my boss questioned my loyalty? Froth is hard on his assistants no matter what we do. That isn't her fault.

"Yes, I did."

Lauren's brilliant smile lights me up inside.

"I'm glad to hear it," says Mrs. Watkins. "Showing mercy like that—it's what God models for us. God forgave us of our sins so that *we* can forgive others when we're wronged." She smiles. "It's wonderful you found such divine forgiveness in your heart, Jeremy."

Whoa. Sometimes this family's religiosity feels over the top to me, but Mama W's words hit me on a deeper level this time. Lauren's transgression was minor and easy to forgive. But forgiveness doesn't come easily to me in other realms, like letting go of my anger toward my boss. Or my father. Maybe I should embrace faith a little more.

As I realize that Lauren and the family are still staring at me, I shift in my chair. "Evan, Coach Froth just asked me to check in on you. When Lauren said she wanted to visit Emma, we decided to drive down together."

Evan lowers his glass of milk and grins with a milk moustache, looking younger than his age.

"I'm curious, Emma..." Lauren turns to her recruit after taking a cautious bite of corn. "Why'd you become vegetarian?"

"Do you want to try it?" Emma almost bounces in her chair.

"Oh, hell, uh, *heck* no," Lauren answers. "I like meat way too much."

I swallow.

"But I do want to know more about my players—what you like and dislike, what makes you tick," Lauren adds.

Emma nods. "Well, I never want to hurt animals."

Mrs. Watkins' eyes crinkle as she gazes at her daughter. "Emma was just crushed when we had to put Bo down."

I think about the golden retriever that died shortly after I started recruiting Evan. He tried to hide his grief, but he suffered one of his only losses as a high-school quarterback the Friday after Bo passed. From Lauren's confused look, I gather she must've started recruiting later than I did and doesn't know this history.

"Emmy cried every night for weeks," Evan scoffs.

Emma and her mother frown at him, and I agree it was bad-mannered to point that out.

After a beat, Emma continues. "And the Bible says we shouldn't eat flesh or drink wine. But I didn't become vegetarian until we went to Peru last Christmas." When she pauses, her lip quivers.

Is the girl about to cry? I have no idea what to say. Lauren gives me a questioning look, but I shrug back at her.

Lauren's voice gentles as she pats Emma's shoulder. "What happened in Peru?"

"We... Gabriela and I—Gabriela was a girl in the host family—were playing with chickens in the yard, and there was this funny one named Lady Gaga who sounded like she was almost singing when she clucked."

I try not to laugh. A chicken named Lady Gaga? Lauren won't look at me, and I bet she's smothering her amusement as well.

Emma sniffs. "Then at dinner that night, they served a whole chicken...with its little feet still attached." Her voice shakes on the last word.

"Lady Gaga sure was deliciosa." Evan smacks his lips.

Mrs. Watkins clears her throat and glares at her son.

But Evan ignores her warning and taps his fork on his plate as he gives Lauren a tight smile. "So now we're stuck eating crap like this casserole every night."

"Evan." My sharp retort is out of my mouth before I can think. Instead of seeming angry that I stepped in, Mrs. Watkins nods at me to continue. "Your mother worked hard on this casserole. You should at least try it. It's really good."

"Seriously?" He blows out a breath. "Vegetarian food sucks. I don't know why you're forcing us to eat this disgusting shit." He gestures toward Lauren's full plate. "I bet the Ohio State coach doesn't even know how to spell *quinoa*." Evan disregards the intensifying heat from his mother's glower.

Lauren's lips part as our recruits stare at her. "Um…"

Apparently, Mrs. Watkins is too furious to speak. Should I rescue Lauren? I sit back in my chair. *Nah.* Let's see how that Ohio State education turned out.

"Um…" Lauren glances at me but finds no help there. "K, e—"

Evan's cackle interrupts her. "Wrong!"

"Evan. Watkins." Harsh words silence the boy's laugh as Mrs. Watkins rises from her chair. Evan freezes as he looks up at her, and even I wither from the venom in her narrowed eyes. But at some point, my manners kick in, and I get to my feet.

"You keep telling your father and me that you're a man now, Evan." Her icy tone nails him to the chair. "Is belittling our guest the behavior of a man?"

His cheeks flush, but he doesn't move.

"Evan." I hold out my palm and wave my fingers to the ceiling. "Stand when your mother speaks to you."

"Mom, I—"

She cuts him off as he scrambles out of his chair. "You didn't answer my question. Was your behavior manly tonight?"

"It's, it's not my fault I don't like your crappy cooking!"

Ooh, bad move, kid. He's digging his grave. Did I ever mouth off like this to my poor mother when I was his age? I hope not.

She shakes her head. "Disrespecting me and our guests, using unacceptable language, failing to take responsibility for your actions—you're not demonstrating the maturity you need for college."

Shit! Evan's parents won't stop him from going to UM, will they? I look at Lauren, whose wide eyes reflect my discomfort.

"I'll be fine once I'm away from *you*!" Evan rails.

"I pray that you will." Mrs. Watkins sighs. "Your father and I will discuss your punishment when he gets home. Suffice it to say that you won't be seeing your phone for quite some time."

Evan's jaw drops.

"Go to your room," adds his mother.

Evan's hands clench into fists. He's about to mouth off, but he glances at me, then at Lauren, and seems to rethink. Maybe he's growing aware of his petulant behavior. He storms off and thunders up the stairs.

Emma scoots her chair back and places her napkin to the side of her empty plate as she rises. I almost forgot she was here. "Thanks for visiting, Coach Chase and Coach Trent." She winces. "Sorry you had to see that." She heads for the stairs, and soon she has disappeared as well.

Lauren gets up from her chair, and we three stare at each other.

"Why did Emma leave, too?" Lauren asks.

Mrs. Watkins seems to deflate as she looks down at the table. She runs her hands through her long brown hair. "Tyler and I read it in a parenting magazine." A crease forms between her brows as she looks at us. "You build solidarity between siblings, especially twins, if you treat them the same. If one's in trouble, the other gets the same consequence. We had to relax that policy in high school or Emma would've never had her phone. But it seemed to work well when they were young. Emma helped Evan behave, and Evan protected her from the mean girls."

Her gaze travels to the window behind Evan's vacated chair, and the crease deepens into a look of guilt. "But then they started having all this athletic success. The attention on them has been insane. When Evan signed his scholarship offer, he changed. For the worse." She grimaces as her eyes dart to mine. "No offense, Jeremy."

"None taken. Everyone treats D-One football players like they're gods, but they're only boys."

"Exactly!" Mrs. Watkins thumps the top of her chair. "Evan started slacking at school, but we didn't find out about it for months, thanks to teachers worshipping him. He's been unbelievably cruel to Emma." The corners of her mouth lower. "Somehow she keeps standing by him. I wanted Emma to have her own opportunities, without worrying about her twin. It's one reason I steered her away from Michigan, toward Ohio State."

Despite the logic of that statement, I have to speak against it. "Okay, that *does* offend me."

"You definitely made the right choice," Lauren says.

Our responses earn a small grin from Mrs. Watkins. "Like my daughter, I want to apologize for putting you through that scene."

"That *was* intense." Lauren shudders. "You got any booze?"

I'm amazed when Mrs. Watkins laughs before she looks at Lauren's untouched food. "No, but I do have a turkey sandwich. Would you like one?"

"Sure! I'm partial to food I can spell."

Mrs. Watkins picks up her plate while Lauren and I grab the others to carry them into the kitchen.

"I guess this is God's great design." Mrs. Watkins places the plates into the sink. "Evan can't wait to move the heck out of my house, and I'm even more eager for him to leave for school." She shakes her head. "All with the goal of increasing independence, helping him grow."

I exhale, hoping her threat about not letting him go to school was an empty one. "Is it okay if I go talk to Evan?"

Mrs. Watkins hesitates. "I think that's all right. Tyler would normally be the one talking some sense into him, but maybe you can give him some fatherly advice."

I tense as I head for the stairs. I know nothing about being a good father.

I've seen Evan's bedroom on a prior home visit, so I know which door is his. After I knock, he calls, "What?"

He's sprawled on his twin bed when I enter, his ankles hanging over the edge. His dorm bed won't be much longer. He stares at the ceiling in the quiet room.

"Thought you'd be listening to music on earbuds," I say.

"She took everything," he grumbles as he scoots to sit up on his bed, arranging a pillow between his back and headboard. "Phone, laptop, tablet, earbuds…"

Damn. Mama W doesn't mess around.

"How're you supposed to study for your AP exams, then?" I take a seat on his desk chair.

He deepens his voice and lectures me. "They're called books, son." He holds up a Spanish Five textbook, and I gather that he's imitating his father. "If I need the laptop to study, Mom

74

or Dad has to supervise me."

I only got through Spanish Four in high school, but I attempt to use the language to ask whether one of his Advanced Placement exams is in Spanish.

"Sí." He squints. "Not that my score will matter."

I lean forward. "Why not?"

"If I get a good score, I'll have to take a more advanced Spanish class next year. Learning the offense will take up all my time, so I don't want to study for a harder class on top of that. Plus, if I get AP credit, I probably won't have a lightened course load till my junior or senior year, right? I'll be gone to the league by then."

He's thought this through way more than I expected from his snarky persona. No wonder he has insomnia. But his logic has some flaws.

"It's good to make a plan for your future," I say. "Your driven, forward-thinking nature is a big reason you are where you are." I tap his knee—even sitting up, his feet almost reach the end of the mattress. "But you're getting out over your skis. You're not living in the present."

His intense focus as he listens surprises me, and for once, he keeps his mouth shut.

"Two aspects of life we have no control over? The past and the future," I continue. "You throw an interception, it's in the past. You gotta let that go. You worry about winning the game, that's in the future. You gotta focus on the play in front of you."

He nods. His stats confirm that he has stellar focus as a QB. It's the rest of his life that needs help.

"Evan, you worry too much about the future. Let the future unfold; let it take care of itself. You'll be in the Spanish class that's best for you, and you'll do excelente. As far as making it to the NFL, you've got the skills—you're the best high-school quarterback I've seen. But—"

"Even better than Adrian Nichols?" he interrupts.

I wish Mr. Watkins hadn't discovered my friendship with him. Sometimes I wonder if Evan wants to play for me only because of Adrian's success. "Hard to compare. Adrian didn't play quarterback till his senior year of high school, so obviously his stats weren't as good as yours."

"Oh, yeah. He played receiver before that, right?"

I nod. "That was my college coach's strength: identifying hidden talent. Coach Hanlon knew Adrian didn't think like a receiver—he was star-quarterback material all the way." And in his wisdom, Coach knew my best quality was helping Adrian achieve that stardom. Coach made sure I was there for every QB meeting, drill session, and video review with my roommate.

Evan gets quiet. "Am I another Adrian Nichols?"

"No. You're an Evan Watkins—you'll forge your own path. But don't get ahead of yourself." I wait for him to meet my eyes. "There's a lot of real estate between high school and pro ball. There're countless things that can go wrong, no matter how hard you try."

His serious brown eyes analyze me, and he pops a question he's never asked me before. "Did you dream about making the league?"

I pause. "Of course. I watched guys around me get drafted, and I wanted that, too."

I worked my way into a starting role my junior year, but I lost it toward the end of senior year when a concussion took me out. My position coach told me I should try out at the NFL scouting combine, but Coach Hanlon steered me toward a graduate assistant coaching position at Central Washington University, where his friend was director of performance. I trusted my head coach, and if he didn't think I could make the league, I definitely couldn't make it. My concussions and back pain cemented the decision.

"But now I'm a coach," I add, "and that's a good place for me." I look at him. "Especially if I can help you become the best quarterback in the country."

A muscle in his jaw ticks as he holds my gaze, and I can almost hear the crackling of the fire in his belly. He wants it. He wants to prove himself.

"Let's get this straight right here." I incline forward in my chair. "If you ever talk to me or Coach Froth like you spoke to your mother tonight, you won't see *one second* of playing time."

His gulp is audible. "Yes, sir."

"Now, I need to get Coach Chase home." I push myself off of the chair.

He springs up from the bed, rising to his impressive height. "You actually *like* her?"

Twatwaffle. I don't want to discuss my potential romantic entanglements with a kid. "She's not bad."

"She's a Buckeye, though."

I cock an eyebrow. "So's your twin."

He grimaces. "Eughh. I'm trying to forget. How could Emma betray me like that?"

"Maybe it's not about you." I think about what Mrs. Watkins said earlier. "Maybe it's *Emma's* turn to shine." I let that sink in. "Emma needs you, you know? She needs your support." I thump his shoulder blade and order him to study in Spanish before I leave.

When I walk into the darkened hallway, I almost run into Mr. Watkins. Was he eavesdropping? He holds a finger to his lips, urging me to keep his presence on the downlow. Then he gestures for me to follow him down the stairs. At the base of the stairwell, he turns to me.

"Well said, Coach."

Was it? "How much did you hear?"

"Most of it, I think. I was coming up to chew him out, but you did it for me. More effectively than I would've, I might add. He actually listens to you."

My chest swells with pride. Evan's family seems more functional than the families of most boys I recruit, and his father praising me for my interaction with his son buoys me. I feel like I did when we crushed Michigan State last year. "You work long hours as athletic director, huh?"

"Too long." He shakes his head, and his eyes look bleary. "But maybe I can step down from being a teacher *and* AD once the kids are off to school."

"I can't imagine many high-school ADs also teach. That's a crazy schedule."

"Yeah, but I had to provide for my twins. Now, most of my friends are trying to figure out how to pay for college tuition." He grins.

The wonder twins' full-ride scholarships have removed that burden.

I hear Lauren and Mrs. Watkins murmuring in the kitchen, and Mr. Watkins must hear them as well, because his grin morphs into a frown. "What Evan asked you... You can't seriously be into to an Ohio State coach, right?"

Staying
Lauren

It's dark by the time Jeremy and I hit the road back to Ann Arbor, and his mood seems to reflect the blackening sky. He hasn't said a word for the past few miles. Was his earlier forgiveness of me just for show? Did I say something wrong? Maybe he's just tired, like I am, after trying to impress our recruits and their parents. I squint at my Mountain Dew bottle and see only one sip left. At least I'll be able to get a night's rest at Alex's place before I drive back to Columbus tomorrow.

"Jenna said they haven't told Michigan Emma's going to OSU yet," I venture. "Jim Dawson was really nice to them—hard to believe—and she doesn't want to let him down."

"He's not a bad guy, actually."

Well, Dawson *seems* like an ass whenever I encounter him. "Will you tell him Emma accepted the OSU scholarship?"

"Hell, no." He shakes his head. "Losing a recruit's one of the worst feelings, and I don't want to be the bearer of bad news. Besides, how am I supposed to know this information?"

I realize he doesn't want anyone to know he's been talking to me. That's probably wise, but it stings. I shrug. "Easy. Evan told you."

"Oh. Right." He turns to me. "What else did you and Mrs. Watkins, I mean *Jenna*, discuss?"

Jenna plied me with discomfiting questions about Jeremy: "*Are you attracted to him? Isn't he cute? Do you want a relationship with him?*" When I stared back at her, mute, or stuttered a few words, she tittered like a schoolgirl. "*Sorry to pry. I've been married over twenty years—I miss the excitement of*

79

the dating game."

There's nothing exciting about dating, lady, I'd wanted to say.

"You guys just make the most interesting couple," she'd added.

Do we? Are we indeed a *couple*? That seems like an overstatement. But the familiar flutter has returned to my body now that he sits so close again. I took off my jacket before I got into the car, leaving the nicotine patch exposed on the inside of my arm. I pick at it. "Jenna wanted to talk about a situation at work."

As it takes a while for Jeremy to respond, I wonder if he detects that I'm leaving out key content from my conversation.

"I've visited the family many times," he finally says. "But I'm embarrassed to say I don't know what she does for a living."

"I'm not surprised. She's super humble. I never knew what an amazing basketball player she was until yesterday, when Emma accepted the scholarship. I felt like an idiot."

He nods. "No doubt the twins get most of their talent from their mom."

"Mr. Watkins looks pretty athletic, too." My mouth twitches. "Even though he played at Michigan."

I feel his glare. "You're lucky you're driving, or I'd give you a noogie."

I remember him knuckling his sister's head back at Woody's. "You are a *child*."

He lets that slide. "So, what does Mama W do for a living?"

"She's director of human resources at a Toledo manufacturing company."

"What'd she want to talk to you about, then? Isn't the head of HR the one who makes life hell for people, not the other way around?"

I give him the stink eye. "Not if you're a woman managing men, and one of the men is a belligerent ballsack who wants to steal your job."

"Whoa." He leans away from me. "Have you ever had that happen with one of your assistant coaches?"

"Thankfully, no. Patrick's been quite loyal."

"He's been with you four years."

How does he know that? In the darkened car, I can make out a glint in his green eyes. "Have you been studying up on me, Coach Trent?"

"I'm good at scouting my opponents, Coach Chase."

His opponent? Is that how he sees me?

"What wisdom did you impart to her, then?"

I exhale. "My advice probably wasn't great. I told her to document everything and try to get closer to her boss, but who knows if that'll help. I'm clueless about corporate America." I consider her eagerness to hear my opinion. "I think she feels a kinship with me as another woman in charge or something."

"She likes you," he concurs. "She's more relaxed around you."

That feels good to hear. "Well, you seem like bros with Evan's dad."

He shrugs and grows quiet. The strain I felt at the beginning of the drive returns.

After a mile or two, I ask, "How'd your talk with the punk-ass go?"

He makes a scoffing sound. "Evan's just scared, that's all."

"*Scared*? He didn't seem that way to me."

"How would you feel if they talked about you on ESPN every night before you've even taken one snap?"

I consider that. Volleyball receives nowhere near the scrutiny of football, but the pressure Evan feels is still no excuse for his behavior.

He folds his arms across his chest. "Mr. Watkins listened in on some of our conversation, and he said I did well. I guess there's that."

I peer at him. "You don't agree?"

He keeps looking ahead and lifts one shoulder, like he's dismissing me.

I rub his arm as I lighten my voice. "You okay?"

Another mile goes by.

"Just thinking about...my dad." He blows air out his nose.

I try to remember our conversation at Woody's. "You said your dad wasn't there for you?"

"Nope." He looks at his lap. "He left us when I was ten." He looks out the window. "Taryn was only five."

I still my hand on his arm. *Wow.* What would it be like to have a parent bail like that? He keeps looking away from me, so I move my hand back onto the wheel. "He hasn't been part of your lives since then?"

Another huff. "He reached out after I got the Michigan job. Guess I was finally worthy enough for his attention. But I didn't respond to his voicemails." He moves his gaze to the windshield, and I notice the roll of his jaw muscle. "I lit into Taryn for giving the bastard my cell number." His left hand squeezes into a fist. "Brother of the year."

He's a big, strong guy, and his anger seems palpable, but I'm not frightened. I see right through the tension radiating off of him. It's not aggression—it's hurt. His father wounded him when he left.

I creep my hand toward his, and I exhale when he allows me to unfurl his fingers and intertwine them in mine. We hold hands for a moment before he looks at me.

"I'm sorry," I say as I stroke one of his knuckles. "You deserve better."

He holds my gaze. When he lifts our enjoined hands to his mouth, my breath catches. I savor the warmth of his lips as they press a kiss to the back of my hand. He watches me, an air of anticipation between us, then kisses my hand again. My skin burns with rising heat, spreading up my arm and into my body like the buzz from a delicious cocktail. Jeremy on the rocks, with a twist of lime.

A honk yanks my attention back to the road. "Shit!" I grab the wheel with both hands and swerve back into my lane. My heartrate accelerates even more. When the right lane's clear, I ease the car out of the passing lane and let the honker fly by us on the left. "Sorry." I wince. "I was, um, distracted."

"Me, too."

The amusement in his deep voice is a total turn on, making

me want to jump onto his lap. We'll be lucky to make it back to Ann Arbor alive.

He points to the speedometer. "You're actually going the speed limit."

"There's a first time for everything." Like the first time he kissed my hand. Will all of his kisses feel so tender? I glide my index finger along my lower lip as I consider the possibilities. *"I'm sure he's full of surprises,"* I told Jenna earlier tonight. When I look back at him, he's staring at my mouth. His eyes slide up to meet mine with a look of hunger. The next thirty or so miles are going to be a challenge.

"You, uh..." I clear my throat. "You were talking about your dad?"

As a muscle tightens near his eyes, I wish I could snatch back that question.

After a silence, he speaks. "I made out fine without him, but it's been hard on my mom. And Taryn. She barely knew him when he left." His lips press into a hard line. "They definitely deserved better."

He doesn't *seem* fine, but I let him hold on to his pride. "Where does your mom live?"

"Chicago."

I remember his coach bio. "That's where you're from, right?"

He nods. "And you're from Cincinnati."

"Stalker much?"

He grins as he scoops my hand back into his. "Scouting, not stalking." My hand feels at home, cocooned in his large paw. I bet he was good at blocking and catching passes with those big hands. "How'd you like growing up in the 'Nati?"

He knows my hometown's nickname? *Oh.* He probably steals recruits from there as well. "It was okay. I still talk to a few club teammates, but I don't really stay in touch with people from home. Except for Alex."

"Alex?"

"My friend in Ypsilanti."

He strokes my hand. "What does he do there?"

"He works in compliance for Eastern Michigan University

Athletics."

"He's an attorney?" asks Jeremy. When I nod, he raises his chin. "Sounds smart."

I love the ease of our conversation. As a college coach, Jeremy gets my world. He knows how lonely and difficult recruiting can be, how nerve-wracking it is to have my job on the chopping block depending on the performance of kids with undeveloped frontal lobes. And, he understands what it means to work in compliance for an athletic department, helping staff and student-athletes follow NCAA rules.

"He's cool with you spending the night at his place?"

I shrug. "I figured I'll call him after I drop you at your car."

He waits a beat. "You don't want me to overhear your conversation?"

"I, uh, don't care about that." I divert my gaze. Alex is an acquired taste.

"You sure?"

"Yep."

He stares at me. "You got something to hide, Chase?"

What? "Fine! I'll call him." I let go of his hand and dial my high-school friend from my steering wheel.

Alex picks up on the second ring. "Lori, darling! I miss your beautiful face. How the shitake are you, bitch?"

Jeremy's eyes widen at the greeting. Ambient background noise fills the car—it sounds like Alex is at a busy restaurant.

"I'm good!" I need to alert him that I'm not alone so that he might at least try to behave himself. "I'm with a..." I glance at Jeremy. What to call him? "A...friend." I wince. That's not the best description—we seem beyond friends now. Besides, I can't be friends with a Wolverine.

"A frrriennnnd?" Alex purrs, and I close my eyes for a second. He's constantly on my case to get a man. "Male or female?"

Jeremy sits back in the car seat and watches me with a fat grin, appearing to enjoy my squirming.

"He's a coach, and we're, uh, recruiting together."

Alex's voice lilts. "Ahhhh."

"I'm in Michigan, actually."

"Cookie crunchfuck!" Alex's tone sharpens. "Why didn't you tell me you were visiting, you whore?"

Thankfully, Jeremy chuckles. *This* is why I wanted to wait till later to call Alex. "It was kind of spontaneous, and I find myself without a place to sleep tonight." I bite my lip. "Is it okay if I stay with you?"

"Exactly why I called you a ho, bitch! I'm *not* in Michigan. I'm in Indianapolis for NCAA meetings. I won't get to see you."

"Oh." I slump against my seat. Why didn't I call Alex on my drive up to Michigan? Probably because I didn't know if Jeremy would accept my invitation. "That's okay. I can get a hotel room."

Alex is quiet for a moment. "I did meet this attorney the other night—girl, he's hawt. I can ask him if he could take you in, but I don't know him all that well, so maybe a hotel is the way to—"

"Lauren's *not* staying in a hotel," Jeremy butts in.

I turn to look at him, and his eyes peg me to my seat.

"She's sleeping at my place tonight," adds Jeremy. "In my bed."

Thump, thump, thump bangs my heart. *Holy shit.* I press the brake so I don't rear-end the car in front of me.

"Well, well, Mr. Coach Man." Suspicion creeps into Alex's voice. "You live in Ypsilanti?"

"Ann Arbor." Jeremy glances at me. "I mean, I'll be on the sofa, of course. But you shouldn't stay in a hotel when I have a perfectly good bed."

Oh. I let out a breath as my heartrate slows. I was freaked out at the idea of sleeping together, but now I'm...disappointed.

Alex jumps into lawyer mode. "What's this guy's name, Lori? What sport does he coach, and where?"

Jeremy and I look at each other.

"He's a good guy, Alex," I blurt. "Listen, I can hear you're busy, so I'll let you go. Don't worry about me. I'll find a hotel tonight."

"We're waiting for the check—I've got some time. Tell me more about yourself, Mr. Coach Man." Alex has dropped his misgivings, and his voice resumes its salacious tone. "You sound like a bigger guy, maybe?"

I can't deal with both of these men at once; I long to dig out a cigarette and light it. Thinking about it makes my fingers twitch. "Good luck in Indy, Alex. Bye!"

"Bitch, you better tell me *everything*—"

The button on my steering wheel ends the call. I keep my eyes on the road, not daring to look at Jeremy. What will *everything* entail after tonight? Is Jeremy hoping we'll have sex?

Should we have sex? If we do, how will it be? I've wanted to get a look at those footballer muscles since I met him, but I'm rusty. And, if I tell him about the last man I was with, Jeremy may want nothing to do with me.

If we do the deed, what will he expect from me? Will he want me to visit him, take time away from my job, take care of him? I'm not sure I want to add another person to my life who needs something from me. My parents, my assistant coaches, and my team seem like enough responsibility on my shoulders.

Somehow I find my way back to Schembechler Hall, despite my emotional turmoil. My car must have known the route since my team plays at this hostile campus every year. I pull up next to Jeremy's black SUV, one of the only cars left in the lot.

I gulp as I feel his eyes on me. Should I take him up on his proposal? Does he really want me in his home? He only offered his place after I said I'd get a hotel room. But I don't want a hotel. I'd rather sleep in my own bed.

His words break my inner monologue. "Thanks for driving."

"Sure." Lights near the building's rafters glitter in his eyes. *Jizzpickle*. There's a stillness in the air between us, like he's about to kiss me, and my lips tingle with anticipation. The tremble in my chest makes it hard to breathe.

Before I know it, I've opened the car door and climbed out. "Thanks for coming with me." My words sound rushed, and with a brisk motion, I shut the door.

I stare with horror at the driver's side window. *I'm so fucked up*. I wish I could shut down my feelings as easily as I slammed the door, but embarrassment floods me.

He sits in my car, unmoving, and I close my eyes. What the

fuck is my problem? I *want* him to kiss me. I want him to hold me. Why did I just haul myself out of my car like my hair was on fire? Why did I get out of *my own car* at all? Why am I such a wuss?

After a beat, he unfolds his muscular frame from the passenger seat. A slight wince crosses his face as he extends to his full height, and I'm not sure if the source of the pain is his back or his ego. But as he leans on the open car door and peers at me over the top of the vehicle, his eyes seem to dance with curiosity.

My cheeks burn, the longer he watches me, and goose bumps prickle my bare arms. He's going to get into his car and drive away, and I'll probably never see him again. *Way to go, Chase.* This push-pull inside is driving me crazy. I need ten cigarettes, smoking them all at once.

He slings his briefcase strap over his shoulder and closes the door. When he hesitates for a moment, my heart sinks. This is goodbye.

But then he crosses around the hood of the car, coming closer as he jangles his keys in his hand. "You don't need to go to a hotel, seriously. You can follow me to my place."

"I'm not getting a hotel room—I'm gonna drive back tonight. I only said that so Alex wouldn't worry about me."

Jeremy frowns. "And make *me* worry about you?"

Fucknuts.

"You won't get to Columbus till after midnight," he says. "I won't sleep well knowing you're out there driving ninety miles an hour."

I study him. "You don't have to worry."

"But I will. Besides, you're out of caffeine." He gestures to my front seat. "You need a new Dew."

It's unnerving how he notices everything. I pat my hair like I didn't understand him. "I need a new 'do?"

"No, I love your hair." When he steps toward me, my heart skitters—just like I felt when he approached me outside the Watkins' house.

But he's not a stranger now. He's not the jerkwad Michigan

coach I thought he was. Why can't I give him a chance? Why can't I give us a chance?

"Sorry," I breathe. He comes closer. "I'm bad at this stuff."

He sets down his briefcase and glides his hands up and down my arms, warming them. "Bad at what?"

My breath catches at his touch, and I lean toward him. "Bad at…" He's so close that the subtle musk of his aftershave floats toward me. Looking up at him, I'm beholden to his deep gaze, the magnetism of his presence. "Kissing," I murmur.

"No way that gorgeous mouth of yours could be bad at kissing." He smirks. "I'll prove it to you."

Yes. I didn't screw up tonight after all. But he hasn't moved in yet. He's still looking at me. What's he waiting for?

I arch an eyebrow. "You said you'd prove it to me, but now I'm thinking you're even slower than your receivers."

A slow grin spreads over his mouth. "There's that sass." He lets go of my arms to comb his fingers through my hair, feathering strands back from my face. His warm palms cradle my cheeks, and my heartbeat soars as he lowers his lips to mine.

I close my eyes, pressing into him. His lips are firm, and I yield to their touch. As he deepens the kiss, my hands slide up his back to hook over his shoulders. Beneath the sheen of his windbreaker, I feel the breadth of his back and trapezius muscles as our bodies meld together. His heat envelops me, an electric charge surging energy up my spine.

In the distance, I hear an engine, but a deep rumble in Jeremy's throat draws my attention back to his pliant lips. It's too easy to lose myself in him. *Hot damn*, the man can kiss.

A car horn makes us both jump, and I yelp as we pull apart. The car's brakes light up the darkness about fifty feet away from our spot, and the male driver yells something about PDA, laughs, then peels out of the lot.

Jeremy covers his mouth. "Shit," he mutters. "I hope that wasn't a football player."

I lift his hand from his mouth, fold it between mine, and kiss the back, mimicking his earlier gesture with me. "If he is, he'll have to get used to it. Coaches are allowed to have lives, too. We can drink vodka, go on a date…"

"A date?" He extends his arm across my shoulders and tucks me into his side, warming and protecting me. "Does that mean you'll drop the crap about driving to Ohio tonight and come home with me?"

He sees through my bullshit, which is tender and frightening all at once. The twinge of uncertainty in my gut fades as I admit to myself that I don't want to go back to my empty house. I want to be with him. "Fuckmuffin, yeah."

His bright smile lights up his eyes.

We're doing this. I swallow. "I'm warning you, though…if you have ugly Michigan throw pillows like the Watkins do, I'm gonna burn them."

Sleeping
Jeremy

When Lauren halts just inside my door, I freeze as well. Does my place still smell like the Brussel sprouts I roasted last night? Is she having second thoughts? Will she abandon me to stay at a hotel after all?

I rush over to the sofa to straighten the navy afghan folded over the corner cushion. My living space is comfortable, but it's not as high-end as it should be given my salary. I've devoted a chunk of my income to paying off Taryn's psychology master's program. I don't want loans hanging over her head as she starts her doctoral studies. I also help out my mom when I can.

"So neat and tidy!" Lauren marvels.

I lower my shoulders and remind myself to be patient with her. I decided back in her car that I've got to stop assuming she wants to run away every time she hesitates. She's touched and teased me too many times to lack any romantic interest. But something is making her skittish. Taryn told me Lauren hasn't dated in years, according to Sam. Maybe she's out of practice due to her hectic coaching schedule.

I haven't had much time for romance, either.

"Well, I'm never home," I tell her. "I'm always on the road or at the facility."

"I work long hours, too, but that makes my house messier, not cleaner. At least that's my excuse for why my house is a pigsty. I just don't have time to clean. How do you do it?"

I set down her duffle bag. I've never allowed my living space to be a mess. "I like my life to be orderly, I guess."

She rubs her thumb over her nicotine patch as a crease forms between her eyebrows. *Why is she worried?* She's staring at my sofa. Taryn bought me the navy-and-red plaid accent pillows.

"No need for a Michigan-pillow bonfire tonight."

"They go well with the color of your sofa." She taps the denim cushions as she looks around. "Do you have any pets?"

I grimace. "I'd love a dog, but like I said, I'm never home."

"Me, too. I've always wanted a Goldendoodle. They're so goofy."

I gesture for her to sit, and she complies.

"What kind of dog would you like?" she asks.

"I like pugs." I join her on the sofa but leave plenty of space between us. She's been the queen of mixed signals, so I'm going to let her dictate any action tonight, even though my lips still burn from that scorching kiss. *Please* make a move. Please don't make me chase you, Chase.

The corner of her mouth angles down. "You know some pugs eat poop, right?"

I recoil. "They do?"

"Yeah. Totally gross. This head coach I worked for had two dogs, and his pug snarfed down the other dog's doodoo, if he didn't stop him."

Okay, maybe I don't want a pug. "You worked for a male head coach? Where was that?"

Her amused smile fades, and she lowers her eyes. "UF."

Her voice is so quiet that I'm not sure I heard her correctly. "Florida?"

"My first coaching job—I was a grad assistant." She aims a tight smile my way. "You were at GA at Central Washington, right?"

So, she's read up on me, too. "Yes. But where are my manners? What can I get you to drink, Coach?"

She taps her chin. "How about a cocktail? I could use one after our recruiting visit."

"I probably have vodka," I offer. But I don't have an icemaker in my aging fridge, so that won't work. "Too bad I didn't know you were visiting, or I would've bought a vat of limes."

She grins.

"Beer, or how about wine? I have a bottle of pinot noir."

"Sounds delish."

I'm back in a flash with two glasses of red. I own only two wine glasses, and it's been almost a year since I've used both of them at once. A fellow assistant coach set me up with his wife's sister, and I had her over after our second date. I consumed almost the entire bottle on my own in an attempt to drown out her vacuous, nonstop chatter. She worked in a jewelry store and kept talking about the size of her sister's diamond wedding ring. It seemed she'd recently realized that football coaches pull in a good salary. She gushed about how big her sister's house would be if her brother-in-law became head football coach somewhere.

I'd jettisoned her after that night because I have no need for gold-digger jock-sniffers. They remind me too much of my college football days.

"Cheers," Lauren says with a smile.

I'm relieved to see she's kicked off her shoes and curled her legs under her as she settles into the sofa. I tap her glass with mine. "To Wolverine wins."

Her eyes narrow, but she takes a sip without questioning whether I've poisoned her drink. We're making progress, people.

"Very good," she says. "I mean, I know jack shit about wine, but I like this. What is it?"

"It's called Meiomi, from California."

Her mouth quirks up on one side. "I didn't know vegans could drink wine?"

The hint of challenge in her expression amuses me. "It's vegan wine, sweetheart."

"No shit?" She holds out the glass and studies it. Then she takes another sip, drawing my attention to her lips curving around the rim. When she lowers the glass, I notice a stain of plummy garnet deepening her lipstick. I want to taste the notes of strawberry and mocha on her mouth. I want those perfect lips on me.

"Like I said, Trent, you're just full of surprises." Her blue eyes sparkle, encouraging me to drum up more ways to keep her on her toes. "You're not the stereotypical football coach, that's for sure. For one, you're vegan—how strange. Secondly, your bachelor pad's spotless. How is that possible? And then you tell me you want a small, yippy dog?"

"Pugs aren't yippy," I retort. I scowl after I take a sip of wine. "But this new information about their nutritional habits decreases their appeal, I have to admit. What happened with the Florida coach's pug? Did his dog ever stop snarfing poop?"

Lauren studies her wine. "I don't know."

"You don't keep in touch with him?"

"*Fuck*, no."

I'm taken aback by the sharp clip of her voice. Her thick swallow, followed by a blush on her cream cheeks, indicates her forceful response surprised her, too.

"He's not a good guy?" I guess.

She turns to stare at a framed image of Sedona, Arizona's red rocks on my wall. I'd love to hike there one day, if I ever have time. "It was as much my fault as his."

What was her fault? What the hell happened with this coach? I attempt to let out the tension building in my chest with a long exhale. "Do you want to talk about it?"

She shrugs. After a beat, she slugs the rest of her wine, and I notice a tremble in her hand. She probably wants a cigarette, and I wonder if I should tell her it's okay to smoke at my place, if she needs it. But she's made it this far tonight, and I don't want to enable her habit if she really does want to quit. I give her a moment by hopping up and retrieving the wine bottle from the kitchen.

"He was married," she says after I pour her a refill. She places her glass on the coffee table, next to mine. Her blush deepens. "But he got a divorce."

I wonder why she won't look me in the eye. "Lots of coaches divorce. All the long hours and travel."

Her eyelids snap shut. "That wasn't it." She shakes her head as she looks at the ceiling. "Or maybe it was the company he kept on the long hours of travel." Her slow swivel to face me seems to take a lot of effort. She watches me for a minute. "He divorced because he and I had an affair."

Whoa. That's some heavy history for her to carry around. Her guilty eyes linger on me, studying my reaction, and she seems so vulnerable that I reach out to stroke her cheek. Her face is hot to the touch, burning with embarrassment. She doesn't lean into my palm, still watching me with wary eyes.

"You were, what, twenty-two?"

She nods. "Old enough to know better." She pulls away from my touch.

"And how old was he?"

She takes a sip of wine. "Forty-two."

I dip my head. "Quite the age difference."

"I'm…" She blows out a breath. "I'm not sure what I was thinking. He's a brilliant coach—he really knows the game. I wanted to learn everything I could from him. But he was a tyrant to his players. Not as much of an ass as my college coach—nobody could top that."

Bill Froth might come close.

"I tried to help him understand female athletes better," she continues. "I couldn't backtalk my college coach if I wanted any playing time, but this time *I* was the coach. I found the courage to stand up for the girls—they didn't deserve his condescending crap. And one time after he was particularly douchey, he and I got into it in his office. We were yelling at each other, and all of the sudden he kissed me. I was shocked." She looks more troubled than enamored, her forehead lined.

"Did you want him to kiss you?"

She flinches. "I…" The line deepens as she stares into space. She takes a peek at me before squeezing her arms around her midsection. "Maybe not?" Her voice is barely above a whisper. Her lips thin. "He had really bad breath."

Gross. The more I hear about this guy, the more I dislike him.

She unfolds her arms. "Who knows what I wanted—I was so young." Her hands twist in her lap. "I did want to win, though. And after he kissed me, he was more relaxed. He was nicer to the team, and they started playing better." Her chin quivers. "I let him kiss me more times. It became exciting, wondering if we'd get caught. He knew so much more about the world than I did.

I was swept up in him, but I couldn't talk to anyone about him, or about us."

The words spill out of her, and I don't want to interrupt. But an uncomfortable knot grows in my gut as she tells me more about this coach. I force my grip on the wine glass to relax as I take a sip.

"Then we made the elite eight, and…" She looks down. "We did more than kiss." Her cheeks flame with color again. "Paul liked to sneak cigarettes in the hotel room—he said his wife would kill him if she knew. I started smoking with him, uh, after we…" Her throat moves. "How cliché."

So, smoking is a reminder of this shameful time of her life? A way to punish herself for her moral imperfections? If I have any say about it, I don't want her smoking another cigarette.

"It wasn't till the next summer that his wife caught us together." She shudders and doesn't speak for a few moments. "I was able to finish my master's degree from afar, thankfully, but it was too late to find another job. I had to go home to Cincinnati and live with my parents."

From her grimace, I gather that wasn't pleasant. "You didn't like living with them?"

"They don't get along." She sighs. "But I was used to their arguments." She chews on her lip. "Her phone calls were what made it so bad."

My eyebrows furrow when she doesn't continue. "Whose phone calls?"

"Paul's wife."

"She called your *home?*" I retract my chin.

"Repeatedly." She rubs her forehead. "She told my parents how I'd wrecked her family. She and Paul had two young children!" Her head lowers, and she curls into herself. "My mom went ballistic—the affair was bad enough, but she berated me more for having premarital sex. My mom's super old-fashioned. But my dad…"

When her lower lip trembles, I want to reach out to her. But she scoots to the end of the sofa as tears start to spill from those beautiful blue eyes. I ache for her. All I can think about is that if some creepy older man seduced Taryn right out of college, I'd want to eviscerate him.

She wipes beneath one eye. "My dad didn't say anything, but I knew he was so disappointed in me. Sports are our thing. Our way to connect. And I'd gone and fucked it up." She sniffs. "I totally lucked out when the UC assistant job came open two months later."

She was at the University of Cincinnati for three years before she became head coach there at the tender age of twenty-seven. After winning the conference and qualifying for the NCAA tournament two years in a row, she nabbed the Ohio State position, leading the Buckeyes to a national championship two years later. I had no idea her triumphant coaching career had such painful origins.

I inch toward her, and she turns to face me. "I'm sorry you had to go through that." I think about how sweet she was in the car after I confessed about my dad. "You deserve better than that lecherous prick."

She angles back from me. "It was my fault. I was a consenting adult."

"He was twenty years older! He took advantage of you."

Her glassy eyes narrow as her lips part, staring at me like I got it all wrong.

"Listen, I understand you did some things you're not proud of." I take a deep breath and try to find the right words to convey the complexity of the situation. "You made mistakes. But this is not all your fault. He had a lot more life experience, like you said. He was in a position of power over you. Did you think you might get fired if you refused his kiss?"

She starts, then frowns. The stillness of her body makes me wonder if she's ever asked herself that question before.

She looks so hurt and confused that I long to comfort her. With my thumb, I slide a tear away from her cheek. This time she leans into my hand. "No wonder you've been so hot and cold with me," I muse.

"Sorry." She winces. "I suck at this."

"He really messed you up, huh?" I clasp her hands in mine.

She blinks at me, and I feel a slight quiver in her hands.

"You haven't been with a man since then?"

Her eyes widen, and I realize she wants to keep that information hidden deep inside.

"I haven't dated much, either," I rush to add. "Like I said, not enough time." The tension in her hands and the taut contours around her eyes tell me I need to articulate myself better. "What I'm trying to say is, I've never been with a woman who intrigues me like you do. Who's as sexy and strong as you are."

One eyebrow cocks. I just complimented her, so why does she look so skeptical? "Is my breath bad or something?"

Her head shake is quick, her smile slower. "You smell yummy."

I chuckle. "I think you smell good, too. Must be pheromones."

"It's just…" She exhales. "You said you like things to be in order." She lets go of my hands and sweeps her arm out toward the room, then down her body. "I'm *not* orderly. I'm a mess."

"Maybe I like some messes." I wait for her eyes to meet mine. "Especially *hot* messes like you."

She squints at me for a long moment. Her tears have dried, and I don't know what she's thinking. In a second, she's on top of me. Her lips mold over mine, and her breasts press into my torso. I cradle my arm around her back as I scoot toward the opposite armrest, pulling her on top of me as we lengthen on the sofa and deepen the kiss. And what a kiss it is. I thought what we shared by her car was exciting, but now the overwhelming closeness of our bodies billows the intense fire of our attraction.

Her fingers slide up my neck and into my hair, sending a tingle down my spine. I clutch the small of her back—she has to know the effect she's having on me as our bodies writhe together—and my other hand combs through her blond locks. The tip of her tongue glides across my lower lip as her warm breath floats across my skin.

Maybe she's been through a dry spell, but her wet mouth on me feels confident and skilled. Her kisses crash through my defenses, and I can't get enough of her. In this moment, there are no more mixed signals.

"Mmm..."

Sweet Jesus. Her little hum of contentment fans the flame of arousal.

Her lips tuck into the corner of my mouth, then skate up my jaw, feathering kisses along my stubble. I feel her hand at my hip a moment before her warm touch slides under my waistband and into my boxers. When she cups my hip bone and her fingers move south to my butt cheek, I almost buck off the sofa.

Her blue eyes, so close to mine, gaze down at me with a questioning look. To reassure her, I reach to her lower back and tug her gray shirt free from her pants. Her coach clothes are much easier to dissemble than the typical frilly outfits women wear. Now I get to feel *her* skin. My hands dive under the back of her shirt and head up toward her bra. She must like my long strokes on her back because she resumes kissing me.

With roving hands, soft touches, and building heat, I'm not sure how long we make out before a vibration between us halts our steamy wriggling.

"Sorry." Lauren reaches into her pants pocket and extracts her phone. "It might be one of my players." But she scowls when she sees caller ID. "It's my mom. Ugh." She sighs as the phone continues to buzz. "If I don't answer, she might keep calling."

"Go ahead." My voice sounds raspy and a little breathless. My racing heart begins to slow as she peels herself off of me to sit up and take the call.

From her clipped tone, followed by a swig of wine, I gather she's annoyed. I notice her empty glass and decide to refill it. There's an unexpected tremble in my legs as I walk into the kitchen to retrieve the bottle of pinot. *Damn.* The woman is undoing me.

"Thank you," she mouths as I pour her another glass. She grabs the wine the second I lift the bottle and downs another sip. Into the phone, she says, "He didn't mean it that way, Mom." Her mother's response seems to irritate her further as she slides down, thumps the back of her head on the top of the sofa, and extends her legs to the floor in front of her.

Our canoodling has pushed one leg of her black athletic

pants up to her knee, revealing the long, lean muscles of her calf. I want those gorgeous legs wrapped around me. Because she's still on the phone, I settle for sitting next to her and reaching for her exposed leg. She watches me as I cup her smooth calf and ease her leg across my lap. I take a few tentative strokes of her shin, adding in some gentle kneading of her sock-covered foot. Her eyes darken as her soft smile grows.

"Of course," she tells her mother. She swivels toward me and lifts her other leg onto my lap to join the first. I push that pant leg up to her knee as well, earning a view of slender, sculpted beauty. My hands glide across her silky skin, over the slight curve of her calves. She lets her head fall back to the pillow on the opposite end of the sofa. When I massage her left instep, she whimpers.

Her eyes pop open. "Um…" She swallows. "Just watching TV." She averts her gaze. "Yeah, I'm at home."

I pause my foot massage. Why did she conceal her whereabouts? Surely her mother isn't opposed to her being with a man at age thirty-six. My mother keeps asking me when I'll settle down with a girl, and I'm three years younger than Lauren.

"Listen, I gotta go—I have to be up early tomorrow." She sits up and gives me a half-smile before lowering her feet to the floor and righting herself on the sofa. "Just tell Dad he has to clean his own bathroom." Her jaw ticks as the call continues. "Mom, I said I have to go." A few more moments elapse, and I hear her mother's voice drone on before Lauren says, "Okay, love you. Bye!"

She shakes her head after she hangs up. "She is *so* exasperating. Impossible to end a call with that woman." With a huff, she gets to her feet and crosses behind the sofa to unzip her duffel bag. Holding her phone charger, her eyes dart around the room, landing anywhere but on me. She seems a thousand miles away.

I sigh and point to my bedroom. "There's an outlet in the other room." As I rise, I ignore a burning stab in my sacroiliac joint. *Huh.* Interesting that I didn't notice one iota of back pain during our make-out session. "You said you have an early morning, right? Let's get you to bed." I pick up the strap of her bag.

"Why don't I sleep out here on the sofa?" she asks as she trails me into the bedroom. Her voice lightens to a teasing tone after I turn on the light. "Figures you make your bed every morning."

I follow her stare to the queen-size bed covered by a light-gray duvet with navy stripes. It's neat, but it's lonely. "I said *I'd* take the sofa, remember?"

She leans down to connect her phone charger to the outlet, then straightens and glances around the room as she fiddles with the edges of her nicotine patch.

"Do you need another patch?" I ask.

She shakes her head. "What about your back pain? You should sleep on the mattress, not the sofa. Tell the truth—your back hurts, right?"

She's asking if *I'm* telling the truth? I set her bag on the bed. "Why'd you lie to your mother about where you were tonight?"

As she steps backwards, she scowls. "I had no other choice. If I told her I was returning to Columbus, she'd worry about me driving at night. Or she'd worry about me driving while talking on the phone. I can't tell her I'm at Alex's because she's homophobic. And if I said I was spending the night with a straight man..." Her hands twist. "She'd worry about my virtue."

I've overheard her lie to both Alex and her mother in the span of an hour. She claimed it was to prevent their worries, but the lies bother me all the same. I inch toward her. "So, if you think I'll worry about you, will you lie to me, too?"

Her eyebrows slant together, and she answers too quickly, "Of course not."

"I don't believe you." She slumps. "If we're going to make this work between us, you need to be honest with me." I gesture back and forth.

"Us?" she squeaks, then clears her throat. "There's an us?"

I inch closer. "I want there to be an us."

After watching me a moment, she takes a deep breath. "Okay. Honesty." Her voice trembles, but a determined look flares in her eyes, and she approaches me. When she starts to unzip my jacket, I grow still. "If we're being honest, I must confess that I want a good look at you." She peels the jacket over my shoulders and down my arms, shucking it to the floor. "Whoops, you like things organized." She scoops up the jacket and hangs it on the closet door. She unbuttons my white shirt. Soon, I stand before her wearing only my khakis.

She traces a line beneath my pectoral muscle, and I fight the urge to pull her into my arms. But my gut tells me to let her run the show.

"Honestly?" She looks up at me with a seductive smile. "You're even better than I expected. Most coaches have dad bods, but you must spend all your free time in the weight room, Coach Trent."

"Pretty much," I confirm. I'm not as cut as I was when I played, but I try to treat my body well.

She rests her palms on my chest, and I wonder if she can feel my heartbeat. "Honestly, I want you to sleep in this bed with me tonight."

My heart thrums double-time.

"Honestly, I, I'm too fucked up, too fucking anxious and worried about screwing this up, to have sex with you right now, okay?" She blinks up at me, and I nod. "But if *you're* being honest, your back is hurting you—you need your bed. And, honestly, you want me to sleep in your bed with you tonight."

I smile down at her. "Honestly, yes."

After the requisite teeth brushing and pajama donning—I'm in my boxers, and she's in a T-shirt and shorts—we climb under the covers. As her back nuzzles up to my chest, we snuggle into an easy spoon. I've felt aroused for most of the night, and her soft skin and clean smell invading my senses doesn't help the situation. But there's also a sense of tenderness and rightness I've never felt with a woman before. I hope this isn't the only night she shares my bed.

She lets out a long sigh. "O-H-I-O."

I squeeze her tighter as I grin. "Go, Blue."

Buzzing
Lauren

Dana's light brown eyes shine with excitement as she describes a new drill she wants to practice today. "I bet Emma will pick it up right away."

I look at my assistant coach, sitting across from me in my office. "The setter spikes the second ball instead of setting it?" My phone buzzes on the desk.

Dana nods.

"We run that play all the time. What's so special about this variation?" I pick up my phone. Now *I'm* buzzing as I see it's a text from Jeremy. It's late May—about a month since I've seen him. Each time we text or video call, I grow more attached. I'm alarmed by how much I miss him.

How's your wonder twin?

I grin. We're both thrilled that Jenna released Emma and Evan from their Toledo home once they graduated from high school. Now that they're on our campuses early, neither of us can get enough time teaching our young stars before the fall season starts. I reply:

Exceeding my expectations, if you can believe that.

Preach. Evan's the real deal.

Emma's gonna help us crush every Big Ten team.

There's only ONE Big Ten team we can't wait to crush.

My grin expands.

"Lauren."

I look up to see Dana's head tilted, her brown hair touching her shoulder. "Have you listened to one word I've said?"

I place my phone face down on my desk. "Sorry. Go ahead."

"This play's different because it's a quick-set, and the setter uses her opposite hand to spike. The defense will never see what's coming." She hops out of the chair and turns to one side, her right shoulder facing me like she's standing at the net. She gets into position. Dana was a talented setter for a small college in Ohio, even though she's only five-foot-five. She jumps, as if to set the ball to the hitter, but instead her left hand slams toward me to mimic spiking the ball over the net.

"Ooh, I like that." My phone vibrates, but I ignore it. "What's the drill you want to run today, then?"

She starts explaining, and I try to listen, but my attention drifts back to my phone. When it vibrates again, I slide it off my desk and peek at the screen, finding two more messages from Jeremy.

Thinking of visiting Taryn for Memorial Day.

Yes! My heart trots a giddy-up as I realize he'll be in Columbus this weekend.

But maybe you're busy.

No! I type a quick reply:

I'd LOVE to see you.

I peer at my text. Maybe I shouldn't have gone for all caps? Am I coming on too strong?

"Who're you texting?"

I gulp as I look up. Dana stands with her hands on her hips, peering at me. "Um...ah..."

"What's going on with you? I've never seen you like this."
She rubs her chin. "Patrick said you've been acting weird—"

"He *did*?" *Fucknockers.* I need to get myself under control.

She reaches for my phone. "Who's got you all distracted?
Let me see."

I scramble to my feet as I slip my phone into my pocket. "Just
my...dad." My pocket vibrates, and I'm dying to read Jeremy's
reply. "My dad, um, he said he was coming up to Columbus, to
visit this weekend. So, I can't be here for practice. Can you take
over?"

A cloud of suspicion still fills her eyes, but she nods. "No
problem." She turns to leave my office and says, "See you in five."

I look at my phone to verify the time, and she's right—
practice starts in twenty minutes, which means that I have to
hustle to the gym to meet Dana and Patrick for our pre-practice
powwow. I'm often late to social events, but I'm *never* late to
volleyball.

I read Jeremy's text:

I definitely want to see you, too.

As I gather my keys, tablet, and Styrofoam cup filled with ice
and Mountain Dew, I voice-text a reply to the Wolverine.

You sure Evan will survive without your tutelage for a few
days?

A glance at my phone reveals the message recorded correctly,
surprising me. Maybe I should use smarty words more often—
voice-to-text gets those right but usually doesn't understand my
curse words. Jeremy swears less and uses a more sophisticated
vocabulary than I do, so I should step up my game.

I'll make the sacrifice to spend time with you.

I pause my speed-walking as I read his text. Oh, God! What

man says stuff like that? My heart melts. As I try to drum up a response, motion to my right catches my eye. One of my players, Cherise Evans, hurries toward the locker room. I smile at her, but she keeps her head down. *Uh-oh.*

"Hey, Cherise."

She halts and looks at me. "Oh! Hey, Coach."

Her big eyes and plastic smile look fake, confirming my suspicion that she was ignoring me. The knot of worry in my stomach that formed during our first few practices with Emma now returns. Cherise, my starting setter, isn't happy that Emma is replacing her.

"Dana's got an awesome new play to practice today," I offer.

Cherise twists a kinky strand of hair between her fingers as she gives me a tight smile. "Great."

"How's the knee?"

Her smile vanishes for a beat, but she recomposes her mask. If I didn't know her so well, I might've missed her true reaction. "Really good." Her eyes dart to the locker room door. "Better get ready for practice!"

After she scurries off, I let out a sigh. I'll have to address this issue soon. Cherise is *the* reason we won the NCAA title four years ago, but since then she's blown out her knee twice. I hate to say it, but she's not the player she used to be. I owe it to her to explain her new role on the team now that Emma has arrived. I wish it weren't so painful to bench an athlete who's done nothing wrong.

As I near the court, I see Patrick and Dana on the opposite sideline huddled over a tablet Patrick holds, reviewing today's practice agenda. I don't want to tell them about my interaction with Cherise. Patrick already told me he thinks Cherise is acting like a petulant child, and Dana's too star-struck by Emma to offer any wisdom. Maybe I can talk it through with Jeremy. I stop and look at my phone.

As I read his last text again, my coaching problems fall to the wayside. He wants to see me. He's coming to visit soon! My fingers fly over the keyboard.

Honestly, I can't wait to see you.

I gnaw on my lower lip as I consider my next text. *Oh, hell.* You only live once.

You're welcome to stay at my house.

When he doesn't respond right away, I add:

If it's ok with Taryn.

Three little dots appear, and my muscles tense as I wait.

Save one side of your bed for me, sweetheart.

My face flushes as I remember the feel of his strong arms cradling me, and I look up from my phone. No players have emerged from the locker room yet, but I catch my assistant coaches staring at me before they pretend to absorb themselves in the tablet again. Another text from Jeremy comes in.

Taryn wants us to be together. She said Sam does, too. So it's fine if I don't stay with her.

Hmm. Sam has been hanging out with Taryn more, especially when I'm out of town recruiting, and I'm not sure how I feel about that. Taryn seems pretty cool, but Sam's *my* best friend. Patrick's watching me again, so I send a last text.

Practice about to start. I have to bench my favorite player to make room for Emma. Wish me luck.

His response comes in a few seconds.

You fucking got this, Chase.

Tingles travel through my chest. I love a man who knows how

to use *fuck* as a noun, adjective, verb, or in this case, adverb. And since he doesn't swear much, the word has even more impact.

I place my items on the scorer's table and smile at Dana and Patrick. "Ready?"

They nod.

"What's our number-one goal for practice today, team?"

Patrick leans away as he squints at me.

I squint back at him. "What?"

"You haven't asked that in a long time."

"Really?" *Is that true?* We always used to start with that question. This is a voluntary off-season practice without the full roster, so I want us to be focused.

Dana, who joined the staff last fall, doesn't know our program's history as well. She says, "We're integrating Emma into the offense."

"Right." I notice a few players emerging from the locker room. "What's an action step for each of us to accomplish that goal? I plan to involve Cherise more. Every skill we teach Emma, I want Cherise to model it for her first."

Patrick frowns. "But Cherise's pouting will slow us down."

I'm glad Patrick has the balls to disagree with me. However, as UC Irvine's best libero in school history, he doesn't know how miserable it is to sit the bench. My coach made sure I got a taste of that experience after I failed a biology exam once...or maybe twice. "Cherise is pouting because she hasn't accepted her new role as mentor. We have to show her how to transition from leadership by example to vocal leadership. And we do that by making her a player-coach."

"She *is* a fifth-year senior," says Dana. "Okay, I'll have Cherise demonstrate new plays to Emma—maybe have her teach them to Emma?"

I point at the tablet. "Good. And help Cherise use the positive language we've been working on as coaches."

Dana's eager nod as she taps the tablet makes me smile. Her enthusiasm kept me going last season, especially after we lost to Michigan in five sets. "So, on this play, have Cherise say, 'Keep balanced' instead of 'Don't touch the net'?"

"Exactly." I turn to Patrick with an expectant lift of my eyebrows.

He thinks for a moment. "I want to get some reps in with Emma on block coverage. Our system's different from her club team, and she's been too deep for covering weak-side hits." He pauses. "I suppose I can have Cherise by her side, directing her where to be on the court."

As a defensive specialist, he's only a tad over six feet, so I don't have to look up far to meet his eyes. "Fucking perfect."

"Cherise better not get too emotional today, just saying."

I pat his back. "Your wife's pregnancy hormones getting to you, Patrick?"

The slump of his shoulders lends him a resigned look. "Way too much estrogen in my life."

"C'mon, you love us girls." Dana elbows him.

As I laugh, I notice that Mariana, my middle blocker from Colombia, is watching us from the baseline. She wheels the basket of balls closer to Emma. After Mariana says something to Emma in Spanish, they both giggle.

"Hey." I perch my hand on one hip. "Are you making fun of me in a language I can't understand?"

"Easy, Coach." Emma twirls a ball and spins it on her index finger. "Mari just said you're in a good mood today."

When Mariana smirks at me, I'm guessing that Emma has given me the sanitized version.

"Don't corrupt my freshman, Mariana," I warn.

She splays her hands to the side, palms up, as her mouth drops. But I'm not fooled by her innocent act. After barely speaking as a freshman at OSU, she emerged from her shell last year and played several pranks on the seniors. I look forward to seeing what she has in store for us her junior year. If her hairstyle is any indication of her attitude, she'll succeed at keeping the mood light. She's braided her thick, black hair into playful pigtails that sway across her shoulder blades as she skips a few feet away from Emma so they can warm up.

I'm not surprised Emma sports the same braided pigtails for today's practice, only she's added scarlet bows at the tips.

Mariana has taken her under her wing. When Emma and her mother visited two weeks ago to scope out the campus, Mariana lit up upon discovering Emma's foreign language skills. Jenna surprised me by allowing Emma to move to campus sooner than expected, but I had to explain that her dorm wouldn't open until June. Less than an hour after I gave them the bad news about the living situation, Jenna told me Mariana and Cherise had offered to have Emma stay with them in their apartment until she moves into the dorm. I'm proud of Mariana's teamwork.

I watch Mariana and Emma pepper—exchanging passes, sets, and hits between them. Emma's effortless sets are a marvel to behold. Her hands are so soft, it's like she caresses the ball with each touch, launching it in an easy arc to its mark each time. But her speed is even more impressive. As Mariana's dig careens to one side, Emma's long legs lope to retrieve it, somehow getting under the ball to execute a usable set. I can't fucking *wait* for our first match.

"I mean it, Mari." I arch my eyebrow at her. "Don't teach Emma swear words in Spanish."

Emma dives for Mariana's spike, then clambers to her feet to hit Mariana's set. I don't know how she manages to snicker, even as she keeps the ball in play. "Don't worry, Coach. Mari told me your dirty mouth is much worse than hers."

"What?" I glare at Mariana. "I never swear."

She grins. "Sí, Coach."

Emma doesn't even breathe hard as she sets another perfect ball. "I won't tell my mom."

You better not.

"Let's warm up!" Cherise hollers at the seven players assembled on the court. They line up next to her, and she leads them up to the net and back to the baseline in a combination of jogging, side-stepping, arm swings, lunges, kicks, and stretches.

Emma's only done this warm-up routine a few times, but she follows her older teammates seamlessly. One time, though, she travels the opposite direction from the group, and my defensive specialist laughs at her. But instead of getting flustered, Emma laughs, too, as she scrambles back into position. Her sunny disposition is already winning them over. Cherise's sour expression, on the other hand, continues to worry me.

***

Three hours later, there's a knock on my office door. I look up to find Cherise. She sure took her time showering after practice. With her wet hair and no makeup, she looks more gaunt and tired than I've seen her before. And I've known her for over four years now.

Cherise had to take a medical redshirt her sophomore year due to a torn knee ligament, giving her another year of athletic eligibility. Then she tore her ACL again at the end of junior year. She limped through her senior year and wanted to leave OSU after graduation a few weeks ago, but I convinced her to stay for a fifth year and pursue a master's degree so she can play for me this fall.

"Come on in, Cherise!" I wave her into the office as I click away from an email.

"You wanted to see me, Coach?"

I wait for her to sit across the desk from me. Feeling a little breathless, I try to calm down. *You fucking got this, Chase.* I hope Jeremy's right.

"How did practice go for you today?"

Cherise shrugs. "Pretty good."

"What did you notice?"

She maintains her blank expression. "Just another practice."

She's not giving me much. "Okay." I let out a breath. "I'll stop bullshitting around."

Adjusting in her chair, she seems to brace herself.

Adrenaline kicks up my nerves. "I want to talk to you about your place on the team. You've given everything to this team as the starting setter, and I see your role evolving this year." Her wary, dark eyes make it hard to get the words out. "I want you to embrace your role as captain, guiding the team, and playing as the backup setter." There. I've said it. How will she react?

Cherise is quiet for a minute. "Emma will be the starter?"

"Well, she'll have to earn the starting position—I won't just give that away. But as a team, we want her to succeed so that the team succeeds. Do you know the only way that will happen?"

She shakes her head.

"The only way this team succeeds is if you help Emma."

She sits back in the chair, blinking double time. Her chin quivers, and she looks away from me. Shitcakes, she's about to cry.

"We need you, Cherise. We need your leadership more than ever."

Sure enough, a tear escapes the corner of her eye. Another follows, and both roll down her cheek. I shift in my chair, wishing she would fight me instead of wallowing in self-pity. Selfishness has no place on this team if we plan to return to dominance.

Despite my frustration with her, my voice gentles. "I know this is disappointing for you."

Her head shakes, and she sniffs. "I'm not disappointed."

Is she lying to me?

"I mean, I want to play…" She wipes her eyes and sits up straighter. "Can I be honest with you?"

"After four years, I think we have that trust between us."

She emits a little sob, but her accompanying smile indicates she agrees with me. "I'm not disappointed I'm losing my starting role to a freshman. I'm…relieved." She ducks her head and murmurs, "I know that sounds awful."

Relieved? This isn't what I expected to hear. "Why're you relieved, Cherise?"

Staring at her lap, she says, "I've tried to be tough, but my knee… It *hurts*. All the time." She sniffs. "I'm not as fast as I used to be. I don't get to the ball like I should, and I miss too many blocks." She peeks up at me. "I'm sorry. I don't want to let you down. I've tried to help this team, to lead the team, but I'm weak. The hitters aren't getting the sets they need, and they deserve better. You deserve better."

Wow. I lower my chin. I can't believe she's admitting all of this to me, her head coach. What amazing humility. How could I have thought her selfish? The girl has fought through two ACL tears, and she agreed to stay a fifth year not because she wanted to, but because I asked her to.

"You're anything but weak, Cherise." I wait until she meets my eyes. "You're a warrior." My words make her cry again, but I continue. "You're one of the hardest workers I've ever coached. You're the one who brought home the national championship four years ago, not me."

Her eyes grow big as she sucks in a ragged breath.

"You've sacrificed so much for this team," I continue. "Your poor knee has been through hell. I knew you weren't at your best, but I had no idea you've been in so much pain."

"I didn't...want to tell you," she sobs.

I think about our athletic trainer. "Have you told Courtney?"

"Courtney's sick of hearing about it. It's been three years!"

I give her a stern look. "So the answer is no, you haven't been truthful with Courtney, either."

Cherise looks away.

"We'll meet together with Courtney to create a pain-management plan for the next six months. I want you to be able to walk after you graduate."

She wipes her nose and nods.

I bite into a Twizzler and offer her one, but she shakes her head. Between chews, I ask, "How're you feeling about Emma living with you? It must've been jarring when Mariana invited her to stay at your place."

Cherise frowns. "Mariana?"

"Yeah." I pause. "She invited Emma, right?"

"No! *I'm* the one who invited Emma. I figured we'd have more time to go over plays that way."

I sit back in my chair. I've completely underestimated this amazing student-athlete. I won't let it happen again. "I don't deserve you, Cherise."

"Probably not." A hint of a smile crosses her face.

"Thank you for staying a fifth year—it means a lot to us. When do your graduate classes begin?"

She tells me about the classes in her master's program, and the easy conversation that has characterized our relationship for years now returns. After a few minutes, Cherise revisits the discussion about Emma.

"She's so talented, and her game's really well-rounded. I could never hit like her! Other than that, she reminds me a little of myself—well, a younger version of myself."

I consider her comment. "Yeah, she's naive, like any freshman. But it's weird, sometimes Emma seems more mature than me."

When Cherise cracks up, I catch a glimpse of the carefree, confident girl she was before her knee injuries. It's so gratifying to see her laugh instead of cry. "Maturity's overrated, Coach."

I smile. "I hope so."

After Cherise leaves the office, I reach for my phone. Jeremy's the first person I want to tell about my day.

Influencing
Jeremy

"**S**tay in there," I whisper as Evan shifts his feet.

Defenders are coming for him, pushing and shoving against the offensive linemen who block them. The pocket collapses around my young freshman. Evan wears a sleeveless red pinny over his T-shirt to tell the defense not to touch him, and no one's tackling or wearing pads during this voluntary practice, so I know he won't get hurt. Still, he's got to feel the hot breath of the players suffocating the small space around him, itching to demolish him before he throws the ball.

Just as the linebacker spins around his blocker, about to mock-tackle my quarterback, Evan pivots and launches the ball in a tight spiral. I watch it float through the air. *Thump.* The satisfying sound of the ball slotting in between the receiver's palms and chest rings true. Talik Jones-Stanton, our best receiver, tucks the ball into his elbow and glides into the end zone.

Evan jogs toward Talik with a big grin, then he leaps and bangs shoulders with the receiver mid-air. They shouldn't do that without pads. But they're not the only ones celebrating— quite a few offensive players pump their fists or high-five as a vibe of hope and potential permeates the practice field.

Mr. Watkins, who I wish wasn't here, also whoops from the sideline. It's still early, but May has brought us a bouquet of *maybe. Maybe this kid's as good as advertised. Maybe we'll beat the Buckeyes. Maybe this is our year.*

Even Austin Hartford, the starting quarterback, cheers from the sideline. "Way to hang in there, Watkins!" he hollers down the field, squinting against the sun. He's probably relieved Coach

Froth isn't yelling at him, for once.

Noticing my boss stalking toward me, one of the muscles in my lower back clenches. Looks like I'll be the target for his rage, not Austin.

"He was supposed to hit the split or tight-end, not the flanker!" Froth spits.

I risk stating the obvious. "They weren't open." I watch the head coach's eyes taper into slits. "Evan got creative—isn't that what we want? Give our QB some latitude to make plays happen?"

"*I'm* the one writing the plays, not an eighteen-year-old kid."

I need to massage his ego. "It was a good play. Your work with the corners is obviously bearing fruit—that was some great coverage out there."

A thousand years ago, Froth played cornerback for a small university, and he fashions himself as some sort of defensive expert. I have to admit our defense has been better than our offense—a trend I plan to change with Evan's arrival and the return of our top running back from injury.

Froth's still scowling at me, so I add, "Want to run it again? I'll have Evan throw it away if his reads aren't open."

After a beat, he shakes his head. "Let's get some handoff reps."

I signal for Evan to practice handoffs with the running back. The more snaps Evan gets with our veteran center, the more comfortable he'll feel come August.

An hour later, we wrap up practice. As I scroll through plays on my tablet to find the pitch play that will need some work, I sense giddy energy permeating the air. When I look up, Mr. Watkins grins at me. *Give me a break.* This is only Evan's second practice.

"My boy's looking good out there."

I slide the tablet into my briefcase. "He did well today. Still a long time till camp in August, though." A long time until we're wearing pads and practicing for real.

"That was definitely worth taking a vacation day from work to see him in action," Mr. Watkins adds.

I was wondering how Mr. Watkins was here on a Thursday. Does Evan's father plan to attend tomorrow's practice as well? He has driven Evan back and forth from Toledo twice this week already, and I'm not sure if that's due to his desire to watch his son play college ball or his mistrust in Evan taking care of himself. Either way, I need to put the kibosh on a parent attending practices. In the midst of chewing out one of our video guys, Froth glares at us from across the field. As I search for the firm yet caring words to kick Mr. Watkins's ass out of here, Evan approaches us.

"Dad—"

"Take off that hideous scarlet pinny," his father commands.

Evan smiles as he rips off the sleeveless jersey. "I've got a solution for you tomorrow. Instead of driving me to practice, you can attend the state track meet. As the AD, you need to be there."

"I already told you I don't want you driving by yourself from Toledo," says Mr. Watkins.

Evan shakes his head. "I won't be in Toledo. One of the receivers said I can stay with him till the dorms open."

Oh, no. I have a suspicion about which receiver made the offer. Glancing to the left, I see Talik joking with a senior, but in between his laughs and playful shoves, he sneaks looks at Evan. Talik has tested positive twice for marijuana—he's hardly the best influence for my star recruit. I tried talking to him about his drug use, but his position coach got on my case for overstepping my bounds.

"I'm not sure that's a good idea." His father's mouth tightens. "Which receiver?"

Evan angles his head toward the two players nearby. "Talik. He led the team in receptions last year, so it's extra important that we connect now. You told me I need to bond with my teammates, right?"

I close my eyes as I remember passing Talik in the facility last year and smelling a whiff of sweet skunk. We're in the weeds now, people.

"Your mother and I want you at home."

Evan scoffs. "I'm going to live here full-time in less than two weeks! What's the difference if I move in now? You're letting *Emma* stay with an upperclassman."

"That's different. She's over two hours away."

"That's not why," Evan huffs. "You trust her more than me. How's that fair? You always preach about treating us the same, but you like her better."

This kid is a guilt-trip master. I search for a way to slink away from this uncomfortable conversation.

"I do *not*..." Mr. Watkins halts and grimaces at the sound of his loud retort, like he's catching himself arguing in the same snappish manner as his son. He sighs and turns to me. "What do you think, Coach Trent?"

Damn. I should've figured out an exit strategy sooner. I'm all on board with removing a reason for Mr. Watkins to attend practice, but I don't want Evan lost in a smoky haze before the season has even begun. "It'd be wiser for Evan to stay with another quarterback. How about Austin Hartford?"

"His girlfriend lives with him," says Evan.

Mr. Watkins frowns. "They live together before marriage?"

Evan rolls his eyes, echoing my internal reaction. Living with your girlfriend before marriage is tame compared to countless players who have fathered children during their tenure at Michigan.

Evan turns to me. "Coach, you wanted me here in January, right? But my parents wouldn't let me, and now I'm behind. I need to learn the offense. You need to teach me." He looks at his father. "There's nothing for me in Toledo now. You said you want me to make Ann Arbor my home. So let me do that!"

Mr. Watkins rubs his hand down his face as he considers for a few moments. "Your mother told me I need to let go. And Pastor Ron said to prepare the child for the path, not the path for the child." He lets out a breath. "We've done the best we can. I suppose I need to let you live your life now, make your own mistakes." He glances at me. "You agree, Coach?"

I hope those mistakes Mr. Watkins mentioned won't ruin Evan's career. "We'll take good care of Evan, sir."

"Yes!" Evan punches the air and jogs over to Talik.

I meet the receiver's eyes, and he winks at me before giving Evan a choreographed fist-bump-jazz-hand fadeaway followed by a hand sliding down the back of the head. *Christ*. They already have a signature handshake. I may need to cancel my trip to visit Lauren so I can babysit, and that thought is depressing as hell.

A little while later, I'm in my office reviewing video of today's practice when my phone buzzes. I set down my green smoothie and find a text from Lauren asking if I can talk. After pausing the video, I call her.

Her phone rings several times, but she catches it right before it goes to voicemail. "Hey." Her voice trembles.

"What's up?"

She pauses, and I think I hear her sniff. "I-I-I didn't think you'd be free."

I bolt out of my chair and close the door to my office. "Why're you crying?"

"Sorry." She lets out a shaky breath. "I thought I could get my shit together before we talked."

What has happened? I pace my office as I wait for her to tell me. Did it go badly with the player she had to bench?

"It's my mom."

My pacing stops.

"She has...breast cancer," she chokes out.

I close my eyes. "I'm sorry to hear that."

"I don't know why I'm crying!" She sniffs. "They think they're catching it early, apparently. And the woman drives me crazy."

"Lauren." I sink into my chair. "She's your mother."

I hear a long sigh. I picture her manicured nail sliding along her eye to wipe away a tear.

"I wish I were there with you," I say. "I want to hold you."

She's quiet for a second. "I want that, too. Long distance fucking sucks."

My lips twitch. Her mother's bad news hasn't depleted her stock of F bombs. "Do you need to go to Cincinnati? I can visit Columbus another time."

"About that." She huffs out a breath. "My mom decided

she's coming *here*. She's trying to meet with an oncologist at the James tomorrow to review her biopsy results, but if she can't get in, then maybe on Tuesday."

"What's the James?"

"It's a cancer hospital at OSU. One of the best in the country—her doctor in Cincinnati recommended it. So, she'll be crashing my place the entire weekend. Yay." Her tone morphs from sarcastic to apologetic. "I can't have you stay with me now. Sorry."

I take a sip of smoothie. At least it sounds like she's stopped crying. "Do you still want me to visit? I can stay with Taryn."

She takes some time to respond, and I imagine her stroking her neck as she contemplates. "I don't know. My mom's a hella handful."

"Sounds like you could use some support."

"That's what vodka's for, and what s…" Her voice trails off. "Listen, I'll be fine."

I've heard that dismissive tone before, and I'm learning it's one of her tells when she's lying. "Hmm. Are you being honest with me, Coach Chase?"

"Ugh." Her little grunt makes me smile. She sighs. "Honestly?"

When she doesn't continue, I prod, "Yeesssss?"

"I was really bummed when I thought I wouldn't see you. Maybe I can slip over to Taryn's when my mom goes to sleep."

"Nope." I shake my head. "If I'm in town at the same time as your mom, I'm definitely meeting her."

She gasps. "No! She's crazy."

I shift in my chair and reach back to rub the base of my spine. "This isn't about her, sweetheart. This is about you."

"You're saying *I'm* crazy?"

If the shoe fits… I grin. "I'm saying you're scared I'll judge you based on your mom's behavior."

She grows quiet.

"Am I right?" I ask.

She waits a beat. "Dick-knuckle."

I sputter a laugh. "What does that even mean?"

Her giggle coming through the phone lights me up. "It's up

to the receiver's interpretation."

"You're calling me a dick-knuckle? My dick is healthy and straight, thank you very much. No bend in sight."

She's full-on laughing now. "Good to know, Coach Trent." Her laugh takes a while to end, tapering off in that little downward sigh I enjoy so much.

"Seriously." I lean back in my chair and prop my feet on the desk. "You don't sound like your mom at all. Well, maybe she's beautiful like you."

"Awww! You say things like that, and I want you here right now. Maybe I'll even let you meet my mom."

She's coming around. "Do you share *any* similarities with her?"

She waits a beat. "She does swear a lot."

"Really?" That's tough to imagine—the woman has to be in her sixties to have a daughter Lauren's age. "Anything else?"

"She..." The humor has dropped from Lauren's voice, replaced by a tremor that characterized the beginning of the phone call. "She used to smoke cigarettes. For many years."

My back yowls its disapproval of my body position, so I lower my feet off the desk and sit up in the chair. "You're worried smoking caused her cancer?"

When she sniffs, I close my eyes. Is she crying again?

"I should tell you something," says Lauren.

I tense. This sounds bad.

"I've been sneaking cigarettes." Guilt laces her voice. "I'm so stupid—I know how awful they are, but I keep doing it. What if I never quit? I'm totally out of control!"

"Hey." Damn, I want to wrap her in my arms. "Quitting cold-turkey is really tough. Everyone has slip-ups. Has the patch helped?"

After a moment, she replies, "I think so."

"Have you been wearing one every day?"

Her voice goes up an octave as she admits, "Um, no?"

"That's it. I'm coming tomorrow, no questions asked. You need me. You need me there to put those patches on you."

"Yeah?" Her breathy response, so soon after she was crying,

surprises me. It also stirs arousal. "Just where will you put the patch?"

"I'll slap it on your ass if you don't start wearing it daily, young lady."

"Ooh. Bossy coach-man." Her sexy lilt is a total turn-on.

I shift in my chair to provide some relief, but instead the movement makes me groan.

"Jeremy?" Her voice sharpens. "Is your back hurting?"

Way to kill the mood, stupid back pain. I'm about to give my pat answer, *I'm fine*, but I stop myself. I just got on her case for not being truthful. "It comes and goes. I just have to deal with it."

"When's the last time you saw a doctor for the pain?"

I sigh. It's been a while. "The doctor said he couldn't do anything."

"Not what I asked. You're evading my question because you don't want to admit how long it's been. Am I right?"

I sulk as she throws my words back at me. "Yes."

"How long?"

"Seven years," I grumble.

"And I'm sure there haven't been any advancements in pain medicine in that time."

I narrow my eyes. "Sarcasm doesn't become you, sweet cheeks."

"Wow, I've gone from sweetheart to sweet cheeks in record time," she teases. "Guess you can give *me* crap, but you can't take it. Typical Wolverine."

"You're not exactly killin' it on caring for yourself, either, Buckeye."

"I don't need to." She pauses. "I've got you to look after me."

My chest swells. If she'll let me, I'll do anything to take care of her.

"Schedule with a doctor, Trent. I mean it."

I grin. "Yes, Coach. See you soon. Maybe I'll even get a speeding ticket on the way."

"Don't do that—one of us needs to be able to drive when they take away my license."

She's going to lose her driver's license? "Lauren—"

"See you soon. Bye!"

I stare at the phone after her abrupt end to the call. Then, my eyes float to the computer screen, and I study the placement of Evan's feet in the paused video. The kid will have to wait till next week to improve his stance. I've got to see my girl this weekend, keep her in line.

A stab of pain tenses my back muscles as I stand. Lauren's right. The first thing I need is to see the team physician about my back pain.

Annoying
Lauren

I freeze, holding a spoonful of coffee grounds aloft in the kitchen, as I hear my mother's growl of frustration from my home office. I hope she doesn't call me in there—my patience is already at its limit. When she arrived last night with three suitcases, her own coffee maker, and a gallon of filtered water, I had a sense this would be a trying weekend. An entire Friday with her has confirmed my fears.

"Lauren!"

Shitcastle. I dump in the last spoonful of coffee and start brewing. I cringe when she calls my name again.

I adopt a cheery falsetto. "Coming!"

"I hate Gmail," she snaps as I enter my office. She glowers at my desktop computer. "I just sent that damn email, and now it's gone!"

"It's not gone. Remember how I told you the emails get stacked on top of each—"

"Then *you* find it." She flings her hand toward the screen. "I sent an email asking Jo about invasive ductal carcinoma, but it disappeared."

From over her shoulder, I look at the screen. I reach for the mouse to scroll through her inbox, but she won't relinquish it to me. I'm forced to shoo her out of my desk chair, and she winces as she moves at a slug's pace to get to her feet. I know her hip hurts, but the drama of her health problems already seems over the top, and we haven't even met with the oncologist in Columbus yet. Lucky for me, they can't see her till Tuesday.

"I thought you were going to see a surgeon about your hip."

123

I settle into my chair.

She purses her lips. "I don't trust surgeons."

Ugh. At least she's taking this cancer thing seriously. I contemplate the words she used as I click on an email: *invasive carcinoma.* Her doctors in Cincinnati told her they caught the cancer early, and it appears non-invasive. While I adore volleyball, jumping to the worst-case scenario is my mom's favorite sport. Still, the uncertainty is frightening. I should be more patient with her—I should be a better daughter.

"See? Here it is."

She peers through her glasses as I get out of the chair. "Oh, good." She emits a cry of pain as she resumes her seat. "But Jo hasn't replied yet."

I'm sure her nurse friend, Joanna, is loving these panicky emails. "You just sent it a second ago."

Her hands fly over the keyboard—she used to teach high-school typing before I was born. She must be firing off another email to Jo. She pauses her typing to ask, "Where's my coffee?"

I close my eyes and let out a breath. Who drinks coffee at six pm? "It's brewing."

"You used my filtered water, right?"

"Yep." *Grr.* "Got plenty of Mountain Dew if you don't want to wait for the coffee."

She flinches. "How do you drink that crap? Way too much sugar."

My mother has dieted all of her life, and therefore, I make sure to eat as much junk food as possible.

"We all need our caffeine fix," I say as I exit the office. Though vodka would probably be a more effective drug for us at this point. Even better: Xanax.

I sink onto my sofa, pull my phone from my pants pocket, and frown. Still no word from Jeremy. He was supposed to hit the road after his practice, meaning he should have arrived at his sister's a couple of hours ago.

As I hear the coffee maker gurgle, I realize I should use this time to text my recruits. Trying to entertain my mom all day has distracted me from getting any work done.

I'm reading a text from an outside hitter in Arizona when there's a knock on my front door.

"Someone's at the door!" my mom hollers.

"No shit," I mutter as I look through the peephole, then gasp. I throw open the door to find Jeremy holding two bouquets of flowers. "You were supposed to text me first!"

He shrugs and flashes a big smile. "Had to be in-person to deliver these flowers."

His hands are full, so I reach for his head to draw his face down to mine. We proceed to kiss the living hell out of each other. His minty taste and sexy smell flood my senses, quickening my breath. He curls his arms around me, and I feel the tickle of flowers on the back of my neck. As I skim my fingers through his short hair, he tucks me closer to his hard body. Long distance fucking sucks, but kissing him after a month apart fucking rocks. We deepen the kiss.

"Who's *that?*" asks my mother from behind me.

I unlock my lips and look up into his troubled green eyes.

"You didn't tell her about me?" he whispers.

I let him go. "Mom." I step back into the house and turn to see her standing in the foyer. "This is Jeremy, my, uh…" I tug his elbow to invite him in. "My boyfriend."

The lines around her mouth stiffen as one eyebrow lifts. Is she also upset with me for keeping him secret? Or shocked that I'm actually dating someone?

"Mrs. Chase." Jeremy offers her the bouquet of pink carnations and baby's breath. It's then I notice that the other bouquet, the one I'm guessing he's about to give me, bursts with blue and gold flowers. Michigan colors.

"I'm so sorry to hear about your test results," Jeremy continues. "Lauren told me how scared she is for you."

I did? Beneath my annoyance is indeed fear, but I don't recall admitting that to him.

My mother's pressed lips still lend her a skeptical vibe, but she accepts the flowers. "Lauren, you didn't tell me you were expecting company! I would've spent more time getting ready." She scowls at her black pants and leopard-print jacket from

Chico's.

Her outfit seems rather hip and flattering for a sixty-four year old, but what do I know? She gets on me all the time for wearing "dikey" athletic garb. "Sorry, Mom. I thought Jeremy was going to text before coming over."

"I'm the one who should apologize," says Jeremy. "I got a late start, and then I had to look all over town to find orchids in just the right color." With a flourish, he presents me with the two-toned blue petals mixed with yellow daffodils.

This is the first time a man has ever bought me flowers, and I can't deny the pleasure zipping through me, despite the ugly color combination. "Thank you, but no one asked you to do that. No one asked you to traipse all over town to find *blue* flowers, especially."

"Lauren!" Mom admonishes. "How ungrateful."

But the amusement in Jeremy's eyes tells me he expected my disdain. "Not a fan of orchids and daffodils?"

"Red roses would be better. Scarlet red."

He nods. "Duly noted for the next time you earn flowers from me."

I dip my chin. "How did I supposedly 'earn' these?" I look at my mother, hoping she doesn't think he's rewarding me for sex or something like that. Her sharp blue eyes study him.

"That has to do with my late start," Jeremy replies. "I—"

"Hey, Mom," I interrupt. I don't want her involved in my relationship with Jeremy if I can help it. "How 'bout you give these flowers some water?" I give her my bunch as well. "I think there are vases under the sink."

She considers my request for a long moment then surprises me when she turns and walks toward the kitchen.

Jeremy must notice her hobbling because he rushes to her side. "Are you okay, Mrs. Chase? Why're you limping?"

His question makes me realize *he's* not limping at all.

"Oh, this fu—" She gives him a side glance. "This damn hip. I probably need it replaced. Maybe I can get a twofer surgery. They can screw in a new hip at the same time they lop off my boob."

When he looks back at me with wide eyes, I think I can read his mind: *We got a live one here.* He better keep his promise not to judge me because of her crazy.

"Let's not get ahead of ourselves, Mom," I say.

Jeremy escorts her on to the kitchen. "I'll help you with the flowers."

"No need." She waves him off. "The coffee's finally done, and I'm going to pour myself a cup first."

We watch her limp into the kitchen, and Jeremy turns to me. "I *thought* it smelled good in here. In addition to the amazing flowers I brought, I mean. You have a coffee maker?"

Based on the eagerness on his face, I decide to buy one for his future visits. I hope this won't be his last time in my home. "My mom brought hers from Cincinnati." I lower my voice and plaster a fake smile. "She'll be here the whole weekend before her appointment on Tuesday. Aren't I lucky?"

He gives a sympathetic cluck. "Was she about to drop an F bomb before she stopped herself?"

"Yep. I learned from the best."

He shakes his head. "Besides swearing, I just discovered another similarity between you two. You both suck at accepting help."

"Not true!" I protest. "I know the value of letting others help me."

"Yeah?" He steps closer. "You wearing a patch right now?"

My heart flutters as I grin. Peering around him, I confirm that my mother is still in the kitchen. I tug down one corner of my pants and undies to reveal the nicotine patch on my butt cheek. "I had to hide it because I don't want to hear my mom's opinions on the subject. I believe you suggested this as a good location?"

His eyes travel from my bottom up to my face and flare as they meet my gaze. Damn, that sexy shade of green with flecks of blue and brown... I feel heat building in my core just from the smoldering look he gives me. He reaches out to touch the patch, and I jump from the tingle of his large hand cupping the curve of my butt.

He catches my little gasp with his mouth, pressing an urgent kiss into my lips. His hand glides up under my shirt to the small of my back and rubs circles on my skin. His tongue action undoes me, and I clutch his shoulder blades with both hands to steady myself, letting my waistband slide back up into place.

"You don't have milk?" asks my mother from the kitchen.

Mother of a monkey. This is the second time she's interrupted us. I sigh as I look up at Jeremy. "Want some coffee?"

He smiles at me. "Sure, sweet cheeks."

I grab his hand and lead him to the kitchen. The flowers lie flat, untouched on the island. My mother peers into the open refrigerator.

"I bought milk just for you." I gesture to the half-gallon on the top shelf. I never buy milk for myself. I eat most of my meals out, so I made sure to grab more groceries before my mom arrived.

She frowns as she picks it up and studies the label. "This is two percent. I only drink organic skim milk."

"You didn't tell me that!"

She shrugs. "Well, you'll have to take me to the store, then."

Oh, *that* should be fun. I wonder if she'll need one of those scooters to get around with her bum hip. I watch her dribble a few drops of bad-for-you milk into her coffee. After I pour black brew into an Ohio State mug, my mother leans away from me.

"About time," she says. "Stop drinking that soda crap and have coffee like a normal adult."

My jaw clenches. "This is for Jeremy, not me. And I don't have soy milk, either—sorry." As I turn to give him the mug, I see that he's taken two vases from the cabinet below the sink and set them on the island. "Oh, thanks!"

"No problem." He accepts the coffee and holds it aloft, eyeing the Ohio State Buckeyes design with an arched eyebrow. "I'll drink it black."

Mom studies him. "Why do you drink soy milk?"

He glances at me as I take one vase to the sink. "I'm vegan."

"That's wonderful!" Mom gushes. "I was just reading an article about a woman who beat cancer by going vegan."

I squint at the water filling the vase. *Is that for real?*

"You know Lauren is the furthest thing from vegan, right?" Mom adds. "She eats all kinds of junk."

My shoulders tense.

"I've never seen someone eat so much candy. She should be a lot fatter with that diet... Lauren! You've got way too much water in there. Here." She bustles over to the sink, her hip pain forgotten. After she steals the vase from me and dumps out half of the water, she demands, "Get me your pruning shears."

I screw my mouth to one side. *What the fuck are those?*

"Scissors, then," she snaps, reading my cluelessness. She rests the vase on the island and begins to unwrap the pink-and-white bouquet.

As I circle the island, I avoid Jeremy's eyes. He must think I'm a complete idiot—I don't know anything about milk, flowers, or how to be an adult, really. But after I extract scissors from a drawer, I feel his hand on my shoulder. I look up, and he winks at me. Since he's blocking my mother's view, I mime a psycho stabbing motion with the scissors. When he grins, I let out a breath and realize how tight my chest has become. Nobody stresses me out like my mother.

As I watch her work on the flowers, I long for a cigarette. Or some candy. Soon she's filled both vases with artful arrangements. "These are really lovely, Jeremy."

"I'm glad you like them, Mrs. Chase." He drains the last drop of his coffee.

I forgot about his suck-up talents. "Mine are missing something, though." I head to the windowsill and pick up a figurine of Brutus Buckeye, OSU's mascot. He's small enough to nestle right into the stems of the blue and yellow flowers, and I like how his scarlet-and-gray striped shirt and red sweatpants clash with the garish colors. "There." I step back to admire my work. "*Now* they're perfect."

His lips scrunch up toward his nose as he stares at how I've *bucked up* his flowers.

Mom tips her head to one side, watching us. "Do you have a notepad, Lauren? I want to make a list for the store."

"Sure." I bend down to grab one from a lower drawer. After I hand it to her, I notice Jeremy has pitched the mascot's head into the water, upside down.

"You're drowning Brutus!" I cry as I right him in the vase.

He shrugs. "Not my fault he's top-heavy. He toppled over." He draws the back of his hand to his forehead in a dramatic gesture. "Said goodbye to this cruel world."

I slug his chest, then remember his sister doing the same thing at Woody's. He sure is annoying sometimes.

"What is *up* with you two?" Mom asks.

I shake my head. "Hate to admit it, but Jeremy coaches for the team up north."

She stills.

I wonder if she understood me. My dad would know exactly which school I'm referring to, but my mom doesn't follow sports or rivalries. "He's a Michigan football coach, Mom."

She hasn't moved an inch. After a beat, she lowers her coffee mug to the island. "Lauren, please help me with an email in your office."

After she strides out of the kitchen, I look at Jeremy.

"What is she mad about?" he asks.

"I have no idea. Sorry, I'll be right back."

He nods. "Take your time."

I spin around and jab my finger toward the vase. "And leave Brutus alone, mister."

He smirks.

Uh-oh. When I enter my office and see her flushed face, I confirm she *is* mad.

"What the hell were you thinking?"

She's hissed that question, but it's still loud enough that Jeremy might overhear. I scowl at her. "About what?"

"You're dating another *coach?*"

Yep, that was definitely loud enough for the whole house to hear. I cringe at the question, which stirs up shameful memories of my affair with Paul. The incessant phone calls from Paul's wife, calling me a whore, Mom screaming at me that I've ruined their family, along with my career, the helpless disappointment behind my dad's glasses—it's hard to breathe.

"Yes, he's a coach. So what?"

"Is he married?"

My jaw lowers. "No!"

Mom juts out her chin. "Is that smart to involve yourself with another coach?"

I close my eyes and feel my nose burn. "Probably not. But then, when am I ever smart in your eyes?"

"Don't try to make this about me. If it were about me, you wouldn't throw this in my face right after a cancer diagnosis! How selfish of you."

Apparently, I'm immature *and* selfish.

"No, this is about you...you and your poor choices," Mom continues. "Are you having *sex* with him?"

Oh, my God. I want to crawl under the desk. My throat constricts. *Don't cry. Don't cry.*

"Maybe this time, you can get pregnant," she rails. "That'd be an even bigger fuck-up."

To my horror, Jeremy pops his head into the room. My lips quiver as I look up at him.

"Hey." He shoves his hands into his pockets. "Think I'm gonna head to my sister's, okay?"

Don't leave! I want to shout. But of course, he doesn't want to stay and witness our argument. After I manage a nod, I hear the front door shut in record speed. He must've run out of here. Guess I won't need that coffee maker after all—he probably never wants to come back.

14

Uniting
Jeremy

Taryn pauses the DVR when there's a knock on her front door.

"Finally." I pop off of the sofa and head for the foyer. I've been texting Lauren all night, asking her to come over after that fracas at her place.

She doesn't even smile when I open the door. Despite her sexy red, form-fitting, long-sleeve shirt and black jeans that hug her shapely legs, she looks awful. Her posture screams *tension*, and weariness has stolen the sparkle from her eyes. Her mother's poor health has infected them both.

Taking her hand, I pull her inside and gather her into my arms. Something breaks in me as she melts into my body. I hate to see her hurting, and I want to protect her, even if it's from her own family. Her mother has no right to yell at her like that. My mom would never be so cruel to Taryn or me.

I brush my hand up and down her back, enjoying the feel of her body tucked into mine. I'm relieved that I don't detect a hint of cigarettes, only a waft of coconut from her long hair fanning over her shoulders. At least her mother hasn't driven her to smoke.

"About time you got here," I say.

She huffs out a breath. "I waited till my mom went to sleep. First time I've ever had to sneak out of my own damn house."

I peer down at her. "You okay?"

She steps out of the hug. "Better now." She waves at Taryn. "Hey, Ryn."

My heart blooms with warmth.

"How's your mom?" Taryn asks as she stands.

Lauren glances at me, then back at her. "How much do you know?"

"Just that she has a health issue and is staying at your house. And that she was really mean to you tonight. That's what Remy told me, anyway."

Lauren's smile lights up her face. *"Remy?"* She grins at me. "That is adorbs."

"No one at Michigan knows that nickname." I narrow my eyes. "Don't go blabbing to my coworkers again."

Taryn laughs. "Oh, I heard about that. They made Brutus Buckeye give a blow—"

"Lauren doesn't need to hear that!" I interrupt. "She's very proprietary about Brutus."

"Damn straight." Lauren's eyes taper with suspicion, then widen as she notices the paused TV show. *"Project Runway!* I love that show."

Taryn nods. "Isn't it awesome? Sam got me into it. Too bad she's out of town or we could play her drinking game while we watch."

"Who needs Sam to play a drinking game?" Lauren says. "I could definitely use some booze right now."

With a little hop, Taryn says, "I'll whip up some drinks!" and makes a beeline to the kitchen.

Lauren circles the sofa and plops onto one corner. "I knew I liked her."

I settle next to her on the middle cushion.

"Oh, want to switch places?" She thumps the armrest. "This side would be better support for your back."

I shake my head as I take her hand in mine. "I'm good here."

She strokes the back of my hand as she smirks. "So, Ryn forced you to watch *Project Runway?*"

Secretly, I can't wait to see which fashion designer wins the unconventional challenge. They have to create outfits using only beach gear in this episode, and one designer was just starting to incorporate orange plastic shovel blades onto dress fabric when Lauren arrived. But I can't reveal my true feelings—she already thinks I'm strange.

I roll my eyes. "It's not too bad. Just trying to pass the time till you arrived." I lift one shoulder. "And it'll undoubtedly get better by adding alcohol. How do you play the drinking game?"

"Sam and I used to drink every time Tim Gunn said, 'Make it work', but now that Christian Siriano is the host, we drink whenever they bleep a designer for swearing."

I smirk. "That fits you well."

She looks around the living room, taking in the crammed bookshelves and modern décor. "This is a nicer house than mine." A line creases her forehead. "Back at my place..." She chews her lip, and I want to nibble that spot. "Why'd you leave?"

"I was furious at your mom for talking to you that way, and I worried I'd say something I'd regret." I unclench my hands. "Also, it seemed like I was making things worse by being there." When her frown doesn't lighten, I add, "Your mom was ripping into you, and I thought she'd stop once I left. Did she?"

She shakes her head.

"That's too bad." Has her mother been that critical of her all of her life? I notice anxious contours still tightening her eyes. "Why did *you* think I left?"

She looks down. "I thought..." Her shoulder pushes up. "Maybe you don't want to be with me anymore."

Her confidence has crumbled like a vegan cookie. Sick or not, her mother needs a stern talking-to for affecting her daughter that way. "News flash, Lauren. You've won me over—you've got your recruit."

She looks up at me.

"I've signed my letter of intent," I add.

Her lips part. "And just what is your intent, Trent?"

It seems a spark has returned to her eyes as they challenge me. What *is* my intent with this feisty woman? I want to hold her close, feel her body pressed into mine. To kiss and explore parts of her I've yet to know. To make her laugh long and hard, ending with that soft sigh of contentment. To lift her up and make her the best coach she can be. To learn from her. To be the person she trusts most in this world. To *love* her, if she'll let me.

But I can't say any of this—she's not ready to hear it,

especially on the heels of her mother's condemnation.

"I want to be the man you trust," I tell her. "I want to be on your team."

After a moment, she allows a small smile to emerge. "So, you want a scholarship to Team Chase. You *are* ranked pretty high at your position."

"Pretty high?" I wrinkle my nose. "I'm number one, sweet cheeks."

She tosses her hair over one shoulder. "Aren't I lucky, then?"

Her coconut smell is driving me crazy. I tug her closer and swoop in to kiss her cheek. "I missed you."

She swivels to face me, her back against the arm rest and one leg folded at the knee. She clutches the front of my collar and pulls me toward her. "Missed you, too—missed you fucking hard."

I feel her lips lift into a smile as she kisses me. Her dirty mouth tastes so good. I smooth my hand down her neck, and she rolls her head to one side, exposing her throat. My lips slide down to feather kisses along her neck. Judging by her rapid breathing, I'm turning her on.

"Maybe we should take this upstairs," she murmurs.

Yes! I've craved time alone with her all month.

But just then, my sister hollers from the kitchen, "The drinks are almost ready!" I'm guessing she's giving us a chance to conclude our hot exchange before she enters the room.

I lift my head from the tender skin at the base of Lauren's neck. "Watch a little TV with my sister first?"

She combs fingers through her hair, weighing her options.

"We have your favorite drink."

"Yeah?"

Taryn enters with a tray of tumblers filled with clear, fizzy liquid, ice, and lime wedges.

"Limeapalooza!" Lauren does a seated happy dance.

"Remy brought the limes from Michigan." Taryn hands Lauren a sweating glass. "Hope they won't be too sour."

I glower at my sister—she's close to earning a noogie—but I accept my drink. After I take a sip, I settle back into the sofa. "Ah.

Fortunately, vodka is vegan."

Taryn raps my wrist with the TV remote. "Wait till the drinking game starts!"

I gesture toward Lauren's half-full glass. "Lauren already drank some, too, and you're not getting on *her* case."

"She's our guest. Okay, let's begin." She clicks the remote, and one of the designers gets bleeped within the first minute. After we all take a swig, Taryn emits a pleased sigh. "This is great. I never had time for TV shows in college."

"You played D-One basketball, right?" asks Lauren.

Taryn nods. "At Loyola. We had zero free time. Grad school's way better."

I remember my time as a master's student at Central Washington. "*My* schedule was packed in grad school." Lauren was probably busy as well, especially with her head coach putting the moves on her at every turn. *How dare her mother throw that in her face?*

There's a bleep from the show when a designer burns her hand on a glue gun.

"Drink!" Lauren orders.

After Taryn lowers her glass, she says, "That's because you were a grad assistant coach. Without sports, I have tons of time. My classmates complain about how much work they have our first year—what a joke. They'd never survive as student-athletes."

I suppose our insane schedules in college prepared Lauren and me for even busier lives as coaches.

We're on our second drink when the judges begin their critique of the fashion designs. Nina Garcia, editor of *Elle*, makes a biting remark about one designer's lack of taste.

"Nina's such a bitchnipple," offers Lauren.

Taryn giggles. "Remy told me about your silo of swear words."

I nod. "It's an art form."

"Hardly!" Lauren snorts.

"What's your secret?" Taryn rarely drinks alcohol, and her eyes have taken on a glassy look.

Lauren shrugs. "Besides a liberal use of *fuck*—the best word ever—I try to combine words in a creative way. *Cumdumpster*, for example. Or *titmuffin. Coochburger. Butterdick.*"

Taryn smacks my thigh as she convulses forward with a silent laugh.

"*Cockschlong*," I try.

Lauren grins at me. "You wish."

"It's true, baby. Do you want to verify?"

She cocks an eyebrow. "You'd probably throw your back out in the process."

"Oh!" I sit up. "I didn't get a chance to tell you earlier. I got a cortisone shot in my L-five today, thanks to you."

"What?" She sets down her drink on the coffee table. "How'd that happen so fast?"

"I know people." My team physician ordered an MRI, fast-tracked the results, and shuttled me to a pain specialist for a guided corticosteroid injection all in the span of a few hours.

"You privileged, fucknut football coaches." But the dance of her eyes makes her appear eager, not angry. She rubs suggestive circles on my lower back and whispers in my ear, "Let's take advantage of that shot. Right now, Trent."

My heart gallops as I nod. I've been wanting this since that night in my bedroom when she admired my chest. I'll show her what my muscles can do.

Lauren pushes off the sofa, grabs my hand, and tugs me to my feet. "Uh, he's going to show me where the bathroom is."

"You'll be okay, Ryn?" I ask over my shoulder as Lauren speed-walks us to the stairs.

"Just don't break Dr. Stevens' bed!" she replies with a drunk grin.

We start frantic kisses on the top stair and somehow stumble into the guest bedroom where I slept the night Taryn moved in. Lauren yanks my shirt free from my jeans, pulling it up my torso as I back toward the bed. I let go of the sides of her face, where I'd anchored myself to kiss her more thoroughly, and lift my arms so she can remove my shirt. She reaches to unbuckle my belt, but I block her approach in order to slide her dark-red top up her body.

My breath catches at the sight of her bra. I didn't expect such a sexy, lacy undergarment on a woman as sporty as Lauren. From the perky swell of her breasts, my eyes slide up the creamy skin of her collarbone to lock onto her heated gaze. "Do you always wear black bras?"

Her hip juts to one side as she pushes up her breasts, highlighting the hardness of her nipples peeking through the silky cups. "You think *this* bra would support me when I jump at the net?"

"Fuck no." I wiggle my hands beneath hers—I should be the one fondling these beauties, not her—as I thank the sex gods for her foresight to wear this for me tonight. "Thank you," I breathe, massaging her soft fullness.

After she inhales a sharp breath, she makes her way back to my belt buckle. I feel her tug and unzip as tightness pools below my waist. Not wanting to fall behind, I unbutton her jeans and shrug them down over her hips. Score! She's wearing matching black panties. Cool air hits my thighs, and I look down to see my jeans falling to my knees. I kick out of them, leaving only my boxers.

To finish peeling black denim off of those gorgeous gams, I kneel before her. As she steps out of one leg, the line of muscle at the side of her quadriceps draws my attention. These long, powerful legs are so different from those on the skinny Oklahoma shorties who bedded me in college. Though I'm still bigger than Lauren, she has more of a presence than those girly airheads. This isn't a college girl's one-night attempt to suck the fame from a high-profile athlete. This isn't a social climber focused on elevating her status without a care for decency or character. This is real—two adults uniting, deepening their connection, finding comfort in each other. Judging by the energy coursing through me, I'm more turned on than I've ever been.

Lauren's busy massaging my hair when I notice a puckered circle at the top of her thigh. "What's this?" I touch the rough skin.

"Scar from my hip scope."

"Right." I see another round scar at the side of her leg, right below the hem of her panties. I connect the dots by kissing one surgical scar, then another. Her fingertips pulse deeper on my scalp, driving me to press upward and lick the soft skin of her belly. I feel her skin quiver beneath my lips as she gasps. Heat emanates from her. I hook my thumbs over the corners of her panties and glance up for permission.

She opens her eyes and looks down at me. The little shimmy of her hips answers for her, and I shuck the black silk to the floor. *Beautiful.* When I kiss the inside of her thigh, she shudders. I believe her trembling is from excitement, not shyness, but I decide to return here later. I don't want to rush; I want to savor her.

I get to my feet. "Any other injuries I should know about before I take you to bed?"

She giggles. As she circles her right shoulder forward, I hear some cracks. "Just an overuse injury on my hitting arm. But I can still do this." She reaches for the hem of my boxers and makes quick work of them. Just like that, I'm naked. I feel her eyes on me, exciting me.

"And I can do this." I circle my arms around her to unlatch her bra. It takes me a few frustrating moments, but at last I figure out the complicated clasps. After letting the thin straps fall over her shoulders and onto the floor, I behold her beguiling body. Before I know it, I've reached for her breasts, cupping their fullness in my palms. She emits a small cry as my thumbs circle her nipples. Her head tilts back, letting her hair tumble over her shoulders. Then she tugs me into her, engulfing me in heated kisses.

As she lifts one knee onto the end of the bed, I lean down to keep our mouths pressed together and follow her. Soon, we both kneel on the mattress while sharing urgent kisses and stroking touches. Her fingertips brush over a scar on the side of my knee, but memories of knee surgery vanish as her hand skates up my leg.

"Cocktastic," she murmurs.

I inhale—it's hard to think. "Prepare yourself for a Wolverine blitz, little Buckeye."

"Ooh, scary," she pants. "Hope that bum knee holds up."

I grin as I pat the nicotine patch on her bottom. "Hope your patch doesn't fall off from the friction."

"You're the only drug I need." She wriggles to the side and reaches behind her to pull down the covers, then scoots on her bottom up toward the pillows. She yanks me forward as she lowers onto her back. I crawl up her body, entwining my legs with hers. I circle my finger over the soft strands of hair near her temple as I hover over her.

Her chest heaves, and her lively eyes glitter. My breath catches in my throat as I stare down at her and feel her very real presence. I've waited for this moment, and now it's here. She's put her trust in me, and I want to do it right. I want to please her. I want to claim her. She sweeps long strokes up and down my back, lighting a fire up my spine. I don't break our gaze.

I've never felt this way about a woman—so drawn to her, bound to her, connected to her. I want to pour those surging feelings into her. I let the scorching energy building in my body take over and flow between us. It doesn't matter who we work for or what divides us; tonight, we are together. United.

***

As pale light filters through the blinds, creating a soft, warm glow, I realize this is the second time I've woken up with Lauren in my arms. This time is even better. My mouth curls into a smile, remembering our night. We've kicked down the blanket at some time during our sleep, leaving only the sheet to cover us. The heat surging between our bare skin is enough to keep us warm.

She doesn't snore, but her deep, even breaths tell me she's still asleep. I close my eyes and relish the feel of her languid body tucked close to mine.

I must've fallen back asleep, because the next time I open my eyes, she's studying me from across the pillow. The sunlight is brighter now, highlighting her halo of blond hair. I brush strands off her face and notice the tense set of her jaw. "What're you thinking about?"

She heaves a long sigh. "My mom."

Not her again.

"She's probably worried about me. I left a note, but she'll

still worry."

"What'd your note say?"

She leans in to kiss the tip of my nose. "Off to fuck a Wolverine."

That dirty mouth turns me on once again. "A tad overconfident, weren't you? How'd you know I was a sure thing?"

She sweeps her arm down her body, which is most unfortunately hidden by a sheet. "As if you'd turn this down."

I give her a broad grin. "Let's give your mom something more to worry about."

About an hour later, we emerge from the bedroom, sexed, showered, and dressed. I expect to find Taryn sacked out on the couch, possibly nursing a hangover, but she's nowhere to be found. I look at my phone and see a text from her.

"Damn." I point at the text. "She didn't wait for me to go to the gym with her."

Lauren shrugs. "You can come to my gym."

"Yeah?" I take out a carton of orange juice from the fridge. "What kind of workouts do you like?"

"I used to run and lift weights. Sam and I even ran a half-marathon, but then my hip pain kicked in. I haven't been back to the gym much since my surgery, until Sam started dragging me there. She thought it would help me quit smoking."

I hand her a glass of juice. "This too healthy for you?"

"Mountain Dew would be better." She takes the glass, though.

How does she stomach that nuclear-yellow soda this early in the day? Good thing I anticipated this request. I grab a can from the fridge and pour it over ice.

She actually squeals. "You bought that for me?" Her hand flies to her heart as her head angles to one side. "I'm in love."

Her tone sounds breathy and sarcastic, but her words make us both pause. A blush pinks her cheeks as she averts her gaze. Over the beat of my heart pounding in my ears, I hear her drink's effervescent fizz settling over the ice.

"I mean..." She still looks at the kitchen wall. "Now that you're caffeinating me, I'll definitely take you to my gym."

"Good." I pour a cup of caffeine for myself—the hot, black, beany kind. "I can make us some breakfast before we go?"

With a frown, she sets down her soda. "I have to get my gym clothes from home. And I should probably check on my mom." Her shoulders slump.

I stir soy milk into my coffee. I want to support her with her mother, but I sense that this is her battle, not mine. "Have you tried standing up to her?"

"That'd probably make her more hostile. And besides, she's right. I screwed up everything."

"Hey." I step closer and tuck her hair behind one ear. "You're not doing anything wrong. Well, except for being with a Michigan coach." That elicits a small smile from her. "You can tell her we practiced safe sex."

Her eyes get huge. "Horrorfuckshow, no!"

"Okay, maybe not." I grin. "But you said it yourself—coaches deserve to have lives, too. Coaches can date. There's nothing wrong with you trying to find love." I used the same word she did, and I don't flinch away from her. I let the word sit there between us, maintaining contact with eyes that convey a hint of fear mixed in with desire. I will never grow tired of looking into her expressive, striking eyes.

"Tell that to my mom."

"Do you want me to?"

She lets out a breath. "No. You're right—I need to stand up to her. I wish she wasn't such a hagbitch sometimes."

"She's just scared." I scrub my freshly shaven jaw. "She worries I'll hurt you like that other coach did."

"But you're nothing like him!"

Thank God. "Glad to hear it. And your mom will figure that out over time. Just be honest with her. You're an amazing woman—stand up for yourself. Stand up for *us*. Fight for us, Lauren."

She listens to my words, then straightens her shoulders. "I will." Then, the corners of her eyes turn down. "Do you have to go back to Michigan tomorrow?"

I feel my eyebrows pull together as I nod. Just as we're getting closer, one hundred and ninety-one miles will soon separate us again. "How 'bout you meet me in Chicago?"

"To visit your mom?"

"Sure, but first I have Big Ten football meetings."

"Oh, in July, right? I heard the OSU coaches talking about it. They were grumbling about traveling to Chicago—they think the meetings should be in Columbus since OSU wins the title every year."

What arrogant assholes! I glare at her. "Don't worry. They won't be reigning Big Ten champs this year."

Her smile is saccharine. "We'll see about that. Sign me up, Coach Trent."

Discovering

Lauren

Sunlight glints off the deep-blue lake, mesmerizing me, while seagulls chirp staccato cries. Though the July sun is hot on my shoulders, a cool breeze off Lake Michigan keeps me comfortable. The spray of sand as a player dives for the ball, followed by a few cheers from the crowd, draws my attention back to the volleyball match I'm recruiting at Chicago's North Avenue Beach.

Not a bad gig. As I sip icy Mountain Dew in the stands, I wonder if I should start coaching beach volleyball. True, Columbus doesn't have beaches, but even the landlocked University of Nebraska has a beach volleyball team that practices on an indoor sand court.

I focus on a sixteen-year-old hitter from Indianapolis. Julia's a pale redhead who looks out of place among the tanned bikini bodies of the other players—I hope she's slathered on sunscreen. She and her partner high-five after winning the point, thanks to Julia's hustle to keep the ball alive. My recruit's awkward moves and gangly limbs indicate that she's not yet at home in her sprouting, six-foot-three body, but she's doing better as a newbie on sand than I predicted. The game sure has changed since I played. Now more indoor players have added beach volleyball to their repertoire in an effort to increase their skills.

Not only is this tournament a good opportunity to watch my top recruits, it's also in Chicago. A giddy thrill vibrates my chest as I anticipate seeing Jeremy. He's busy attending Big Ten football sessions and media events at a hotel near O'Hare Airport, but he plans to meet me here soon.

Since Memorial Day, we've managed to spend three

weekends and a couple of weekdays together. We're trying to squeeze in as much time as possible before our seasons rev up in August. Heaviness weighs down my heart as I think about going weeks, maybe even months, without seeing him. It's becoming harder to say goodbye each time we're together. I freaking cried last week as I drove away from the hotel in Findlay, Ohio—our halfway meeting spot. WTF? I'm turning into a total sap.

Between sets, I study myself in the restroom mirror as volleyball fans enter and exit the stalls. My dark-gray sleeveless polo shirt and black skort don't look too wrinkled, but my wind-blown hair is wild. I take time to gather it into a neat ponytail before sliding my black visor back into place. Despite the visor, my face and exposed shoulders appear pink, so I reapply sunscreen. But now, my face looks shiny. It takes several minutes to touch up my makeup. After I press my lips together to distribute lipstick evenly, I scoff at my reflection. *Peckerbucket*. I never paid this much attention to my appearance before I met Jeremy.

After I emerge from the bathroom, a middle-aged man and woman approach me. "Coach Chase?" the woman asks.

The Ohio State logo on my shirt and visor have given me away. Her short, carrot-colored hair and freckles give *her* away. "You must be Julia's mom." I smile.

"I'm Ashley, and this is Julia's father, Walt."

I shake both of their hands. "Julia's playing well. I like her hustle."

"She's much better at indoor." Her tall father's facial muscles barely move.

"Well, it's only her second beach tournament."

Her mother lights up at my words. A Division One coach knows details about *her* daughter! Then, the woman's eyes expand as she looks to my right. "Oh, dear."

I follow her gaze to see Jeremy standing near the concession stand, looking yummy in a navy polo and khakis. The shirt is tight across his pectoral muscles and tucked in smartly at his lean waist. I want to get those clothes off of him.

"Is that the Michigan volleyball coach?" my recruit's father asks.

I'm so accustomed to seeing the tasteless yellow M on his shirts that I didn't even notice it at first. There are also yellow stripes running over his shoulders that echo the design of their football helmets. I have to admit the shirt looks badass, especially on him.

Jeremy takes a few strides toward us and removes his sport sunglasses as he looks at the man. "I coach football, sir."

"But you're not far off, Walt," I say. "Michigan's volleyball coach is also a man, whereas *my* players appreciate playing for a woman. They say I understand them better."

A narrowing of Jeremy's eyes makes me want to laugh.

"What's a football coach doing at a volleyball match?" asks the mother.

Jeremy and I exchange nervous glances.

"I'm in town for Big Ten meetings," Jeremy explains. "Had to check out the lakefront, but I didn't realize I'd run into Ohio State fans." He wrinkles his nose as if he smells a foul odor. "I'll be leaving now."

We watch him walk in the direction of the lake.

"I'm also heading out." I feel a gravitational pull toward the navy-shirted man striding away from me. I reach into my little backpack-purse. "Here's my business card—let's keep in touch. Julia's high on our list, and she'll love smashing sets from the nation's number-one recruit."

A spark of interest flashes in Walt's eyes. "Emma Watkins committed to OSU?"

I grin. The fact that a volleyball dad in another state knows Emma is testament to her talent. Recruiting became much easier the day she signed with us. "Yes. We're thrilled Emma's a Buckeye."

"Not bad." Walt nods like I just earned his respect.

"Good luck to Julia—not that she needs it." I give a little wave as I walk away from them, parallel to the water. Once I see that they've returned to the stands, I jog toward the blue expanse of the second biggest Great Lake. I find Jeremy's powerful physique silhouetted against the water and skyline as he faces southeast.

Skipping up to him on the sand, I take his hand in mine.

He gives my hand a squeeze. "I miss this view."

The reflection of skyscrapers on the shimmering water *is* impressive. Traffic from Lake Shore Drive provides a broad, humming soundtrack for the vibrant city. Chicago in the summertime is a place to behold.

"Got rid of those annoying parents?" asks Jeremy.

I knock my shoulder into his. "Their daughter's in the bag now that they know Emma Watkins is my setter."

"I hear you. Every QB coach in the Big Ten wants to know how we acquired Evan."

"How were your meetings?"

He removes his sunglasses and slides them into a pocket. Then, he leans across me to clasp my other hand, pulling me to face him. Smiling down at me, his gaze roams over my face until it lands on my eyes. "I missed *this* view." He nudges below my visor to kiss me, and I close my eyes as I feel his warm mouth on mine. He lets go of my hands and cradles the sides of my face as he deepens the kiss. All the stress of airports, flights, ride shares, and recruiting melts away when I'm in his arms.

He presses a smooch to the side of my nose. "You have the cutest little freckles here, sweet cheeks." His lips skate across my face and peck at my jaw before nibbling my earlobe, and a purr escapes from my throat.

Suddenly self-conscious, I glance to the side and notice three older women staring at us from the bike path nearby. Once I step back from Jeremy, they resume their speed-walk north.

"Whoops," Jeremy laughs as he puts on his sunglasses. "Caught gettin' busy on North Avenue Beach."

"Gettin' biz-aaayyy," I echo.

His smile fades. "How's your mom?"

I tilt my head toward the city. "Want to walk?"

"Sure."

As we stride down the bike path, hand in hand, I tell him about my recent visit to Cincinnati. The OSU oncologist confirmed the treatment plan outlined by my mom's hometown doctors, so a Cincinnati surgeon performed a mastectomy two weeks ago.

"How's she doing? That's gotta be tough for her," Jeremy

says.

I grimace. "She's been in some pain, of course, but she wanted her breast removed instead of having to get chemo or radiation. And her oncologist says it looks good that she won't need more treatment, if the scans turn out like they expect."

He lets go of my hand and extends his arm across my shoulders, tucking me into his solid body. I feel cocooned against the light wind swirling off of the lake as we continue our stroll. "How're *you* doing?"

I consider his question. "My mom's actually been nicer to me lately. Maybe this health crisis has made her reexamine her life or something, and she's less worried about the things that usually stress her out." I look up at him. "She loved the suck-up flowers you sent, by the way. White lilies, nice touch."

His grin is smug.

"She even said, 'Please thank Vegan Boy for me.'"

His grin vanishes. "Vegan *Man*."

I smirk. "I guess it's my dad I'm more worried about. Before I left, he gave me this begging look, like *please don't abandon me*."

"Because he didn't want to be left alone with her?"

"Yeah, but this was different. He has no fucking clue how to deal with his emotional fallout from her cancer. He's totally freaked out." I picture him fidgeting by the kitchen island as he watched me spoon takeout Chinese onto plates. Sitting at the table, Mom read aloud from her iPad about side effects from the medication her oncologist prescribed. The entire time, Dad said nothing, just watched with wary eyes. He seemed so helpless.

I snuggle the crown of my head into Jeremy's shoulder. "I know my dad doesn't like when my mom bitches at him, but he's still scared of losing her. It's like they need each other in some dependent, dysfunctional way." I stop walking and turn to him. "I don't want us to be like them, okay?"

He watches me. "You're not like her, Lauren. You know that, right?"

I see my reflection in his sunglasses, and my screwed-up eyes look skeptical.

"Sure, you give me shit about where I work," he says. "But I like that. I like your sass. You keep me on my toes."

My shoulders lower a notch.

"You're way more critical of *yourself* than you are of me." He takes my hand, and we resume our walk.

After a minute, I ask, "Will you let me know if I'm acting like my mom?"

He doesn't respond.

"I mean, don't compare me to her," I clarify. "That might piss me off. But let me know if I'm being too harsh? Too unfair?"

"I can do that." He nods. "But only if you'll tell *me* when I'm being a jerk. When I'm distant, or make things all about myself." His lips press together. "I don't want us to be like my parents, either."

From the muscle ticking in his jaw, I surmise that he doesn't want to expand on that topic. I'll wait to learn more about his parents when we visit his mother tomorrow.

A pair of rollerbladers brake as they pass us, then reverse direction on the path and skate up to us.

"Well, lookee here," the woman says.

The balding man laughs as he points at our shirts. "A Wolverine and a Buckeye, hand in hand." His southern drawl sounds mocking.

Jeremy and I halt, and I feel him brace next to me like he's expecting verbal abuse.

"Coexist!" the man says before he folds the petite woman into his side.

I squint at them.

The woman shakes her head. "This idiot—" She tosses her thumb over her shoulder at him. "—went to Alabama, but I graduated from the much better school: Auburn."

"Roll tide!" bellows the man.

"Good to see we're not the only bi-rival couple." She winks at me.

Jeremy nods. "Bi-rival. I like that."

A gray-haired man stares a little too long at us as he jogs by. He's not a Big Ten football coach discovering our bi-rival romance, is he? The woman must read my consternation because she cups my left shoulder and says, "Relax, sugar. We won't tell anyone."

I notice a wedding ring on her finger.

Her husband's eyebrows furrow. "You two haven't come out to the world yet? But then why y'all wearing your school colors?"

"To antagonize each other," I answer.

Jeremy shakes his head at me, then looks at the couple. "Any tips for 'coming out', as you call it?"

"You'll be fine," says the husband. "People will be surprised at first, give you some hell, but they'll get over it."

Jeremy adjusts his sunglasses. "Our employers might not."

"Oh, shoot." The man dips his chin. "You both work for your schools?" Our silence answers for us. "Better keep those chickens in the coop, then."

I chuckle. This man is just like the father of one of my former players at University of Cincinnati. She was from Mississippi, and her dad would holler the most endearing Southernisms from the stands, like, "Y'all fryin' their ham to-*night*!" or "Flim flam, bim bam, Cincinnati, by damn!"

"Thanks for the advice." There's wry amusement in Jeremy's voice.

The wife tugs at her husband's shirt. "Richie, we gotta go. Nice to meet you two."

"You as well," I say.

The husband drawls, "Bless your heart."

We watch them rollerblade north. Jeremy rubs his thumb over my knuckles. "Better keep those chickens in the coop," he mimics. "Speaking of chicken, want to head back to the hotel before we grab some dinner?"

I smirk. "Soy chicken, Vegan Man?"

Jeremy laughs. "Do you realize you just said, 'I am chicken' in Spanish?"

"I guess that's right—I *am* chicken about people discovering our secret. Let's get you out of these Michigan clothes right away."

He lowers his sunglasses a notch to let me see his eyes. "Yes, you need to take off that ugly gray shirt, Coach Chase. Dinner will have to wait."

***

As Jeremy hands his car keys to the hotel valet, I realize we didn't think this through. We've booked our own rooms on separate floors, but there are Michigan coaches on Jeremy's floor and Ohio State coaches on mine. The OSU travel office decided to add me to the large block of rooms for the football staff when I submitted a recruiting trip request.

I whisper, "Maybe we should go to our own rooms and change clothes first."

"Hells, no!" He gestures for me to enter the revolving door. After we emerge into the lobby, his lips brush my ear. "I can't wait that long."

Heat blooms up my spine.

"Besides, there's a football coach social in the conference center right now," he adds in a low voice.

"Shouldn't you be there?"

He holds up his phone. "I just *had* to call a recruit in Texas."

He punches the elevator button and rocks on his heels, seeming proud of himself for setting up this clandestine tryst.

My heart pumps excitement through my bloodstream. It's all I can do to keep my hands off his belt. "My room?" I propose.

"Your room have a jacuzzi?"

My mouth drops as I shake my head. "Football coaches," I mutter.

His grin is huge as we step into the empty elevator. He presses the button for the sixth floor, and I give him a puzzled look. "Didn't you say you're on the fourth floor?"

"My room's by the stairs, so we'll take a couple of flights to avoid detection." His large hand pats my butt cheek. "Gotta protect your virtue for Mama Chase."

"Fuck my virtue."

His eyes smolder. "Exactly."

The elevator dings, and we pull apart. I wait a beat before following him out, but the hallway is empty. He opens the stairwell door, sticks his head in, then looks back at me. "C'mon, sweetness."

151

When he takes my hand and tugs me down the stairs, I giggle. The thrill of getting caught is a sensation I haven't felt since sneaking out to party with my friends in high school. We're almost to his floor when I hear someone coming up the concrete stairs below us. Jeremy stops cold, and I lunge for the side railing to avoid careening into him.

On the landing below, another Michigan coach stands stock still, holding the hand of a leggy brunette. His craggy face appears thirty years older than hers—what a womanizing cad. As I look closer at him, I draw in a quick breath. *Shitbiscuit.* He looks like the head coach. The older man jettisons the woman's hand from his grasp, but Jeremy tightens his grip on mine.

"Coach Trent." The man scowls at Jeremy, then at me.

Jeremy swallows. "Coach Froth."

Yep, he's Jeremy's boss.

"After you, sir." Jeremy holds out his arm in the direction of the fourth-floor exit.

Coach Froth opens the door for the woman, and it clangs shut behind them.

We're both breathing hard as we stare at each other on the stairs. "How'd that just happen?" I ask.

He shakes his head. "The conference center is on the third floor. I should've known—should've kept you on the elevator, damn it." We wait a bit before hustling into his hotel room.

He paces the expansive room as he grips his skull. My throat tightens as I watch his distress. Did I just make things hard for him? He's told me a little about his boss, and the man sounds like a dickhead. But Jeremy won't get fired just for being with a Buckeye, right?

"Guess your boss didn't want to take the elevator just one floor up," I muse as I remove my visor and toss it onto the dresser.

Jeremy lets out a grunt. "They were sneaking around, just like us. That woman's not his wife."

"I gathered that." My mind goes to Paul in an instant, and I feel my stomach turn. I sink onto a chair. "She's not an assistant coach, right?" *No, it's unlikely for a woman to coach football.* I untie my running shoes. "A staffer?"

He sits on the bed. "Never seen her before." He looks at me and must read the disgust on my face. "Hate to tell you, but he's not the first coach to have something on the side."

I cringe as I kick off my shoes and socks. "I know."

He nods. "The seedy side of the big-time college football, like I said. Sometimes it feels like you're selling your soul to do this job."

"It's not just football that's seedy. Ethical breaches can happen in any sport."

He studies me. Neither of us mentions my affair with my head coach, but it's there all the same.

"Anyway," I continue, "I hope you don't get into trouble with Froth."

He sighs. "Like that 'Bama guy would say, the chickens have done flown the coop."

"Maybe not." I sink back into the chair with my legs straightened in front of me. "Don't worry about your boss. He's got a secret to protect, too. He's fixin' to keep that chicken locked up tight."

"I hope you're right."

A question pops in my head, but I chew on my lip, wondering if I want to know the answer. "Have you...?" He meets my gaze, and the depth of honesty in his eyes propels me forward. "Have you ever had...something on the side?"

When his mouth twitches, I realize the jealous undertones of my question, and my face warms.

"I have to admit I wasn't a saint in undergrad. Girls threw themselves at us..." He winces before he looks at his feet. "Not that it's an excuse. I was young and stupid."

I fiddle with my silver necklace. "Was this when you were injured?"

He angles his head to one side. "Mostly, yeah. Why do you ask?"

"I've watched some of my players go off the rails after injuries. Their grades tank, they make dumb decisions, alcohol, depression...well, except for my setter. She's been golden for us despite blowing out her knee twice."

153

"Huh." He stares at the wall. "The knee injury and concussions *were* some pretty dark times for me. Maybe I thought girls would make it all better. But they didn't." He looks at me. "That's not what I want in my life, Lauren. I want what Adrian Nichols has."

He's told me about his best friend, one of the best quarterbacks in the NFL, who married young and has three children.

"Screw Bill Froth," he says. "Screw 'em all." His eyes blaze. "No matter what people think, I want *you*. You're the only woman in my life—you know that, right?"

I pop off the chair and lift my shirt over my head before chucking it next to my visor in a heap of discarded OSU gear. "Scoot back," I demand, and Jeremy barely gets into position before I try to climb up his legs onto the bed. The minimal give of my skort limits my leg spread, however, so I wiggle out of it and straddle him in only my sports bra and panties.

His warm hands stroke my back as he looks up at me with a twinkle in his eye. "Beautiful, sugar."

His poor attempt at a Southern accent makes me smile. I tug his shirt free of his pants and slide it up and off of him. Tracing my finger over the band of muscle on one shoulder, I admire his powerful body. He sure has power over me. He's become even more cut now that his decreased back pain allows him to run. After a series of steroid injections, he got a nerve ablation in his L5 that's really helped him. But even if he weren't so fit, I'd still be drawn to him. He's intelligent, insightful, steady, and strong. With him in my world, I feel like I can do anything.

"Am I the only man in your life, Lauren?" He glides his fingers up and down the nape of my neck.

I lean back into his touch. "As if you have to ask." But his eyes still bore into me, waiting for my response. "Absofuckinglutely."

"Good answer. I'll reward you by sharing my jacuzzi."

"What generosity, you entitled cockschlong."

He kisses me, and I feel his lips spread into a grin as they mold to mine.

16

Driving
Jeremy

"**H**ow much longer?" asks Lauren from the passenger seat of my SUV.

I see through the swishing windshield wipers that we're about to merge from I-57 South onto I-80 West. We left the hotel two hours ago, luckily avoiding further confrontations with rival coaches on our way out, and we had brunch downtown before heading to my mom's. "Ten minutes or so."

She fiddles with her hands in her lap, looking like she wants a cigarette. After four months, she's kicked smoking—she doesn't even use a patch anymore—but the cravings are probably still there in times of stress.

"Nervous?" I ask.

She glances at my speedometer. "You could drive faster, you know."

I smirk as I scoop up her fidgeting left hand in mine. "My mom's going to love you, sweetheart."

Her narrowed eyes express doubt, but she squeezes my hand. The mournful Fleetwood Mac song on the radio delivers ambience that matches the gray, wet farmland scenery on both sides of the highway.

"This doesn't look much like the big city."

"No one's heard of Frankfort, Illinois," I say. "It's easier to tell people I'm from Chicago."

"What's the population of Frankfort?"

I look up to the right. "A little under twenty-thousand."

"Was it hard to get recruited from a town that small?"

"Not if you're from Lincoln-Way East High School." I puff out

155

my chest. "We were state champs my senior year."

She grins. "Still stuck in the glory days, I see."

"I plan to move those glory days from the past to the present this year."

With a shake of her head, she says, "Then you'll need to coach for a different university."

Grr. "Button your lips, Buckeye."

We listen to Stevie Nicks sing about thunder and raining.

"You said Adrian Nichols quarterbacked for your high school?" she asks a few minutes later.

"Yeah, though not till we were seniors. He played receiver before that." The summer rain slows to a drizzle, and I let go of her hand to adjust the speed of my wipers.

"That's weird. Why'd he switch positions?"

Because I told my high-school coach that if he didn't let Adrian try out for quarterback, I'd quit. I was sick of three years of anemic passes from our starting QBs, and I knew Adrian had a mighty arm after throwing the ball around with him in the off-season. But it seems egotistical to take credit for his amazing performance now. Adrian is the one who worked his butt off to earn his success, not me.

I shrug. "My coach finally saw the light."

She takes that in. "You followed Adrian to Oklahoma, then?"

I lean away from her. "He followed *me*. I committed my junior year. D-One schools weren't even looking at him until he had such a great senior year. I told the Oklahoma coaches how talented he was, and they snatched him up before other schools could get him."

"Wow. He should pay you part of his NFL salary."

I laugh. "He probably should."

My phone rings, and the embarrassing caller ID flashes on my dashboard console. After I let the call go to voicemail, Lauren asks, "Who's Hair-Bear?"

I wait a bit before admitting, "Harry Stevens, our offensive coordinator. He's got back hair like you've never seen."

"Nice image." She shudders. "So, you're ignoring a call from your boss?"

"Technically." I love that she understands the football-coaching hierarchy. "Though Froth's such a micro-manager that he doesn't give Harry much authority."

"You call him Hair-Bear, but you don't like him?"

I look at her. "No, he's a good guy. Why do you say that?"

"You didn't answer his call."

"I don't want work to interfere with our time together."

"Uh-huh." She gives me a knowing look. "Nor do you want an OSU coach to overhear you talking to a Michigan coach."

Bingo. "Jeez, you're paranoid, Chase."

Before she can reply, her phone buzzes, and she looks at a text. "My libero's freaking out about her organic chemistry exam."

I've learned from Lauren that a libero is a defensive specialist; a shorter player among giants. "She's a pre-med major?"

Lauren nods. Her fingers fly over her phone as she replies to the text.

"How does she have time for all the labs?"

"She's taking orgo in the summer because it's tough to fit it all in. But she's wicked smart—if anyone can pull it off, she can. Patrick says she knows way more about the game than he did in college."

After she finishes her text, she returns her phone to her lap.

"What advice did you give her?"

"I told her I know jack shit about chemistry, but I do know she's smart as shit, so she'll ace the test as long as she studies her ass off." She aims a sweet smile at me, and I know she texted those exact words to her player.

If I played volleyball, I think I'd very much like to play for Coach Chase. There's no pretense there—just a blunt belief in her players' potential, and a crass, fiery passion to push them out of their comfort zone. I know *I'm* uncomfortable with Froth discovering I'm sleeping with the enemy. How will this bi-rival, long-distance romance play out? Is it sustainable?

I take a peek at Lauren's tanned, sculpted legs extending from white jean shorts, and my eyes glide up to her royal blue, flowy shirt, which brings out the sapphire of her eyes. Somehow, we need to make this work. I want this relationship to endure. I want Lauren to be the first *and* last woman I take home to meet my mom.

When my phone rings again, I frown. It's unlike Harry to call me twice unless there's a problem. But I can't tell him Lauren is with me—unless Froth has already ratted me out—and I don't want her to overhear our conversation.

She cups my shoulder. "C'mon, Hair-Bear can't be as bad as Alex."

As I fondly remember her obnoxious friend, I answer the call.

"Where are you?" asks Harry.

I tense. "On my way out to Frankfort." That's not a lie. I wonder if he's upset that I'm skipping morning meetings. "All the QB stuff was yesterday, so I didn't think I needed to be there today. Sorry I didn't run that by you first."

"Nah, today's agenda's a waste of time. It's good you're visiting your mom."

Hearing his affable tone, I let out a breath.

"I didn't see you last night at the social or dinner," Harry says. "And then I got a text from Rafael Diaz's dad—he's on my case about them not hearing from you."

The Texas recruit I was supposed to call. *Crap.* I close my eyes.

"Just checking to see you're okay," adds Harry.

I glance at Lauren, and she's looking down at her hands. "My bad, Hair. The OSU quarterbacks' coach was up my butt all day, pumping me for info about how we landed Evan. I wanted to avoid him last night."

Harry makes a sound of disgust. "He's almost as bad as the head coach. Damn, that Malone's such a pompous prick. Shady, too."

Lauren sports a small smile as we trash-talk the Ohio State head football coach, Sean Malone.

"Swear to God that entire staff cheats," Harry rails. "How else do they land five of the nation's top-ten recruits in one year?"

"Yeah, something's off," I agree. "Good thing Evan's father is a Wolverine, or the Buckeyes might've swept up six of the top ten this year." We vent about the OSU staff for a while before I say, "Sorry Diaz slipped my mind—I'll make sure to call him soon."

After we hang up, I notice Lauren no longer smiles. She's grown quiet as she stares out at the houses of my mom's neighborhood.

"You okay?"

Her eyes pinch at the corners. "What Harry said... Is it true? We're not cheating, are we?"

I give her credit for asking that. I'd feel defensive in an instant if someone suggested our recruiting wasn't above board. "You're an Ohio State coach. What've you heard?"

She rubs her collarbone.

When she doesn't respond, I say, "Probably sour grapes. Harry played for Michigan years ago, so he hates losing to you guys especially."

"If Harry thinks Malone's a prick, how does he feel about Froth?"

"Harry toes the line in public, but we both think the same thing: Froth's a total ass." I pull into the driveway of my modest childhood home. "The good news is, Harry didn't ask anything about you. Maybe you're right that Froth will keep his mouth shut."

We're approaching the front door of the ranch house when Lauren freezes. "We forgot to do a swear-word exorcism."

I grin, recalling her barrage as we sat in the Watkins' driveway. "No need—my mom will love you, swear words and all." I kiss her hand. "You're very lovable."

She bumps her hip into mine. "You too, Jer-Bear."

My mother opens the door before I can decide if I like that new nickname. "Jeremy!" she cries, holding out her arms. "It's been too long."

With a stab of guilt piercing my chest, I wrap her in a hug. Mom gets lonely, and I should visit her more often.

After we let go of each other, I introduce Lauren. I view my mother through my girlfriend's eyes. Anna Trent is taller than average, but shorter than Lauren and me, with a light-brown bob and warm blue eyes. She complains about her round belly, but she keeps herself in pretty good shape for a fifty-six year old. Twelve-hour shifts as a nurse help preserve her fitness.

"You're right, Jeremy." My mother beams at me. "Lauren *is* beautiful."

Lauren laughs. "I like you already, Mrs., uh, Ms. Trent..."

"Call me Anna." Mom invites us in.

I still don't understand why she kept my father's name. He left us twenty-three years ago—why the loyalty? Equally perplexing is why she never remarried.

Mom leads us into her kitchen, painted the same drab light yellow from my childhood. I offered to pay a contractor to spruce up the joint, but my mom wouldn't hear of it.

"Are you hungry?" Mom gestures to the spread of food almost spilling over the table.

She shouldn't have gone to all this trouble on her day off. "Mom, I told you we went out for brunch in the Loop. You didn't have to do that."

She removes a glass and cup from the pantry. "I'll just get you something to drink, then."

Lauren smirks as she notices the two-liter of her favorite beverage and other items of questionable nutrition on the table. "Jeremy knows the best restaurants in Chicago, but I'm never too full for candy." She plucks a Twizzler from the open bag and slides it into her mouth. When those plump, red lips suck the licorice, I find myself gawking. Too bad we already checked out of the hotel.

"Jeremy."

I turn my attention to my mother and realize I missed her question. "What?"

"I asked where you took Lauren for dinner last night."

"Oh. Big Bowl. Lauren likes Chinese food, and it has great vegan options."

Mom hands us beverages and shoos us into the living room. The space is neat, but the dark paneling and worn plaid sofa feel depressing.

After Mom sits in the rocker lounge chair and Lauren joins me on the sofa, Lauren asks, "Are you vegan too, Anna?"

"Egads, no. Jeremy didn't start that craziness until after he moved away from home."

Lauren leans toward my mom and holds her hand up to one side of her mouth, but I hear her all the same. "He ordered kung pao *tofu*." She and my mom convulse together.

"Ladies." I jut out my chin. "Don't judge."

Mom and I sip coffee while Lauren swigs her nuclear-yellow drink.

Lauren eyes me. "I never asked before—why'd you go vegan?"

I shrug. "Because I want to be a head coach."

She peers at me.

I set down my coffee. "There's a sports dietitian I worked with at Arizona State—he's amazing. He understands performance nutrition like no one else. He told me that plant-based diets bring on all kinds of benefits, like improved blood flow and endurance." In the presence of my mother, I omit the scientific finding about increased sex drive from veggies. That perk has felt like a disadvantage due to living so far from Lauren, anyway. "When I'm working fifteen-hour days, my diet's a good way to keep my energy going."

"I learn a lot from our sport dietitians, too," she says. "They're great. Well, except for one of them."

The dark cloud crossing her face indicates she's thinking of her boss, Rhonda, a former sports dietitian. I try to take her mind off her troubles. "Proof's in the soy pudding. Once I started a vegan diet, I landed the Michigan job."

"Hardly a performance improvement, I'd say."

Lauren's jab makes Mom laugh.

"Mom," I whine, "Don't egg her on."

"Oh, this silly rivalry." Mom shakes her head. "You know, Jeremy, with the sheer number of schools you've coached, you could have just as easily landed at another Big Ten school like Ohio State."

"Blasphemy," I say.

But at least Lauren and I would live in the same town if we coached together. Would we have started a relationship if we both worked at the same school? Would I even know her? We football coaches rarely have time to attend the all-staff coach meetings. Since I started at Michigan, I've come to recognize a few coaches from other sports, but we're so siloed that it's not a meaningful connection.

Mom rocks in her chair as she looks at Lauren. "Jeremy has always been competitive—don't take it personally. He felt the same way about Mount Carmel."

I notice confusion on Lauren's face, so I explain, "That was our rival high school, up in Chicago. A Catholic all-boys school."

"You absolutely hated Mount Carmel, but you could've easily gone there yourself, if—" Mom catches herself and stops speaking.

If Dad hadn't left us for another woman. My father used to talk about saving money to send me to the selective high school. But after the divorce, Mom applied for a nursing job in Frankfort and moved us here. The cover story was that it was too expensive to keep living in the city, but I think there's more to it than that. Chicago holds too many painful memories for my mother.

I try to pull her out of those memories. "Adrian hates Mount Carmel, too," I offer.

Her expression lightens as I knew it would at the mention of his name. "How *is* Adrian?"

"Haven't spoken to him since he started camp." NFL preseason tends to slurp up all of his time. "But I plan to call him on my drive home, after I drop Lauren at the airport."

"I wish you could stay longer." Mom sighs as she rocks in her chair. "So, Lauren, Jeremy tells me you're from Cincinnati?"

"Where I attended Catholic school."

I arch one eyebrow. "Didn't take, apparently."

She doesn't blanch. "Right? What a waste of my parents' money. But we did have the best volleyball team in the city."

"How long have you been coaching?" Mom asks.

Lauren pauses. "Fourteen years—that sounds like a long time. Not much to show for it."

"Didn't your team win the national championship?" Mom asks.

"You know about that, too?" Lauren gives me an appraising look. She didn't mention me one time to her parents, but she's all I can talk about when I call my mother.

"That must've felt like a lot of pressure to win the title early in your career," says Mom.

Lauren exhales as she looks down. "So much pressure." She sighs. "I'm not sure how we did it. Well, my setter was a big reason. Cherise was a special player before her knee injuries took her out. Also, my athletic director's great." She glances at me, then back at Mom. "He gave me everything I asked for. I didn't like our strength coach, so I got a new one. And my recruiting budget's off the hook—OSU spares no expense at helping their coaches win."

"How nice for you," I growl.

She ignores my sarcasm. "I just threw myself into coaching, into my team, that year. I loved those girls. I'd do anything for them. If something crappy came at me, I pushed it away and refocused on volleyball. I was so hell-bent on proving myself."

"Proving yourself to whom?" Mom asks.

Lauren starts. After a beat, she looks at me. There's torment in her eyes, and I realize she's thinking about her head coach. Will she tell my mother about the affair?

"Lots of people," she says. "I've made mistakes, done things I regret." She closes her eyes and shakes her head. "But I didn't let it bother me. My team was all I cared about. At the tournament, we got lucky when the top two seeds got beat in the semifinals. It just clicked for us that year."

"What a high," I say.

Lauren frowns. "The high didn't last long. Some coaches might build on that success, but I choked under the pressure. I let the stress beat me down."

Mom tilts her head. "It's hard for all of us to deal with stress."

Lauren harrumphs. "I *suck* at it."

I consider her response. She's tried to push away stress by smoking and swearing, and maybe drinking, too. I wonder if walling herself off from men has been one of her strategies as well. I hope she doesn't push me away.

"You've already proven yourself to me, sweet cheeks." I wink at her.

She seems to let go of her sad funk as she smirks. "You're not there yet with me, Jer-Bear, but keep trying."

Mom laughs.

"Anyway," Lauren adds, "Coaching has felt way more fun this year. Our second national title will be even sweeter."

Huh. She's gone from thinking she'll get fired to plotting another championship. I guess that's what Emma Watkins can do for a program. I'm optimistic about this fall as well, but not as cocky as Lauren. As a head coach, she has a lot more control over her program than I do.

Lauren's ice cubes clink in her glass as she takes another sip.

Mom says, "I love your nails."

"Thanks!" Lauren extends her arm and shows off her red, sparkly fingernails.

"But how do you have time for manicures as a coach?"

Lauren reaches for her purse-backpack. "I do them myself. Have you seen these nail polish strips before?"

Mom examines the package Lauren has handed her. "Well, look at that!"

"I can show you how to apply them, if you like. They're fuh—" She blushes. "Super easy."

Mom smiles. "I'd love that."

"But choose a different color for my mom," I order.

Lauren rolls her eyes.

This seems like a good time to leave them to their girlish pursuits. I stand. "Mom, why don't you sit next to Lauren, and I'll go call a recruit."

Mom usually complains when my coaching duties encroach on our time together, but she scampers over to the sofa with barely a glance at me. I wait for Lauren to send me a pleading don't-leave-me-alone-with-your-mother look, but she seems absorbed in showing the nail strips to my mom. They've only just met, but the ease of their interaction makes them seem like old friends.

***

A few hours later, we drive to airport after a tearful goodbye with my mother. The lump in my throat from watching her cry took several miles to subside. Mom stocked the backseat of my car with leftovers and made Lauren promise to visit again soon. I don't know how that will be possible with our seasons about to begin.

"I knew I'd like your mom," Lauren says.

"Yeah? How'd you know?"

She leans over to kiss my cheek. "'Cause she made you." She nods. "And Taryn."

Taryn has told me she hangs out with Lauren and Sam all the time. Now that *Project Runway* is between seasons, they've been binge-watching *The Bachelor*, drinking every time someone says the word *journey*. They get so sloshed some nights that they have to sleep over instead of making the short walk home.

"Your mom told me you're a big reason Taryn earned a basketball scholarship," Lauren says. "You used to coach her all the time."

I remember our arguments on the neighborhood court. Taryn didn't like it when I pushed her to practice more, but she had no one else to encourage her. I didn't want her to miss out on realizing her athletic potential just because Dad left when she was young.

It sounds like Mom really warmed up to Lauren. "I can tell my mom likes you, too," I say.

"Well, she's much easier to get along with than my mom."

I twist my mouth to one side. "I could probably say the same thing about our fathers, in reverse."

A mile or two go by as the easy-listening station plays from my satellite radio.

"Your mom told me your dad's a cop—a detective, I mean."

I let that sit between us. After I finished the phone call to my recruit, I did notice a more somber vibe in the room. But then they giggled as they showed off my mom's scarlet nails.

"Did you ever want to become a police officer?" she asks.

I nod. "I used to worship my dad. He was a big part of my life. He coached me in football and basketball and baseball—until he left."

"He stopped going to your games after the divorce?"

Tension spreads through my body. "He'd show up randomly, and it'd tense me up, searching the stands every time to see if he was there. I started playing badly. Mom said she could talk to him, but I didn't want to drag her into it—she always cried after he yelled at her. So, I was the one who told my dad in no uncertain terms to stop coming to my games. And he listened."

She rubs my shoulder. "I'm sorry."

I focus on the outline of the city ahead of us, noticing low clouds obscuring the upper levels of skyscrapers.

"When I asked your mom why she never remarried, she said she was so busy working and raising you two and she didn't have time to date. And now she thinks she's too set in her ways to be with anyone."

Wow. Lauren coaxed some good intel from Mom.

"She's worried about you living alone, though, being single."

That I already know. "Does your mom get on your case about not being married?"

She pauses. "You know, not really. She hasn't pressured me once about dating, or about giving her grandkids, either."

My mother hasn't said anything about me having children, but I know she would love to be a grandmother. She often mentions her friends' grandchildren when we talk.

I let a mile go by and ask, "Do you think you want to have kids one day?"

"You mean other than the twenty children I coach?"

We share a rueful smile.

She rubs her thigh. "When I was young, I definitely thought I'd be a parent. I wanted to bond with my kids over sports, encourage them instead of criticizing them. But then..." She looks ahead at the concrete jungle in the distance. "Well, I'm pretty old. It probably won't happen for me." After a moment, she looks at me. "What about you?"

I know my answer right away, even though I haven't had the

best role model when it comes to fatherhood. "I want kids. I just don't want to screw them up."

She studies me, and I try to figure out what she's thinking. Does that scare her off? Might she want to have children, too? Possibly with me?

A Christopher Cross song starts playing, and she scowls at the radio. "Okay, what the buttertwat is this station?"

"Yacht Rock Radio."

Her lower lip pulls down at the corners. "That's for real? I mean, it's a station people under the age of eighty can listen to?"

"Easy, sweet cheeks. It relaxes me after a long day at work."

"Oh my God. Another weird thing about you." We take the exit for the airport, and she slumps in her seat. "Another thing I'll miss about you."

I slow my speed as I think of a thousand things I'll miss about her. The summery smell of her hair. Her playful, snarky teasing. The challenging sparkle in her eyes. Her long legs. The dedication she shows for her craft.

As we pull up to departures and I put the car in park, sadness fills the vehicle.

"How long is your drive home?" she asks.

"About four hours." When she frowns, I add, "I've got yacht rock and recruiting calls to keep me company."

"And calling your friend Adrian."

I nod. "Thanks for the reminder, though he probably won't be free." I turn to her. "You haven't asked me much about him. Most people want to know what a famous person is like in real life."

She shrugs. "He's just a person."

"He is." I have no doubt that Adrian will feel at ease with her, just like my family does. That's yet another thing I'll miss about Lauren: her down-to-earth nature. She doesn't fawn over the glamour of revenue sports. Instead, she fights for women's volleyball. After catching a glimpse of Lauren's intensity and Emma's athleticism, I'm beginning to view their sport as every bit as important as mine. Each of our sports has unique difficulties, but we both try to claw our way toward excellence. The struggle of the fight makes it all the more worthwhile.

She sits motionless, staring at her lap. I hope the airport police won't harass us for lingering.

"Maybe you can catch a later flight?" I suggest.

Her lips press together. "But you have to be at work early tomorrow."

I have to break down video tonight, actually. I try not to think about the endless tasks awaiting me now that my season's knocking on the door.

"Maybe I could skip my flight and drive with you?" She still looks down.

"I'd love that." I don't blink at the idea of adding five hours of driving to my trip if I could spend more time with her. "But I'm guessing you have even more work than I do waiting for you at home."

She gives a perfunctory nod, then squeezes her hands into fists.

I dip my shoulder to try to see her face. "Lauren?" She averts her eyes. "Look at me, sweetheart."

As she looks up, I detect a sheen of unshed tears that hits me in the gut. I gather her in my arms as best I can in the front seat. Pressing her to me, I murmur, "It'll be okay. We'll figure it out." How, I don't know.

The traffic cop rapping on the window pisses me off, but the interruption motivates Lauren to let go of me and climb out of the car. I circle to the rear cargo hold and retrieve her roller bag. Her suitcase is light, but it's still amazing that my back doesn't hurt one bit from the motion.

She squares her shoulders and stares up at me with clear eyes—it appears she has won the battle against her tears. She even manages a smile. "Hope to see you soon, Jer-Bear."

The sexy curve of her mouth as she speaks makes me decide I like my new nickname. "Not if I see you first, sweet cheeks." Neither of us wears our school colors today, so I plant a hot, heavy, very public kiss on those sassy lips of hers. I hold her close and encode the feel of her into my memory. This kiss will need to last a while.

Leading
Lauren

I drum my fingers on the wooden armrest of an expensive-looking chair in the administrative suite of the athletic department. Now that it's August, I need to get back to my team, pronto. Every practice counts with only two weeks until our first match.

In an obvious power play, Associate Athletic Director Rhonda Childsworth is making me wait to meet with her. I don't know why she called me in here, but I'm certain it's not good. A tendril of unease works its way up my spine. *Rhonda doesn't know about Jeremy, right?* Sam told me her boss wants to meet with her today as well, so maybe it's just a one-on-one meeting with all head coaches.

Too bad I can't capitalize on the waiting time by saying hello to the big boss: the athletic director, Andy Hunter. He appears to be away from his corner office, probably shaking down boosters for donations to the latest construction project. An astute businessman, Andy is the one responsible for building the new high-tech arena I call home. The only downside of his frequent fundraising is that I rarely interact with him. Instead, I have to deal with his underling.

And here she is, at last, emerging from her office with a plastic smile.

I once heard about a study correlating physical attractiveness with life success. With her slender physique, shiny black hair, and polished power suit, Rhonda is testament to that research. For damn sure, her hostile people skills haven't vaulted her up the corporate ladder. Though she's seven inches shorter than me, she wields her threat of firing me over my head like she's a six-footer.

"Coach Chase." She ushers me in and gestures to the chair across from her massive desk.

Does she expect me to address her as Ms. Childsworth? "Rhonda."

She maintains that little fake smile as we sit. "We're checking in with our female head coaches before the school year begins. We care about you, Lauren."

Give me a fucking break.

"We want to encourage a healthy work-life balance," she continues. "How's that balance going for you?"

Is she trolling for information about Jeremy? No way I'll disclose details of my personal life to this bitch. "This is *your* initiative?" Yikes, I need to watch my tone. That question sounded way too incredulous.

Her lips thin. "Well, Andy is the one who charged us with this task, actually. He read an NCAA study about the struggles of women coaching at this level." Her dark eyes peer at me. "Tell me about your struggle."

"I'm...good." I shrug.

As she waits for me to elaborate, the silence extends several moments. "How're things socially for you?" She leans closer, dips her head, and peeks up at me with a coquettish flair. "Anyone special in your life?"

What the fuck is this? My romantic life is none of her damn business. I wonder again if her true motivation is getting me to spill about Jeremy. Then, a chill of fear grips my chest. She hasn't heard about my history with Paul, has she? She continues to stare, so I match her synthetic smile. "It's just me." I used to think taking care of myself was hard enough without adding a romantic partner to the mix. Now I feel lucky to know Jeremy has my back, even though he lives miles away. He takes care of me, too.

"Is there anything the administration can do to help you?"

Stop threatening to fire me, bitchnipple. I need to end this conversation. "Listen, Rhonda, I love coaching. I especially love coaching at Ohio State. It's been my dream to return to my alma mater. And I knew the demands of coaching at this level long before I took this job, so you won't hear me complaining about the insane hours. I want to win—I want to bring home another championship to this department—and that won't happen unless I completely devote myself to my team."

She shifts in her seat.

I look at my watch. "Speaking of my team, we start our next practice in fifteen minutes. Is there anything else?"

Her mouth purses. "There's one more topic I'd like to discuss."

Uh-oh.

"We're reviewing the recruiting process with every coaching staff member. How are your prospective student-athletes coming along?"

Why is she asking this? "You didn't receive my July report?" Rhonda is the only associate AD requiring her coaches to submit a monthly summary of recruiting activities—a total waste of my time.

She bristles. "Of course. What I'm asking is if you have any recruiting violations to tell me that didn't make it into your report."

Landing Emma increases our chances of success, thereby decreasing Rhonda's ability to fire me, so now it seems she's moved on to a different tact to shit-can me: accuse me of recruiting violations. "Absolutely not."

"No impermissible contacts to self-report?"

She won't let this go. What is she digging for? The NCAA rule book is a thick document that changes every year, and once or twice I've committed an inadvertent error that I made sure to report, but nothing major. Alex and the OSU compliance office keep me well-informed.

"No. But you'll be the first to know in the unlikely event that a violation occurs."

She scrutinizes me. "Good. I'll let you get back to our student-athletes, then."

As I take the elevator down from the tenth floor, I notice the extreme tension in my shoulder blades. This would typically be the best time to light up a cigarette. Instead, I shake out my muscles and send Jeremy a text. The athletic department no longer pays for our phones, so I feel freer to speak my mind.

Just met with FuckYouRhonda. STRESS! But no cancer sticks, I promise. Hope your bosses are nicer.

I'm surprised when he replies as I reach my car. He must be texting me from a meeting.

Sucks about the bitchboss. Froth in a MOOD. Let's commiserate tonight over a glass of vegan wine.

I grin. Sexting with Jeremy every night helps me get through every day. My phone vibrates again.

PS. You don't need cigarettes. You're already smoking hot.

I giggle at the fire emoji, and I can't deny the happy buzz I feel as I jog into the arena.

***

Two hours later, it's easy to see how fatigued my players are. The strength coach demolished them in the weight room before our morning practice, and they're all dragging ass toward the end of our afternoon practice. I remember the sore, leaden muscles of the preseason back when I played. But this isn't the time to go easy on my team. When they're fighting through set five of a close match, they'll need to pull from reserves of energy they didn't know they possessed. And August practices fuel up those reserves.

As Patrick tells the team to grab some water, I approach my athletic trainer and ask, "We've got a tough drill next—how's Cherise's knee holding up?"

Courtney's dark-blond hair sways as she shakes her head. "She's toast."

"Thought so." I observe Emma's rapt attention on Cherise as the older setter gives her corrections from the serving drill we just completed. They're both breathing hard. Emma nods and takes a swig from her water bottle.

"Your nails look great," Courtney says. She sold me the nail polish strips last week.

I waggle white fingernails with black polka-dots. "Of course you think that." I knock my hip into hers. "Gotta grovel before your best customer."

Courtney wears the standard red polo and black shorts of athletic trainers, and I compliment the perfect match of her plaid nail design.

Then I realize this water break has extended long enough. "Burpee bitch drill!" I holler.

Cherise cuts off one player's groan with a clap of her hands. "C'mon, let's do this!" She and Emma part ways as they assume the setter position on either side of the net, with hitters and defensive specialists filling in the court around them.

I gesture for my third-string setter to take Cherise's place. "Cherise, come join me and help me coach. I want Holly to get some reps."

Cherise's eyes taper as she shoots Courtney a look—she knows her substitution has nothing to do with Holly and everything to do with her worn-out knee—but she jogs over to my side nonetheless.

I'm about to yell instructions when Cherise interrupts me. "What's the play, Coach? I'll tell 'em."

Her eager tone tells me she's recovered from her initial anger over her removal from the drill. I cock my head as I study her. Is she ready to lead the team? "Quick-set to middle is the only acceptable play."

"Listen up!" Cherise shouts. Her chest glistens with sweat, and her clunky knee brace has to weigh her down, but her strong voice conveys energy. "Five-one's the only play that's allowed. If you have to run another play, your side has to do a burpee and get right back into defense."

My backup libero, Tatum, scowls. She mutters something to Kaylee, a freshman outside hitter, and Cherise is on her attitude right away. "Tatum, will you explain to the freshmen why we do this drill?"

Tatum, a junior, perches her hands on her hips and snaps, "Transitions."

"That's right." Cherise nods. "Faster transitions are the best ammunition."

I meet Dana's eyes across the court, and she smiles at me. I've emphasized the importance of quick transitions between defense and offense countless times, and it's edifying to hear my player recite that from memory.

"Also, this drill puts pressure on us to run the exact play we want," adds Cherise. "Let's see who's up for the challenge, Buckeyes."

Yep. I smile. She's ready. Watching Cherise blossom as a player-coach reminds me of a memoir I read. The author was a famous coach who built a winning dynasty by hiring his former players as assistant coaches. They knew his systems well and could convey consistent messaging, allowing him to become more of a visionary instead of dwelling in the day-to-day details. Patrick and Dana are excellent assistants, but I would love to add Cherise to my staff one day, if she becomes a coach.

Cherise points at the server on one side, and Tatum jump-serves the ball over the net. My starting libero passes the served ball to Emma, who executes a beautiful quick-set to Mariana. Tatum somehow digs Mariana's spike, eliciting a cheer from Patrick, but her pass is off target. Holly has no other option than to salvage a high set to Kaylee, the outside hitter. Because they didn't execute the required quick-set to middle for the drill, all six players on Holly's side drop to the deck then jump up to complete a burpee. Too bad another wicked hit from Mariana hits the floor before they're back on their feet.

"Excellent." I pump my fist. "Again."

The side that didn't do the burpee serves this time, and my libero serves a floater. Holly quick-sets the second-string middle blocker, who hits the ball at a vicious angle. Somehow, Emma digs the ball and shouts, "Help!" since she's unavailable to set the second ball. Mariana fills in with a wobbly set to the weak-side hitter.

"Burpee!" reminds Cherise, and Emma's side drops to the court for a pushup followed by leaping into the air. My libero barely lands back on her feet before she has to dive to dig the spiked ball careening to her side, and I hear Emma laugh as she improvises a set. She and her five teammates hustle to execute another supersonic burpee.

About ten minutes into the drill, laughter has ceased, replaced by the sounds of hyperventilated breaths from this cardiovascular challenge. "Again," I order. Kaylee musters the energy to glare at me, and I hope she channels that anger into blistering spikes. She'll thank me come October.

From the corner of my eye, I notice someone in the stands. I turn and smile as I recognize Jenna Watkins.

She waves, then points at herself, mouthing, "Okay?"

I nod.

As the drill resumes, players on both sides pump up and down, scrambling to transition and somehow keep the ball in play. Shouts and squeaking shoes fill the air—I'm loving this effective communication on the court. The chaotic back-and-forth volley finally ends when Mariana's spike hits Tatum's ass before she can peel herself off the floor.

"Oomph!" Tatum cries, rubbing her butt cheek after she pushes up to her feet.

Mariana points at her through the net. "Sorry for the booty ball, chica."

Tatum's chest heaves, and she appears too tired for a retort. I glance at Emma, whose eyes plead with me to stop the drill from hell.

Cherise laughs, however. "Now the freshmen know why Coach calls this drill *burpee bitch*."

I cringe, knowing Emma's mother is in the stands. I hope she didn't hear that.

"Great effort," I say. "Five more burpees for everyone, and we're done."

I place my phone to the side and hit the court for a pushup, joining my players and assistant coaches. When I spring up for a jump, I see Jenna pumping up and down for burpees as well.

After the players stumble to much-needed showers and I wrap up the practice with Patrick and Dana, I smile at Jenna as she approaches.

"You didn't have to do the burpees, too," I tease.

She holds out her hands. "You said *everyone*, Coach. Besides, we do them in CrossFit all the time. I love how hard you're working the girls."

Given her fit frame, it doesn't surprise me to learn she's a CrossFitter. "I've thought about trying CrossFit. How do you like it?"

"It's a perfect way to get out aggression before the workday."

I nod. "What's up with the..." *Don't say cocky cumpster.* "... uh, *guy* you manage at work? He still jonesing for your job?"

She sighs. "Poor Tyler gets an earful from me every night. I'm lucky I married a good listener."

I think about the text exchange I just had with Jeremy, complaining about bitch-puss Rhonda. He's also a good listener. I look up to find Jenna studying me. "What?"

"How's Coach Trent?"

I drop the smile that's crept onto my face. "I'm guessing you're not here to talk about *him*."

"Well, I'm here to check up on Emma before I take her to dinner, but this sounds way more fun to discuss." She leans closer. "Are you two still talking?"

We're doing a hell lot more than that. Oh fuck, I can't hide my grin.

Jenna gasps. "I knew it! You're so cute together." Her hand flutters to her heart. "And to think you met outside my house. Must've been divine intervention."

I'm not sure about that, though I have cried out thanks to my higher power every time Jeremy brings me to the cusp of climax.

"But you live so far apart," she coos as she pats my shoulder. "Sounds tough."

I notice Dana and Patrick watching us from across the court. When my shoulder tenses, Jenna looks in their direction.

"They don't know about you and Jeremy?" After I shake my

head, she winks. "Don't worry, I won't tell Emma."

"Thank you. By the way, your daughter's killin' it at practice."

She lets go of my shoulder for a giddy clap. "Wonderful to hear. I'm so impressed by Cherise Evans and the way she's mentored Emma. You've got yourself one heck of a fifth-year senior there, Coach."

"Don't I know it." I'm pleased that Emma feels the same way about Cherise as I do. Since I'm always hungry for information about the freshmen to integrate them better into the program, I pump Jenna for more details. "How's Emma enjoying Ohio State?"

"She loved her summer classes, and like I said, she speaks highly of Cherise. Mariana, too. She's not too happy with you at the moment, though."

I take a step back.

She grins. "Which means you're demanding a lot from her, working her hard, just like you should."

I relax. "How's it going with her roommate?"

Jenna's expression sobers, and she seems to hesitate.

Hmm. Kaylee Stenstrom has seemed standoffish to me, and now that I think about it, I haven't seen much closeness between her and Emma at practice.

"Emma would kill me if she knew I was telling you this, but she's not getting along well with Kaylee. I keep encouraging Emma to try harder, but Kaylee doesn't seem to like her, no matter what she does." Her shoulders press up for a moment, then fall. "We invited Kaylee to dinner tonight—she said she's busy."

I frown. "I'll talk to Kaylee."

Jenna holds up her hand. "Please, don't. This is Emma's battle. She's dealt with drama from other players before, and she'll figure it out." Her hand returns to her chest. "Evan's supporting her through this, which warms my heart."

The punk is helping my Emma? Hard to believe.

Her brown eyes crinkle. "But enough about Emma. Tell me more about that handsome Coach Trent."

18

Spiraling
Jeremy

I wipe sweat off my forehead as I bark out commands to the quarterbacks doing footwork drills. Steamy August days like these make me wish I were bald like some of the other coaching staff. But then I wouldn't have the pleasure of Lauren running her hands through my hair—I freaking love when she does that. I *miss* that. It's been over three weeks since we've been together, with no meet-up scheduled for the near future.

Evan's tall body crashing to the grass breaks my musings. He must've gotten his cleat caught in the agility ladder he's been side-stepping to the beat of my directions. Before an athletic trainer or I can reach him, he's back on his feet, with a scowl visible beneath his helmet. He raises his right arm and cocks the ball in a ready-to-throw position as I resume my commands to hustle right or left.

"Hartford, get in there," I order, and Austin switches places with Evan. I guide my backup QB through the drill, but from the corner of my eye, I see Evan tearing off his helmet and squirting water over his red face. The panting grunts of linemen drift over as they collide with blocking sleds and push them down the field. It's got to be brutal baking in the sun wearing a helmet and pads. My players better get used to it, though. This is Big Ten preseason football.

I'm supervising a graduate assistant coach's placement of cones for our next drill when there's a commotion near the practice field's entrance. As I notice short, tightly-coiled dreads emerging above the heads of our security guards, I grin. Just about everyone in America recognizes him, and I'm not surprised when security lets him through. I lift my hand to wave, and after he sees me, he jogs over.

"Yo, Adrian!" I bellow, mimicking Sly Stallone from the *Rocky* movies and earning an easy laugh from my college roommate.

His hug is perfunctory considering I'm a sweaty mess. Somehow, Adrian looks cool and fresh. He's always been cooler than me.

"I thought playing the Lions would give me a break from the Florida heat," he complains. "What's Michigan's problem?"

"Stick around—it'll snow tomorrow." I gesture for Quentin Hill to weave through the cones for the next footwork drill. It takes a while for him to get started, though, because my four quarterbacks stand slack-jawed in the presence of NFL royalty. Evan fidgets with his helmet strap as he stares at Adrian. "Move it, Hill!" I order.

The fifth-year senior's back problems must have vanished given the sudden quick feet he demonstrates in the drill.

"How'd you get away from Ford Field?" I ask. Adrian's team arrived yesterday to prepare for a preseason game between the Jacksonville Jaguars and Detroit Lions.

Adrian shrugs. "Coach wants to start our backup QB. He needs *lots* of reps. So I got the afternoon off."

"To rest your aging body?"

"Heh," he grunts.

Adrian's thirty-three, like me, but he's been in the league eleven years already. His diligent work in the off-season has kept him healthy, for the most part, but the ferocious attack of countless defenders has taken its toll over the years. NFL careers have a limited shelf life. I motion for Austin to take Quentin's place, then ask, "How's your shoulder?"

Adrian quiets his voice. "Coming along."

I nod. At the college level, we guard player injuries like national-security secrets, not only to avoid giving the opponent an advantage, but also to protect players' personal health information. In the NFL, this injury secrecy is on steroids.

"How's your back?" he asks.

I told Adrian about Lauren cajoling me to see the doctor.

Thinking about her bossiness, I smile. "Surprisingly good."

He elbows me. "So when am I gonna meet this lady of yours? Nichelle is dying to meet her, too."

Adrian started dating his eventual wife, Nichelle, our senior year at Oklahoma. She was a triple-jump Big 12 finalist on the track team, and their three children will no doubt age into athletic superstars. I bet Lauren and I could combine our gene pool to create some studly jocks as well. But, I grimace as I dream about the future. How will we make babies when we don't even get to see each other?

"Must be tough to do the long-distance thing," says Adrian. "I'm lucky Nichelle and I never went through that."

He *is* lucky. His wife worked in marketing for a few years after graduating, but she is now a stay-at-home mother who manages her husband's brand.

I sigh. "I can't lie. It's been rough being apart from her."

"Have some faith, Jeremy." Adrian gazes at me. "If it's meant to be, it'll happen."

I try to soak in his calm, steadying presence.

"Coach Trent?" the GA coach butts in. "Want Watkins in there next?"

I realize Hartford has been stuck quick-stepping through the cones for too long, and his bent-over form appears on the verge of collapse. I point at Evan.

Adrian calls, "Good effort, Austin."

Austin snaps up and beams at us. Compliments are foreign to him.

Once Evan starts shuffling through the cones, holding the ball at the ready to fire down the field, Adrian asks, "How's the kid?"

"Not too sharp today," I grumble.

"Looks like he's put on some muscle—maybe that's slowing him down."

I consider that. Evan's throws during camp have packed an extra zing, and some receivers haven't been able to pull down the high missiles.

Adrian looks at me. "Are you questioning him as the starter?"

I shake my head. "Evan locked up the starting role his first week here. He's gifted as hell." I frown as I watch him. "His progression has stalled lately, though."

"Want me to talk to him?"

I aim a grateful smile at my friend. "Absolutely."

But before Adrian has a chance, Bill Froth sidles up next to us. Froth pumps Adrian's hand like they're BFFs. Adrian's congenial demeanor shields his knowledge that I can't stand my boss.

"Appreciate you visiting us," Froth tells Adrian.

He's visiting me, not you, buttdumpster. Lauren has fully infiltrated my mind. Froth hasn't said a word to me about our July stairwell encounter, though his glares have seemed extra pointed since then.

"Run some one-step fades," Froth orders. "Let's show the NFL QB what we got."

We ran those yesterday, and I had different plans for today's practice, but I have no choice but to follow his demands. *One day,* I promise myself. One day *I'll* be the head coach.

The GA coach crouches to mimic the center and snaps the ball to Evan. Though our defense is otherwise engaged in another part of the practice field, the GA coach starts to come at the quarterback to mimic the pass rush. Long before the coach reaches him, Evan passes the ball to Talik near the sideline. When Evan's throw zooms over Talik's outstretched hands, Evan punches toward the ground with a frustrated snort. Another receiver, AJ, jogs up to the line, and this time Evan's pass is on the money, floating into the AJ's hands with just the right timing.

"Better." Adrian waits for Evan to look in his direction. "With fades, you want to float like a butterfly. You can sting like a bee later."

Evan grins. He proceeds to take a quick step before launching the ball in a perfect spiral for subsequent snaps.

"Quick release for a freshman," Adrian murmurs.

I nod. Evan's release time rivals that of pro quarterbacks, and he's only just beginning.

After the other quarterbacks have their turn, Froth barks, "Play-action five step."

I stifle a groan. We did this yesterday, too. Our offensive coordinator, Harry Stevens, has joined our group on the sidelines, and he and I share a quick eye-roll. Adrian looks about as bored as I do while each quarterback fakes a handoff before stepping back to pass.

"Gun screen," says Froth.

This time Evan backpedals into the shotgun formation as a running back stands close to him. After the snap, the running back steps in front of the quarterback to hide him before Evan launches a throw. Evan's passes are accurate, but I have to admit, Austin's smooth movements make him the better quarterback.

When Froth announces the next drill, my eyes bug. He's skipped from easy reps to one of our most complex plays, and it's clear he's trying to impress our guest. Adrian's smirk tells me he also sees through Froth.

I've only taught this play to Evan once, though his grasp of intricate progressions has impressed me. I'm confident he'll get it right; it's the receivers who might screw it up.

Four receivers line up on the right side, with only the tight end on Evan's left. After the snap, Evan evades the GA coach's pass rush. Instead of passing to the right receiver, his throw careens into the back of the tight-end's helmet. *Whoops.*

"What the FUCK?" screams Froth. "Did you take the short bus today, Watkins?"

Evan gives me a confused look—he must not understand the unkind reference.

Froth spits, "What's the definition of a flood play?"

All of the offensive players hover on the field, frozen by the head coach's tirade.

"Um, we flood one side of the field with receivers," Evan answers.

"Fucking genius. If you're as smart at Coach Trent says—" Froth's venomous eyes turn to me, then back to Evan. "—then why the fuck you throw to the other side?"

Evan's throat moves as he swallows. "I thought it was a trick play?"

"Looks like *you're* the one who's tricked!" Froth's fists perch on his hips. "You might be the dumbest quarterback we've ever recruited. First you mouth off to my staff, then you act like you've never played the game before. You're skating on thin ice, Watkins."

I don't remember Evan mouthing off to me or any other coaches. *What's Froth talking about?*

Froth huffs a breath out his nose. "Hartford!"

Austin jumps in to take Evan's place. I try to focus on the drill, but I sneak peeks at Evan to see how he handles the verbal abuse. *Not well.* The face-mask of Evan's helmet dips so low that it rests on the front of his shoulder pads.

Once the drill ends and Froth stomps off, Adrian whistles softly through his teeth. "*Whoa.* If Coach Hanlon spoke to us like that, I probably would've quit. No way I'd make it to the league."

And no way would I have become a coach if I played for the hack I'm currently working for. I feel dampness as I rub the back of my neck. "If you hadn't gone pro, what would you have done instead?"

Adrian sports a faint smile. "Coaching, I think."

I whip my head in his direction. "Really?"

"There's nothing like a good coach—a good teacher. I had so many amazing mentors, starting with Coach Hanlon. It'd be gratifying to try to be like him one day." He looks down. "I mean, I'm nowhere near the coach you are, of course, but I could learn. Maybe after I retire."

His uncharacteristic nervousness as he discusses a career change is interesting to observe. "I hear a lot of pros suffer after they retire."

Adrian nods. "The divorce rate skyrockets. That won't be me, though. Nichelle and the kids are everything. I want to keep providing for them after I retire, maintain a sense of purpose and contribution."

"I've got a great idea." I slide my hands into my pockets. "Once I become head coach somewhere, you can be my QB coach."

He looks up with a grin. "Deal."

"And your first job interview is to help my QB get his head

out of his butt."

"Will do." Adrian scrubs his smooth jaw as he eyes my four quarterbacks taking a water break. "What do you think's going on with Evan?"

I shake my head. "Trying to figure that out. He knew that play."

"At this point, you've focused more on teaching him defense than offense, right?"

"Right." Coach Hanlon taught us that quarterbacks need a keen understanding of defensive formations before they can even start to understand offensive plays and passing lanes.

"Maybe he's overwhelmed," says Adrian.

"True, but the kid's smarter than he looks. It's like his brain suddenly fogged up." When I hear myself say those words, I pause. Maybe I do know what's going on with Evan. It seems my stern lecture about avoiding social influence from Talik and other players has fallen on immature ears.

I watch Adrian talk to Evan, marveling when he gets the morose freshman to laugh. But from Evan's steady gaze on Adrian, it also looks like he's intent on his mentor's message. *Good*. The kid needs direction. And I intend to give it to him.

I approach our head athletic trainer, Mario Costa. "I want a drug test tomorrow."

"No can do." He shakes his thick head of black hair. "Froth convinced the ADs to delay the test till September."

After our opening game against Notre Dame, I realize. *Convenient.*

"Why you want a test?" asks Mario.

"Watkins seems off to me."

Mario snorts. "He's probably beat after this morning."

"This morning?"

"You didn't hear? Watkins mouthed off to Tony at weights— bad move. Tony had him run suicides till the boy almost passed out."

I close my eyes. Tony Masten's our strength coach, a bald tyrant. He's been Froth's director of sport performance for years, and no one questions his mistreatment since he's in the head coach's back pocket.

"Even more reason to test my QB for weed," I say.

"Yeah?" Mario looks unconvinced.

"Fatigue, trouble retaining information, and now irritability—" I tick off each reason on a different finger. "What does that sound like to you?"

The athletic trainer's mouth slants down. "He'll be on our list come September."

A defensive lineman goes down and cradles his ankle, leading Mario to run out to the field to examine him. Watching the trainer's retreating form, I shake my head. It's not only Tony who's in lockstep with Froth.

I need to help Evan before it's too late—before our goal to beat the Buckeyes and his dream to go pro both vanish up in smoke.

Missing
Lauren

With our seasons about to start, Jeremy and I have been desperate to see each other. His team travels to South Bend, Indiana, tomorrow for a tough opening game, and he needs every second to prepare. My team hosts two non-conference teams that we should crush. Therefore, we decided I would drive to Michigan. Driving six hours to spend a few hours together is worth it, especially if he visits me next time.

But I've been sitting in the Schembechler Hall parking lot for fifteen minutes with no sign of my hunky coach. His brief texts apologizing for getting stuck in meetings have tapered off, and both my temper and body are stewing in the early-evening August sun.

"Screw this," I mutter. Then, I have an idea. I make a phone call and drive out of the parking lot.

Alex dances a little jig as I enter Ann Arbor's famous Zingerman's Deli. He presses a kiss to my cheek before ordering Reuben sandwiches for us at the counter.

Once we find a table and sit, his eyes peg me to the chair. "Spill it, bitch."

I enticed my friend to come straight from work to meet me by promising to fill him in on the mystery coach-man he's hounded me about all summer. But now that the moment has arrived, my throat feels dry. I sip water (they don't have Mountain Dew, damn it) and study Alex.

His cornflower blue dress shirt and slim purple tie make him look every bit the debonair attorney. The artful way he's gelled his blond hair into a peak above his forehead completes the look. Alex played volleyball for our brother Catholic school in Cincinnati, but since he's only about my height, he didn't get to play in college.

I skim my hand over the spikes of his short hair. "I've missed my gay husband."

"Uh-huh." He folds his arms across his chest. "You better stop interfering with this investigation, or I'll charge you with obstruction of justice."

"You're not a district attorney, dipshit." As he keeps glaring, I give in. "Turns out I'm dating a college football coach."

He leans in, his eyes shining with intrigue.

"For, uh, Michigan, actually." I add.

His jaw drops, and then he cackles. He's still laughing when a waitress delivers our sandwiches.

Between bites of a pickle spear, Alex shakes his head. "Your life's a complete car crash, Lori. I just can't look away."

"Shut your pickle hole." As I try the pastrami, I suppress a moan. This is the best Reuben I've ever eaten. But since its origin is Ann Arbor, I won't admit it.

Alex doesn't bother to hide his moan as he bites into his sandwich. "Deliciogasm, right? So, how'd you meet your Michigan football coach?" He sits up. "Wait a minute. Your star recruit—her twin's Evan Watkins!" His eyebrows scrunch. "That makes...the quarterbacks' coach your paramour?"

I giggle. "Stellar investigative skills."

Alex whips out his phone and finds Jeremy's online coaching profile in a second. "Nooiiice." When he turns his screen to me, I notice Jeremy's face looks younger and happier in the photo, which was likely taken before he started coaching for Bill Froth.

Alex's eyes widen and his lips part as he looks up over my shoulder. "Even nooiiicer in person. A tall drink of tequila."

The man under investigation arrives at our table ten minutes before the deli's closing time.

"You got my text," I say.

Jeremy slides into the chair next to me. "Sorry I'm late, sweetheart."

His passionate kiss makes me forgive him an instant. It's so good that I plan to write him a thank-you note later. I'm still in a daze when Jeremy reaches his hand across the table.

"Good to meet you, Alex."

My friend's unhinged mouth closes and curls into a smile as he shakes Jeremy's hand. Alex's gaze bounces back and forth between us before landing on me. "Never hold out on me again, bitchcakes."

As the waitress brings over an entrée that Jeremy must've ordered at the counter—some stinky vegan hash—Alex nudges toward me. I prepare myself for another insult.

"I'm really happy for you. Way to go, kid." His gleaming eyes and heartfelt tone bring a lump to my throat.

***

A few hours later, I drive back to Columbus. I should think about the game plan for tomorrow night's match. Instead, I glide my fingertips along my collarbone, replaying Jeremy's touches at his place. He seems drawn to kissing and stroking the hollow of my neck, and as far as I'm concerned, he can spend all night there. My extra-sensitive skin burns from his focused attention. Good thing it's dark outside so the other drivers can't see me brushing my fingers along my skin in a horndog trance.

When I start singing along to the radio, crooning about sailing away to Key Largo, I wince. I can't believe Jeremy got me to listen to Yacht Rock Radio. However, I would love to lounge next to him on a sailboat in the Florida Keys. Maybe we can fit that into our schedule ten years from now.

The ring of my phone interrupts the smooth voice of Bertie Higgins. My mother is a night owl, like me, so I'm not surprised she's calling me at 11:02 pm.

"I haven't heard from you."

Her voice is clipped. I frown as I set cruise control to nine miles over the speed limit. Was I supposed to call her? Preparing for tomorrow's match and squeezing in a trip to Michigan have monopolized my brain today. The second I remember, my stomach sinks. "The results from your scans! You got them today, right? What'd they say?"

"Great news, honey. I'm cancer free!"

My hands begin to tingle like they do after a rush of adrenaline. The long breath that leaves my body, followed by the same lump in my throat from earlier, surprise me. I didn't realize I was so nervous about the scans. "That's *awesome*, Mom. Just amazing."

She launches into more details about follow-up treatment, then pauses. "Are you driving this late at night?"

There's no way to hide the telling hum of tires on the pavement. "Yes."

"You're not recruiting, right? Your father told me your first matches are this weekend."

I chew on my lip. Should I be honest with her? She'll probably rip into me, but I'm sick of lying to her. I'm sick of keeping my visits to Jeremy secret. "I'm driving back from Michigan."

Silence.

Fuck it. "I went to meet Jeremy." She still hasn't said anything. "I miss him. I had to see him."

"You're sure that's a good idea?" she asks.

"No?" I shrug. "I don't know if it's good or bad—all I know is I can't stop thinking about him. It's...kind of scary, actually."

Her voice softens. "I remember feeling that way once. With your father."

I tuck my chin, finding it difficult to imagine my parents feeling infatuated with each other. If they ever were in love, that love now seems long gone.

"We met at a Bengals' game, you know."

That's right—I forgot about that. My dad's still a die-hard fan of Cincinnati's NFL team, despite their sucky record.

"My friends thought he was damn handsome," Mom continues. She's quiet for a beat. Then she sighs. "I shouldn't criticize him so much."

A rare moment of self-awareness for the momster. "So, why do you?"

"Because he's incompetent!"

And, moment over.

"Do you know I caught him putting a dirty knife back into the drawer?" she rails. "No wonder I get sick all the time." She launches into a diatribe about his latest failings.

"Mom?"

But she keeps going, now complaining that he never cleans Furlock's litter box.

"Mom!" My shout gets her to shut up, and the ensuing silence jacks up my heartbeat. "Would you stop it with Dad already? I don't want to hear you bitch about him."

"But he just makes me so fucking mad!"

"And I feel fucking *sick* listening to it!" My chest rises and falls with rapid breaths. My fingers itch as they grip the steering wheel. I need to do something, hold something—like a cigarette, maybe. I imagine bringing it up to my lips, inhaling the soothing heat, forgetting about my stress... *Crap!* Here I am, thinking about smoking while talking to a woman who just beat cancer caused by the very substance I crave. What a fucked-up urge.

"You don't have to yell at me," says Mom.

I stare at the dashboard console, feeling drained. "I know." I jolt when another call comes in. What is Emma Watkins doing calling me at this hour? She should be asleep.

"Mom, sorry, I gotta take this call. We'll talk later—great to hear about the scans." I click over to Emma before my mother has a chance to prolong our conversation with countless stall tactics. "Emma? Everything okay?"

Her sob straightens me in my seat.

"What's wrong?"

"It's Kaylee," she cries. "We're at the ER."

My stomach drops. "Why?"

"She took some pills. Sorry, Coach. I should've known she was upset."

Holy shit, a suicide attempt by one of my players? Emma's wrong. *I'm* the one who should've known.

"But I was at Cherise's," Emma adds. "When I came home, I f-f-found her on the floor..."

I close my eyes, feeling tremors rip through me. "Was she conscious? Will she be all right?"

"I-I think so. Our RA called nine-one-one, and the paramedics kept Kaylee talking as they took her away."

"Is anyone with you?" I demand.

"Courtney."

Thank goodness our athletic trainer is there.

"And Cherise," says Emma.

My cheeks burn—I should be there, too. "I'm two hours away. I'll get there as soon as I can."

"Okay. Hold on." There's a rustling sound.

"Coach?" My captain's voice is now on the line.

"Yeah, Cherise?"

"Should we tell the rest of the team?" she asks.

I shake my head. "No. Don't do anything until I get there. Actually, you two should get to bed. Courtney will take care of it."

"I'm staying, Coach. I'll make Emma leave, though."

"*No!*" I hear Emma huff in the background. "*I'm not going! She's my roommate!*"

I roll my eyes. God damn caring, responsible teammates. "Fine. Just stay put until I arrive."

A look at my speedometer shows I'm going eighty-five. The cops better stay away from me tonight.

* * *

A dribble of charcoal blobs on Kaylee's chin, but I don't have the heart to tell her. She looks miserable enough in the emergency department cubicle without knowing there's evidence of her stomach being pumped all over her face. She's over six feet tall, but she somehow seems small, engulfed by the hospital bed and monitors around her. Her skinny legs extend from a floral hospital gown.

"I just want to get out of here," she mutters.

That's not going to happen. In the waiting room, one of our sport psychologists told me they're trying to coax Kaylee toward voluntary admission to the psychiatric unit. But if she refuses, they'll enforce a 72-hour hold—standard procedure after a suicide attempt, evidently. I haven't had to deal with this before, but our psychologist said suicide attempts are on the rise in student-athletes. My stomach is so twisted in knots that I can't imagine enduring this awfulness again. Kaylee's going to be okay.

But what if one day an athlete of mine isn't? I shudder.

I wait until her roving eyes meet mine. "This is some serious shit, huh?"

"It was just my antidepressant. I accidentally took too many—no big deal."

Hmm... Twenty-six pills combined with a lot of booze don't sound like an accident. "Have you been unhappy, Kaylee?"

She scratches her ankle, where I notice for the first time a tattoo of a volleyball. Her lower lip juts out in a pout. "I want to go home."

"Home as in your dorm room, or home as in Arizona?"

As she slouches, dyed red hair covers half her face. "My parents can't find out about this."

Whoops. "Your parents are on their way."

Her head whips up. "You *called* them?"

"I had to call them, Kaylee. You tried to...kill yourself."

"No, I didn't! I—" She clutches the sides of her head as she huffs out a breath. "Great, just great." She lets go of her head and stares at her lap, lowering her voice. "This'll make them even more disappointed in me."

I pull a chair closer to her bed and sit. I'm feeling the effects of the late hour. I'm frustrated that I couldn't convince Emma and Cherise to go off to bed once I arrived. My two setters, along with Dana, Courtney, and the sport psychologist, are still in the ER waiting room. They only allow one visitor at a time, and I insisted on going first. "Why would your parents be disappointed in you?"

She glares at me. "Because you won't give me any playing time. I'm not stupid. I see the writing on the wall."

My coaching decisions made her want to off herself? Guilt deflates my lungs.

"And Emma throws it in my face." Her mouth trembles. "The famous Emma Watkins is a starter, but her loser roommate won't ever get off the bench."

I scrunch my forehead—her perception of the situation is whack. "Are you aware that Emma and Cherise are still in the waiting room? I told them to go home, but they refused. They're really worried about you."

"Is Tatum here?"

When I shake my head, the hope in her eyes vanishes.

"Tatum probably doesn't know," I explain. "Emma involved the captain, of course, but nobody else." I think about my players. "What do you want me to tell the team when you're not there for the matches this weekend?"

"What do you mean? I'll be there. I'll act like nothing happened."

I brace myself. "Hate to break it to you, Kaylee, but they're not going to let you leave the hospital for a few days."

The news propels her back into the mattress. "Awesome." The IV in her arm makes it difficult for her to lace her arms across her chest. "Now I'll never be a starter."

I'm growing annoyed by her petulant attitude. "Volleyball is the fucking least of your problems right now!"

That gets her attention. She sits up.

"Do you realize you could've died? Dead players don't have a great hitting percentage, you know."

Her widened brown eyes blink at me.

"Listen, I get it. I wasn't a starter my freshman year either. It sucks to be the very best on your club team, then find yourself riding the bench when you've done absolutely nothing wrong. It hurts. But most freshmen don't get any playing time—that's just the way it is."

"*Emma* does."

"Do you know that Emma would *die*—" I cringe at my poor choice of words. "—to be your friend? She thinks you don't like her."

Kaylee leans back. "*She* doesn't like *me*! She's never in our room—she's always at Cherise's."

"Has she invited you to come with her? Have you accepted any of her invitations?" When she doesn't reply, I lean closer. "Have *you* asked her to do stuff together?"

Her silence answers for her.

I have to end this conflict now, or we won't reach our goals as a team. I try to step into Kaylee's shoes to see how she got it so wrong. "It must be humiliating to room with the number-one recruit in the nation."

She freezes. *Bingo.*

"It's okay to feel jealous—it shows your fire, your desire to be the best. But don't get stuck in jealousy, Kaylee. Recognize the opportunity you have with Emma on your team. Hell, I wish *I'd* had a setter like her when I played."

I hope the pucker of her eyebrows means she's thinking about what I'm saying.

I keep going. "I've seen Emma's sets to you, hanging up there like they're gorgeous peaches, just waiting to be smashed."

Her eyes tighten at the corners as she stares at the wall, like she's visualizing those perfect sets.

"You've had some killer hits during camp, Kaylee." She meets my gaze. "You've got speed and grit. Where're you getting the idea that you won't get any playing time?"

She looks down. "Because I'm not starting tomorrow." She sniffs. "I'm a total failure."

"Get your head out of your ass. Just because you're not starting our first match doesn't mean you'll never play. Keep working hard, and you'll get your chance."

She swallows as she takes in my words.

After a moment, she looks away from me. "Do you...?" She sneaks a look at me. "Do you think I'm any good?"

Oh my God. I'm going to kill her myself. "Kaylee, I recruited you for two years—of course you're good. I chose you because you're gutsy as hell. How could you think of giving up like that? That's not like you."

She ducks her head.

"I brought you all the way from Arizona because you're such a talented outside hitter. I brought you here—I'm responsible for you." My hand covers my heart and feels its rapid thump. "I had to tell your parents tonight that you could've died on my watch."

She cringes.

"You're new here, but I can't wait to get to know you on a deeper level. We need you, Kaylee. Get better so you can come back to the team stronger and even more determined. We need you with us on our hunt for a national title, okay?"

***

How does Dana look so bright-eyed as she sits in my office before our pregame meal? Probably because she's younger than me. I pulled some all-nighters out drinking with friends in college, but my thirty-six-year-old body isn't too impressed by the three hours of sleep I managed last night.

While Patrick runs down our opponent's best hitters, I'm grateful I let him stay with his pregnant wife instead of joining us in the ER. At least one of us will be sharp for tonight's match.

A knock on the door shakes me out of my sleepless haze. I grin as I see what the deliveryman carries: a bouquet of red roses. He sets the vase on my desk, and I ignore the curious looks from my assistants as I read the card.

Scarlet roses for my Buckeye beauty. Kick ass tonight, Coach.

"Who sent the flowers?" asks Dana.

I hide my smile. "Oh, no one special."

"Nope, nope, nope." Patrick inclines forward with a defiant set of his jaw. "Not going to cut it, Coach. You've been swooning over someone since May. We deserve the truth."

"Yes, we do." Dana nods.

I chew my lip. Sam and Taryn already know, of course, and Alex took the news well. But will my assistant coaches look at me differently when they find out?

"Don't you trust us?"

Dana's question hits me in the gut. "Of course, I do." Too tired to keep hedging, I take a deep breath. "I'm dating a Michigan coach."

Patrick's mouth sags open, but Dana jumps off her chair. "No way!" she squeals. "Who?"

I scroll through the photos on my phone to find my favorite one of us together at Big Bowl in Chicago. We're both flushed from sun, sex, and alcohol. I can still feel Jeremy's strong arm across my shoulders, holding me and steadying me. I miss the sense of security I experience in his arms.

"He coaches Emma's brother," I say as I show them the

photo. "Jeremy Trent. We met in Toledo when we recruited the Watkins twins. But please keep this to yourselves, okay?"

"No problem," says Dana.

Patrick shakes his head. "Can't believe I'm saying this about a Wolverine, but he seems like a good guy. I can see how happy he makes you, Lauren."

Shining
Jeremy

Energy surges through my veins the second our offense takes the field. On one side of Notre Dame Stadium, a sea of green undulates as the students cheer on their defense. Though their colors are blue and gold, similar to ours, their fans wear green T-shirts in deference to their Irish heritage. Visible over the other side of the stadium is the top of a haloed Jesus with his arms in a victory pose—a mural on the side of the library. *Touchdown Jesus*, he's called. Even the Savior roots for Notre Dame.

But I hope Jesus shines more light on the Wolverines than the Irish on this cloudy day. Notre Dame deferred after they won the coin toss, so my much-hyped freshman quarterback gathers the offense in a huddle. For this nationally televised game, every camera points at Evan as he crouches behind our center. He's about to take his first snap of his first game—the beginning of a storied career or a fantastic flop. The crowd roars. Ten feet away from me, Bill Froth eyes me up and down. I feel like I've just eaten an order of vegan nausea nuggets.

Evan hands off the ball to our running back, who makes it only two yards before a defensive tackle wraps him up and throws him to the ground. The crowd goes apeshit. I look at Harry as he signals a pass play to Evan. It was smart to start off with a run, but now it's time for our star QB to show his stuff.

Evan drops back in shotgun formation. The offensive line provides great protection, giving Evan all kinds of time to find his receiver. Too bad his pass rockets over the receiver's outstretched hands. Again, the crowd thunders its approval of Notre Dame's defense.

Now it's third and long, an unenviable way to start the first offensive series. What the hell is that jangling noise? "Key play!" booms the announcer, and I see the glint of metal held aloft by every Notre Dame fan—oh, they're shaking their key rings. Ridiculous.

After faking the handoff, Evan scrambles as he searches for an open receiver. Notre Dame's All-American linebacker is in hot pursuit. I tense as the linebacker lunges for my quarterback, but Evan spins and shakes him off. *Throw it away*, I plead. Just as the linebacker is about to sack him, Evan launches a pass downfield. I cringe as the Notre Dame cornerback sprints around Talik to pluck the pass from the air and fall with the ball held in a tight cradle.

"Irish interception!" the announcer yells.

And a Michigan fail. The deafening cheers make it hard to hear the coaches on my headset as they respond to Froth's expletives. First, Froth yells at the coaches sitting in a booth far above the field, then he stalks over to Harry to rip him a new one. Before Froth finds me, I take off my headset and search for my star recruit.

Evan rips off his helmet and slumps on the bench. An offensive lineman bumps his fist into his shoulder pad, but Evan ignores him. What an effing disaster.

Will Lauren give me shit after we lose, or will she stroke my bruised ego? I don't plan to find out. I slide my sunglasses to the top of my head as I crouch in front of Evan.

Fear. Above the slashes of eye-black on his cheeks, his brown eyes emanate fear. They also look tired, and I wonder if he was too nervous to get any sleep last night. How can I get him back on the right track?

"How you feeling out there?"

He swallows. "Fine."

I frown. "Want to try that again?"

After a long exhale, he admits, "Freaked out."

"No shit. You look like you're about to poop your pants."

That earns a small grin from him. "NBC would probably like that. Boost their ratings."

I glance at the TV camera downfield and notice a closer camera aimed right at us. When I return my focus to my QB, I forget about the media coverage. "Screw NBC, Evan. They don't know you. They certainly don't care about you. This isn't about them. This is about you and your amazing arm." I squeeze his bicep beneath his shoulder pad. "Damn, son. You've got some guns there."

He squints at me, probably wondering where I'm going with this pep talk. I wonder, too. From the corner of my eye, I notice the hyperkinetic moves of a short guy with a red beard, green vest, and green pants.

"Look at that dumbass leprechaun," I say. Evan's gaze follows mine to our opponent's mascot. "You want to let Lucky Charms over there beat us?"

Despite the tension of the game, Evan snickers. "Hell no."

"Okay, then. That was just one series, and we have a lot of game left. What'd Adrian Nichols tell you during camp?"

His shoulders pull back an inch. "One snap at a time."

"Good advice. Remember what I said about staying in the present?" Evan nods. "That interception's history. The touchdowns you're about to throw—they're in the future. None of that matters...only right here, right now."

His cheeks puff as he blows out a breath.

I tap Evan's thigh and recall the mindfulness skills I read about in a book by Pete Carroll, coach of the Seattle Seahawks. "Tell me some colors you see right now."

He cocks his head with a skeptical furrow of his brow, but he answers me. "Green." His stare moves from the spectators to the field. "Maize stripes on blue helmets." I glance over my shoulder at our defense. At least the interception occurred in Notre Dame territory, and their offense doesn't appear to be going anywhere this series.

"What do you hear?"

He pauses to listen. "It's quieter than it was when I was out there."

The Notre Dame crowd stopped screaming once their offense took the field. "Just slightly louder than Toledo high school games, huh?"

He smirks.

"You'll get used to the noise at away games," I promise. "And home games, too. It can get rocking in the Big House."

We tick through what he notices with his other three senses, then I say, "Do you know how Adrian Nichols played in his first college game?"

Evan shakes his head.

"Well, there you go. Nobody cares about those stats, including you." I wait a beat. "I happen to remember, though. Adrian threw for only seventy yards, with three interceptions."

His eyes bug.

"Don't believe your own hype, Evan. This is only one game, and you're brand new to college ball."

The muscle in his jaw ripples.

"Think back to your first game as QB. How old were you?"

"Eleven." He shrugs.

"What'd you love about being a quarterback then?"

His eyes take on a faraway look. "Leading the team. The guys listened to me, followed my lead. It was my team."

I nod.

He sits up a little taller. "But the best feeling? When I evaded a defender…" His shoulder dips like he's replaying his jukes to break free from the defense.

"By the way, that was a good spin move, making their linebacker miss," I note. "He's All American, you know."

"So Coach Froth keeps telling me." Evan scowls.

No wonder the boy's as tight as a corkscrew—Bill Froth's in his head. I prompt, "You were talking about after you evaded a defender…?"

His head bobs. "Yeah. My receiver would finally get open, and I'd launch a freaking bomb. Watching the ball float into his arms before he glided into the end zone, and my O-line looking back at me like I just performed a miracle, like I'm Adrian Nichols or Tom Brady or something—it's the most amazing feeling. It's like crack. Quarterback crack."

I hope he's talking about crack in the metaphorical sense.

"Tom Brady played backup quarterback for two years before he started for Michigan," I remind Evan.

"That's right." He seems calmer now. Then his eyes narrow. "I thought you wanted me to focus on the present. Why're you asking me questions about the past, when I was a kid?"

Punk. "That feeling you just described? Recreate it when you go out there. Take risks and launch your 'freaking bombs'. Throw *ten* interceptions—I don't care."

He pulls back from me. "Coach Froth will care."

"I'm your position coach. I'm the one who dealt with your pain-in-the-ass father for the three years I recruited you. Listen to *me*."

Evan smirks again.

"Just take one snap at a time, have fun, and lead your team. This is your team. Not my team, not Coach Froth's team. *Your* team."

After he sits motionless for a moment, he cracks the biggest smile I've ever seen from him. "You got it, Coach."

***

I'm still puzzled as to why our athletic communications director asked me to attend the post-game press conference with Evan. Typically, only the head coach and maybe a star player or two provide a postmortem of the game. I'm unaccustomed to the buzz of the crowded media room in the bowels of the stadium. But once Bill Froth finishes his analysis and reporters start zinging questions at Evan, I understand why I'm here. Just about every question centers around our conversation that preceded Evan throwing six touchdown passes and rushing for his seventh.

"Evan, you seemed much more relaxed after your QB coach talked to you," the first reporter begins. "What did Coach Trent say?"

Evan somehow sticks out his chest while at the same time slouching back into his chair. Following his first college victory, he's like a different person than the scared freshman I counseled on the sidelines. I hope he doesn't let one game go to his head. "Coach Trent told me to throw ten interceptions—he didn't care."

Surprised laughs fill the room, and the lines etching Froth's face deepen as he glowers at me. *Touchdown Jesus.* That was Evan's one takeaway from our powwow?

But Evan grins at me as he continues, "That was just what I needed to hear, actually. I was really nervous, and I wasn't playing my game. Coach Trent told me to go out there and have fun, and that's what I did."

When a few reporters smile at me, I start breathing again.

"Evan," another reporter starts. "You set a record for the most yardage by a Michigan freshman quarterback in school history..."

My eyebrows lift. I wasn't aware of that stat.

"...in only your first game," the reporter adds. "What helped you today?"

Evan shrugs. "It was all Coach Trent."

I don't dare look at Froth—he's got to be fuming after that statement. My balls retract as I can almost hear the furious scratches of Froth's pen on paper when he writes my termination letter.

"I mean, of course the offensive line and receivers did an amazing job," Evan explains. "Shout-out to my receivers—they made easy targets out there. Then our defense holds the number-five-ranked team in the nation to only six points? That's dope."

My balls loosen a little. At least the kid remembered his media training. However, he still hasn't thrown a bone to his head coach.

"But Coach Trent knew just what to tell me," says Evan. "He made me remember when I started playing QB back when I was eleven—what a blast it was to lead the team and connect with the receivers. And he reminded me of some advice Adrian Nichols gave me about staying in the moment and taking one snap at a time."

This kid has remembered our conversation almost verbatim. I'd better be mindful of what I say to him in the future.

"What about Coach Froth?" a different reporter asks Evan.

"How have you responded to his coaching?"

When Evan hesitates, I clench my jaw.

"Oh, uh, great." He couldn't sound faker if he tried. "But Coach Trent told me this isn't Coach Froth's team."

Holy shit. This press conference needs to end right now.

"It's not Coach Trent's team, either," adds Evan. "It's my team…our team—the players' team. We're the ones who need to work our butts off to win the game."

There's silence in the room, and one reporter looks at Froth. "Coach, this has been one of the most lopsided victories in the history of the Michigan-Notre Dame game. What do you credit for the W?"

Froth mentions his preparation of the team, his game plan, and his coolness under pressure. It's clear he takes all the credit for the win.

An hour later, I'm on the road heading back to Ann Arbor. Instead of riding on one of the team buses to northern Indiana yesterday, I decided to drive my car with the idea of continuing on to Chicago after the game. However, taking time off work to visit my mother doesn't seem wise after that press conference from hell.

A text arrives from Lauren:

Congrats on the big win! I'm so happy for you (but not for the team up north).

Since I had to wake at five for my noon game today, I didn't get the chance to call her last night after she texted. Her text thanked me for a bouquet with the RIGHT color of flowers. I glance at the clock and wonder if she's free before her match.

She answers my call right away. "Is this the famous quarterbacks' coach?"

I grin at her saucy tone. "For now, anyway. Haven't been fired yet."

"*Fired?* Why would you get fired after that awesome game? ESPN loves you too much."

I'm not sure what she means by the ESPN comment. "You

didn't see the post-game conference?"

"No, we were practicing. The girls are resting in the locker room before warmup. What happened during post-game?"

"Evan happened. He told the reporters I'm the only reason he played well, and that this isn't Froth's team."

She inhales. "Uh-oh. Fuckstick Froth didn't like that so much?"

"He hasn't said a word to me. But he sure looked pissed off."

"Between that and all the nonstop clips of you talking to Evan, no wonder you're worried about getting the boot. Rabid Frother will hate you for stealing his thunder."

I scrunch my lips up to my nose. "Clips?"

After a pause, she says, "Oh, you've been too busy with the game to know. You're all over the news, Coach Trent."

I sit stock-still.

"They're calling you the QB Whisperer. They keep playing the conversation you had with Evan followed by all of his touchdown passes. He set a Michigan record or something? What'd you say to him?"

I recall her text to her player when we were together in Chicago. "I stole some advice from another coach: I told him I know jack shit about the future, but I do know he's skilled as shit right now, so he'll ace the next series as long as he focuses his ass on one play at a time."

Her low, sexy laugh tells me she got the reference to her words. "Brilliant. Who knew I'd make you so famous?"

I'm not sure what to make of my TV exposure. If it helps me land a head coaching job one day, I'll realize my dream. But if it gets me fired... I don't want to think about it. I turn my attention to *her* coaching career. We've already discussed the horror of her player's suicide attempt, so I focus on a happier topic.

"I saw you crushed your opponent last night, like you thought you would. How was the match? Emma do okay?"

"A pretty good start. I played all three of my setters, so no freshman record for Emma just yet."

Maybe *I* got the better twin. "How'd Cherise's knee hold up?"

"Great. She's been more diligent with her rehab, and she gets better rest with Emma here." She's quiet for a moment. "My assistants were in my office when your flowers arrived. They grilled me about who sent them, and I, uh, told them."

Maybe she'll have more time to talk to me without hiding our relationship from her staff. "How'd they take it?"

"Surprisingly well. Everyone who finds out totally takes it in stride, almost like they're rooting for us. Maybe this whole rivalry thing is a nothingburger."

"It's a sexy burger, that's for sure."

She grunts. "Don't say sex. You'll distract me from my match. Speaking of matches, I should probably go."

A text comes in, and I almost veer off the road as I read it.

"You still there?" asks Lauren.

"Uh…" I let out a breath. I can't believe what I'm reading.

Her voice lifts an octave. "Are you okay?"

"I'm, um, guess you could say, *stunned* by this text I just got."

"Who's it from?"

"My dad."

She's quiet for a second. "Whoa."

I see an exit coming up. "You got a minute? I want to pull over and try to make sense of this, figure out if I want to respond."

"Of course. I'm an expert in crazytown parents, you know."

I shake my head. Her mother's a piece of work, but at least she's been there for her daughter. My dad hasn't seen me for over twenty years. After I pull into an Arby's parking lot, I read the text to Lauren:

Jeremy, it's Dad. You told me not to contact you, and I have to say I don't blame you. I deserve that after how I've treated you and your sister. But Taryn has allowed me to call her every week, and—

"She has?" Lauren interrupts. "I didn't know that. Did you?"

I sigh. "No. But I asked her not to bring him up after the last time she gave him my number. I knew I should've changed it."

"That would be hard to explain to recruits, though."

Exactly. The woman gets me.

"Keep reading," she orders.

And I'm trying to apologize to her for missing out on her life. I want to apologize to you, too. I don't expect your forgiveness, but you need to understand that my leaving had nothing to do with you. It was about my immaturity, my selfishness, and my failure at relationships. Nicole left me years ago—

"Who's Nicole?"

My throat's so tight that it's difficult to speak. "A police officer. His partner." I swallow. "The woman he abandoned us for."

Her voice lowers to a soothing tone. "That's awful you had to go through that."

My hands have curled into fists, and I unfurl my fingers. "His text keeps going."

"Let's hear it."

I'm a hard man to get along with. I had given up on any sort of relationship with you until I started therapy with a police psychologist. He helped me see how wrong I've been. How much I hurt you, Taryn, and Anna. Then I saw you today on national TV. I don't deserve to feel proud of you, but I do. You've become a good coach—not because of me, but despite me. You should be the head coach, not that idiot Froth.

"On this we can agree," says Lauren.

I'm too riled by this text to smile at her comment. "There's only a little bit more."

It's unfair of me to ask, but will you text me? Will you call me? I'll be here.
Dad

"Wow," she says after a beat. "That's a long-ass text."

"Yeah."

"A fucking good text," she adds.

I chew the inside corner of my mouth. It *was* good. I've waited twenty-three years to hear stuff like that. My nose burns, and I shake my head to clear it.

"Do you want to contact him?"

I crack my neck from side to side. "Thanks for listening to all of that—I know you have to go. I'm not sure what to think right now. One text doesn't make up for what he did to our family."

"You're right. He can't go from jerkfuck to father of the year in five seconds. Take some time to think on it. You'll do the right thing, Jer-Bear."

How does she get me to grin at a time like this? "Thank you, sweet cheeks. Get out there and crush the Redhawks." Her team plays Miami University tonight.

After we end the call, I drive for thirty miles, thinking about Evan and his father. I decide to call Taryn, and she fills me in on her latest conversations with our dad. She's not pushy, but I can tell it will be easier for her if I thaw the ice between Dad and me. Then I call Mom, and she surprises me by encouraging me to reach out to my father.

I'm almost to Ann Arbor when I make the call. "Hey, Dad."

21

Reuniting
Lauren

Project Runway All-Stars is halfway over by the time I make it to Sam's house the following Thursday night.

"Sorry," I mutter as I set down my bag and sink onto a lounge chair.

From the sofa, Sam pauses the show. "No worries. I know you have a big match on Saturday." She heads into the kitchen.

As I dip a chip into guacamole, Taryn taps her fingernail on her glass of white wine. "You need to catch up," she tells me.

"Amen." After Sam returns, I accept wine from her and take a long sip. "But I have to stop at one glass because we have a match tomorrow night, too." The long weekends of competition have begun, but at least we don't start traveling till next weekend.

"How's your freshman?" asks Sam.

I know she's referring to Kaylee. "Back at practice today. She seemed pretty upbeat, but I'm going to keep my eye on her." When Taryn gives me a confused look, I explain, "My player had a, um, mental health crisis."

Taryn opens her mouth, like she wants to say something, but she sips wine instead. "Suicide attempt?"

I frown at Sam. "You told her?"

"Of course not. Taryn studies clinical psych, remember?"

I simmer down. One reason Sam's such a good friend is that I trust her to keep secrets. And I did already tell Jeremy about Kaylee. I turn to Taryn. "Got any advice?"

"Is your player seeing a therapist?"

I nod.

"They'll take care of her," Taryn says. "The therapist can

help her figure out what to tell the team."

"She sent them a group text before practice," I say. "I was surprised she told the team what happened because she was so damn mad when I called her parents. But two of my players already knew, so it would've been tough to keep the whole team in the dark." One reason my workday ran so long was the individual meetings I had after practice with players shaken by the news.

"That's good." Taryn runs her hand through her brown hair, reminding me of her brother's same gesture when he's thinking hard. "She took pills?"

I lift my chin. "How'd you know?"

"Number-one method for girls and women."

I shudder. "She ODed on her antidepressant. I didn't even know she was taking one."

"Lots of college athletes take meds these days," says Taryn.

Sam rolls her eyes. "Yep."

Sam's athletic trainer said her swimmers have more mental health issues than most athletes, but Sam's good at dealing with them. I, on the other hand, don't really know how to handle these situations. Kaylee avoided eye contact today—I hope she isn't angry with me.

"Don't worry if your player takes some time to come around," Taryn tells me, almost like she's reading my mind. "She's probably embarrassed."

I nod, grateful for her insight. "She told me it wasn't a suicide attempt."

"Maybe it wasn't." Taryn shrugs. "But it's not uncommon to deny it at first."

Twenty minutes later, we laugh at a judge's snide remark about a dress's V design drawing attention to the model's girly bits.

"Remember that white dress with splashes of red that Tim Gunn called 'an homage to the menstrual cycle'?" Sam says.

Taryn snorts. "I missed that episode!"

She's younger than us and was probably in college when it aired. My phone dings with a text from her older brother.

Need your ear

To lick, or to listen? ;-)

Can I call you?

Hmmm... It appears he's not in a mood for sexy times tonight. "Okay if I take a call in your breakfast nook, Sam? Jeremy needs to talk."

"Sure." She grabs the remote, but I shake my head.

"No need to pause the show. I already know who's gonna win."

Sam groans. We both dislike the cocky designer the judges have been favoring.

As I near the kitchen, my phone rings.

Before I pick up, Taryn huffs from behind me, "Tell the QB Whisperer he owes me a call!"

I smile as I answer. "What's up, buttercup?"

"I keep trying to get fired over here."

The buzz from my glass of wine zooms away like a frightened bee when I hear his anxious tone. "What's happening?"

"Got a coaching situation—a, uh, crisis."

The tremble in his voice alarms me. *Has he already been fired?*

"This needs to stay between us," he says.

I don't hesitate. "You got it."

"I mean it, Lauren. You can't tell anyone at Ohio State."

My face flares with heat. How dare he accuse me of snitching to my colleagues? "I already said I'll keep it quiet! You didn't tell anyone at Michigan about my freshman, right?"

"Of course not. This is a bigger deal, though."

I scoff. "Bigger than an athlete trying to take her own life?"

His exhale is audible. "No. Sorry. Higher profile, maybe, but not as bad as what you've had to deal with." He sighs. "I'm losing perspective. This bullshit job presses down on my chest like a hundred-pound weight."

I get it. In the heat of the season, every coaching decision can feel like the difference between life and death.

"Just don't know if I've got the balls to do the right thing," he says.

A smile spreads across my face. *I know.* "This is about Evan?" I guess.

"Yeah." Another sigh. "The punk tested positive for weed."

No wonder he made me promise secrecy. "You sort of saw that coming, huh?"

"I wish I was wrong."

"Well, he doesn't have to miss the game on Saturday for his first positive, right?" I say. "They just get counseling. At least that's how it works at OSU."

"Right. That's what our policy says, and it's what Froth wants. But coaches can enforce stricter consequences if they need to."

Wow. I sit back and extend my leg to the opposite chair under the kitchen table. Jeremy's thinking of benching his star quarterback for smoking pot. That *will* take balls, especially if the head coach is against it. "But how will you suspend Evan if Froth wants him to play?"

"It'll be tough, but Harry wants to bench him, too. My saving grace is that Hartford—my backup QB—can definitely beat Saturday's opponent. We were only going to play Evan for the first quarter, anyway."

I mull that over, considering additional arguments to present to his boss.

Jeremy must mistake my silence for judgment because his voice takes a defensive edge. "We're talking Evan's entire career, Lauren! He keeps using, he can kiss the pros goodbye. Hell, he won't start for Michigan, either. I've already seen his performance decline since he got here."

"I agree with you!" I realize I sound defensive, too, and I lower my voice. "It's what I'd do."

"Oh." A long pause. "Okay. That's all I needed to hear." When he returns to his typical deep, smooth tone, I relax. "Enough about the punk. How're you? How's Emma? Preparations for Saturday going okay?"

I catch him up on my day.

***

Sitting in my office Saturday afternoon, I reflect on the pregame practice we just finished. Although we won three sets to zero last night, our jump serves sucked, so Patrick and I helped our players improve the consistency of their tosses. As Dana ran the setters through the paces, I noticed tension replacing Emma's characteristic sunshine. She wasn't quick or fluid with her sets. Tonight's match against Brigham Young University will be Emma's first big test as a college player, and I've never seen her so nervous.

My attention drifts from my tablet to the TV that plays OSU's football game. We try to lure volleyball recruits by taking them to home football games, but we don't have recruits on campus this weekend. I'm glad our new arena is on the outskirts of campus, though finding parking was still difficult amid the home-game hoopla.

Ohio State is crushing the smaller school—another reason I chose not to attend the snore-fest football game—and I return to video of BYU's recent matches on my tablet. But my eyes snap back up when the TV coverage switches to Michigan's stadium and a closeup of Evan gesticulating at Jeremy on the sideline.

"Shit." I set my tablet aside and lean in toward the TV screen.

"Whoa, Nelly," the TV announcer says. "Freshman quarterback Evan Watkins is giving his coach an earful. Maybe it's because he hasn't played the entire game."

The announcer's sidekick chimes in. "The Wolverines obviously don't need his arm today, but still, you gotta wonder why he didn't get any snaps after his smoking start against Notre Dame."

Smoking start? I half-close my eyes and mimic taking a hit from a doobie. A good description of the reason Evan's riding the bench.

"You wonder how the quarterbacks' coach will respond to this insubordination," says the announcer. "Looks like Bill Froth is letting his assistant handle it."

I watch Froth turn from Jeremy and Evan back toward action

on the field—not that he needs to supervise his team. It's the end of the fourth quarter and Michigan is up 35-3. Jeremy was right that they didn't need the starting QB for this game. But Evan isn't having it. His hands flay in wild circles as he barks in Jeremy's ear. When a muscle ticks in Jeremy's jaw, I draw in a breath.

In a flash, Jeremy jabs his pointed finger down the sideline. Evan freezes. Jeremy says something else to him. Evan doesn't move until Jeremy takes a step toward him. Then, Evan turns with a scowl and storms off in the pointed direction, probably toward the locker room.

"Looks like the coach just ejected his own player!" laughs the sidekick announcer.

His partner muses, "Huh. Never seen that before. What's going on with these Wolverines?"

Whatever it is, it looks bad. Jeremy seemed like he was seconds away from punching a player, Woody Hayes style. Talk about getting fired—his career would be toast.

When Patrick comes in to ask a question, it takes me a moment to reorient to my office. TV coverage has returned to the Buckeyes. Patrick and I resume our game prep, but worries about Jeremy distract me.

After our pregame meal, I'm back in my office. I answer Jeremy's call on the first ring. "What the hell happened?"

He's quiet for a second. "Just left Froth's office. We met with Evan." His voice sounds defeated.

"What'd the punk say to you on the sideline?"

"He was furious I'd suspended him for the game, and he kept demanding to be put in. Froth didn't back me up, of course. He told Evan the suspension was my idea."

"What an assgiblet."

He huffs a breath out his nose. "But the real kicker is that Froth's letting Evan's ridiculous behavior on the sideline go unchecked. You can't let a player get away with that and maintain any authority. But Froth's giving into Evan's threats."

I squint. "Threats?"

Jeremy exhales again. "At first I agreed not to tell Mr. and Mrs.

Watkins about Evan's positive drug test, but after his behavior at the game, I told Evan I had to let them know. I need his parents to talk some sense into him. But Evan went off the rails when I said that. He threatened to transfer if I told his parents."

"Wow." What would I do if Emma threatened to transfer to another university just because I didn't give her what she wanted? There's no way she would do that, though. I got the good twin—the reasonable one. "How'd Froth respond to that?"

"His job is on the line. All of ours are. We play a good team next week, and Froth wants Evan in there. So, Froth ordered me, in front of Evan, not to say anything to his parents."

I shake my head. Jeremy is in such a rough spot, having to kowtow to his cockmuffin boss.

"Evan was crying by this point," Jeremy adds. "I think the pressure finally got to him. He kept saying, 'I need Emma.'"

What can his twin do for him? I frown. She's got her own life here, anyway.

"Froth looked pissed that Evan was crying, and he asked me who Emma was. Classic—he doesn't even know his players. When I explained that Emma's Evan's twin who helped him in high school, Froth demanded I bring her to him right away."

My eyebrows pucker. "What do you mean?"

"Evan needs Emma. He needs her to talk him down."

I shake my head. "Then he can call her. We have an hour before we go on the court."

"No, he said he has to see her. Talk to her in person."

"How about I drive Emma to you right now, and we'll both miss the match?" I suggest in a snide tone.

"Would you?"

My jaw drops as I see scarlet. I cannot fucking believe he would expect me to do that. "What the *fuck*, Jeremy? I was being sarcastic. This is an important match tonight! No way we'd miss it."

"I get it, but this is about Evan's entire career."

Who gives a damn? "Don't give me that. We both know this is about *your* career. You're scared of your star recruit leaving you."

"So, you won't bring her up here?"

I'm so enraged that I can't see straight. "If he needs to see her so bad, why don't you drive him down here?"

"I can't leave the facility that long—Froth would kill me."

"And I can't sacrifice my career for yours," I hiss. "I have a big match tonight—not that you care—and I need to focus on my team. I can't worry about your shit on top of that." I don't even say goodbye before I end the call.

My chest heaves. Did he really just ask me to miss my match for him? All that talk about him admiring me as a head coach—I should've known he didn't mean it.

Dana pops her head into my office. "You okay?"

How much did my assistants overhear? My body is shaking. "No." *This* is why I didn't want stupid rimjob romance in my life. It's always a disaster.

***

A few hours later, I'm in the locker room with my team after the third set. We're down two sets to one. We need to take sets four and five to win the match. Emma has settled in and played well, probably because I didn't tell her about this Evan mess. Her parents didn't, either—they're in Michigan taking care of Emma's grandfather after he fell off a ladder last night. He's okay, but they're just making sure.

I'm still ticked off about the phone call with Jeremy. I survey my team. They don't look tired, but their jumpy gazes seem scared. BYU's middle blocker is one of the best in the country, and we haven't figured out a way to contain her.

"You know," I begin, "some people don't think volleyball is a *real* sport."

Mariana's head pops up. I figured that would flare up her Colombian temper.

"They think only men's sports like *football* matter." The word drips off my tongue like cocktail bitters. "That girls like you can't be accomplished athletes. They think we should only pay attention to male athletes in revenue sports."

Mariana's eyes blaze.

"Know what I think?" I pause. "I think they're full of *shit*."

Emma's mouth quivers. Kaylee, on the other hand, lets out a full grin.

"I've seen you play. I've seen you train." My hands find their way to my hips. "Remember when Cherise hit her target for *sixty* serves in a row?" A few players nod. "Or when Tatum made twenty-five pull-ups?" I look at the short, wiry defensive specialist. "Damn, girl."

Tatum laughs.

"And we all remember drills like burpee bitch." I ignore someone's groan. "I bet BYU didn't do that drill. Fact is, we're the more prepared team. We work harder than any team out there." I make eye contact with every player. "We're making a statement tonight: The Buckeyes are back." More nods. More fiery stares. "The Buckeyes are back!" I pump my fist. "We're poisonous nuts, and we're gonna poison your dreams."

My absurd ending line earns some giggles before we jog back into the arena.

***

It's after 10 pm when Emma emerges from the locker room after the match, her wet hair looking more black than brown. When she sees me, she lights up in a smile and says, "That was so fun!"

Her bubbly spirit lessens the lingering anger I feel toward Jeremy. He's one reason I have such a talented player on my roster. "Competition seems to bring out the best in you."

"Can we play more top-ten teams?" she begs. "The other matches are boring."

I laugh as I shake my head. Her growth mindset is a thing to behold. "How're you spending your Saturday night?"

She studies me. "I know I should probably go to bed, but Cherise is having people over to celebrate the victory. Don't worry; I won't drink."

That makes *one* of the twins who's responsible. "You're in college, and you have a day off tomorrow. You *shouldn't* go to bed right away. But I wonder if you'll come with me on a drive instead of hanging with your teammates."

"A drive?"

Once I explain, she's on board with the plan. I text Jeremy.

We arrive at the Findlay hotel around midnight. After I pull into the space next to his black SUV, I shake Emma's shoulder to wake her.

Two coaches and two athletes emerge from the vehicles. Evan yawns—he probably slept in the car as well—and I marvel at the change in his physique. He's not as built as Jeremy, but he's definitely put on some muscle.

Jeremy watches me with wary eyes.

"Hey," Emma says as she steps into her brother's arms. It's a sweet hug from a sweet girl. I hope she can infuse some of her light into his darkness, at least for Jeremy's sake. "What's going on, Evvy?"

Evan looks at Jeremy. "Can we talk in your car, Coach?"

Jeremy nods at the vehicle. "It's open."

Evan and Emma slide into his driver and passenger seats where there's plenty of room for their giraffe legs.

My shoulders tense as Jeremy approaches me.

"Want to sit in your car?" he asks.

"No." I press my lips together.

Fluorescent light from the hotel sign reflects in his eyes. His handsome green eyes. "Thanks for bringing Emma here, meeting us halfway."

"I wouldn't have agreed to come here if your shitnanigans had made us lose tonight."

"My shitnanigans?" He grins.

Don't give me that sexy smile. "We better not be here too late—I don't want Emma up all night. She has to study tomorrow."

"Eh, she'll be fine. I'm sure those Ohio State classes aren't too rigorous."

After the long day I've had, I don't find his teasing funny at all. Instead, my resentment starts building again. "Evan's the one who should worry about studying. Is he getting *any* supervision up there in Ann Arbor?"

Jeremy bristles. "You're saying I don't take good care of him?"

I shrug. "Looks like his career's imploding. And you may

not care about Emma, but I do. I don't want her sucked into his fuckstorm."

"I care about Emma! What're you talking about?"

"You *care* about her? You wanted her to miss her match tonight, all for Evan!"

His forehead creases. "Listen, I—"

"You think your sport's the only one that matters! You're so smug up there in your TV tower, wrinkling your nose at the little loser sports playing their trivial, meaningless games, deluding themselves that they're important when we all know they only exist because of their football team."

"Are you done?" His nostrils flare.

"I'm just getting *started!*" I roar. "I—"

He crosses over to me in a second, engulfing my next words in an impassioned kiss. I place my hands on his chest to push him away, but when I feel the vibration of his rapid heartbeat, I let go of my resistance and massage his muscles instead. He cradles my face in his hands as he deepens the kiss. The flush of anger on my cheeks morphs into arousal as I inhale his strong, masculine scent.

He tucks me into his solid body. "I'm so sorry," he murmurs into my ear. "That was really douchey of me to ask that of you." He pulls back and looks down at me. "I don't know what I was thinking. I *wasn't* thinking. That was one-hundred-percent desperation. But there's no excuse."

Damn straight.

"Volleyball *does* matter. And you're a fantastic coach." He swallows. "This kid…" He angles his head toward his car. "He just drives me insane. So much talent…but if he doesn't pull it together like his sister, he's going to wash out."

Is that explanation good enough? Should I let Jeremy off the hook? His solid arms holding me feel so right. I've missed him, and I don't want to have to leave him.

In Jeremy's car, I notice Evan looking down as Emma talks to him. Evan's made mistakes, just like I did when I was his age. I wish I'd had a twin to talk me out of my ill-advised relationship with Paul. Though Evan's a punkass, there's no doubt I want to see his amazing arm in action for years to come.

"It would suck if Evan doesn't realize his potential," I agree.

We let go of each other but still stand close.

"But Evan doesn't matter as much to me as you do, Lauren. I'm so sorry I put him ahead of you today. I promise I'll never do that again. You come first with me, okay?"

Something shakes loose inside of me as I listen to his words. I realize he's the most important person in my life, too—ahead of my parents, Sam, Alex, and my assistants. Here I was, so scared to let any man in, worrying he'd hurt me like Paul did. And somehow this Michigan Wolverine has burrowed his way into my heart, inch by inch. His prominence in my life is the very reason his earlier actions hurt so much. But his apology seems sincere. I can see the fear in his eyes as he begs for my forgiveness.

"Evan told me Emma had fifty-three assists tonight, close to Cherise's record from her freshman year."

I'm touched that Evan looked up that stat and shared it with Jeremy.

"Evan and Emma brought us together," Jeremy says. "But I won't let them pull us apart." He gathers my hands in his, warm and firm on a cool September night. His eyes crinkle at the corners. "Will you forgive me, Coach Chase?"

I think about how relieved I felt when he forgave me for tattling about his sister attending OSU. *"Forgiveness is divine,"* Jenna told us then. The naughty thoughts I'm having about this man are anything but holy.

"Do we have enough time to get a hotel room?" I ask.

Exposing
Jeremy

Thank God Lauren accepted my apology. It would crush me if I'd let Evan interfere with our relationship. I allowed my concern for his career to cloud my judgment, and it was an awful thing to say to her. Evan will be in my life for only two, maybe three years more. I want Lauren with me for the long game.

We've been driving north for ten minutes without a word from Evan. I hope he got what he needed from his twin—he seems calmer, at least. He hasn't bitched about my music like he did when we left school. I tap my left foot to the beat of Little River Band's "Cool Change."

I drink coffee from a to-go cup and grimace at its cool temperature. Evan and I stopped for beverages at a gas station before meeting up with Lauren and Emma. Buying Lauren an ice-cold Mountain Dew underlined my apology. After our shouting match in the parking lot, she allowed me to sit with her in her car. She guzzled the entire bottle as we waited for Evan and Emma to ignite their wonder-twin powers. The longer Lauren and I talked, the more we seemed back to normal. Recalling the flare of passion in her eyes as she shared the highlights of her match deepens a cavern of longing in my chest.

Evan knocks back a drink of Gatorade, and then he frowns at me. "Can't believe you didn't let me buy a Mountain Dew. You got *her* one."

"Coach Chase doesn't have to perform at a game this Saturday."

"Does that mean my suspension is over?"

I exhale. "Depends on how you behave at practice this

week."

He shakes his head. "Emma's right."

I look over at him. "About what?"

"About our coaches. We saw you dry humping, you know."

I tense. I wish Lauren had allowed us to talk it out in her car at first, but she was too mad. When she went off on me, obviously hurt, I had to correct her misperceptions. I *do* respect her and her sport. I wanted to let her know how I really feel about her, and the best way to do that was to kiss the living hell out of her. As her plump, pliant lips molded to mine, I knew I was inching back into her good graces.

"Emma said you're like our parents, only younger." He shudders. "Mom and Dad still make out all the time."

I take that in. "You don't know how lucky you are to have them as parents, Evan."

"What, because they're super strict?"

"Because they're in *love*. You're lucky your parents are still married, even. I don't have that—lots of people don't." I think about the conflict between Lauren's parents.

Evan looks out at the black night on a desolate stretch of 75 North. "Emma said her coach is nothing like Mom, though. She swears a lot."

I smirk.

"Coach Chase even *smokes*," he adds.

"She quit," I reply on reflex. I wonder how Emma found that out. "And cigarettes are different from marijuana, but you shouldn't use either."

Evan snorts. "You sound like my dad." He shakes his head. "That's what I told Emma—her coach may be different from Mom, but you're just like Dad."

A sense of pride inflates me. I've second-guessed myself throughout this drug-test tornado, but I must be doing something right if Evan's comparing me to his father. "I know you meant it as an insult, but I take that as the highest compliment."

He's quiet for a moment. "It's not an insult."

My eyes widen as I glance over at him.

"Emma reminded me how great I played with Dad's support—

how many times he helped me learn plays, practiced with me all night after school, taught me how to talk to college coaches... He was so freaking proud of me when I signed at Michigan." He looks down. "Then I screwed it all up. Emma thinks I should tell him about the weed, but he'd be so disappointed in me." His voice quiets. "I'm an ungrateful piece of crap."

I need to hire Emma Watkins as head of player development. "Hey." I wait for him to look at me. "You're *not* crap. You're a good boy on his way to becoming a great man. But weed isn't part of that journey. Drugs will derail your dreams."

He sighs.

"Everybody makes mistakes," I say. "The great ones learn from them. That's why I suspended you—to teach you there are consequences for breaking team rules. To get you to stop using weed." *To dump the teammates who got you into trouble.* I give him a pointed look. "Have you stopped smoking?"

"Yeah." He sits up a bit. "Yes, sir."

He addresses me the way his father told him he should. I hope Evan's grateful for his supportive family full of role models. Talik isn't so lucky—he grew up in foster care. "How's that going?"

"Fine."

I don't believe him, so I wait for him to elaborate.

He yawns. "Except I can't fall asleep. The athletic counselor said my sleep will get worse before it gets better."

I'm glad he's getting expert advice.

"And he told me to get new friends." He scowls. "That's so unfair."

This athletic counselor needs a pay raise. "It's hard to let go of your bros."

His lips purse.

"Talik's a fun guy," I offer. "A cool dude. He's very talented." After Evan nods, I add, "He could be so much better."

"How do you know that for sure?"

"I saw it in my teammates. Three guys got drafted from my class. The only one who's still playing eleven years later?" I pause. "The guy who never used weed."

The corner of his mouth turns down. "Adrian Nichols."

"Yes, sir."

A few miles go by, and Evan asks, "How much longer till we're home?"

It's a good sign he just referred to Ann Arbor as his home. "About eighty minutes."

He reclines his seat. "I probably won't be able to sleep. Especially with your annoying senior-citizen music in my ear."

I turn down the radio and hope this cold coffee will keep me awake.

In less than five minutes, I hear Evan's breathing shift into a steady, deep cadence. I look over at him in the moonlight. At the sight of his slack jaw and relaxed, long limbs, a sudden tenderness floods me. *Sleep well, my little punk.*

***

I rub my bleary eyes as I walk into the facility the next morning. Since we're supposed to arrive by seven the Sunday after home games, I eked out only three hours of sleep. I was so tired that I nicked my neck shaving. This spinach smoothie I'm drinking better deliver its promised Popeye power, or I'll fall asleep at my desk.

While the rest of campus still sleeps off their hangovers, the football training room buzzes with activity. An athletic trainer tapes Evan's ankle. *Good, he'll be ready to run some drills soon.* When he meets my gaze, he smirks. I'm pleased to see him bounce back from yesterday's drama.

But on the padded table next to him, Austin Hartford's expression isn't so jovial. He downright glares at me. I watch an athletic trainer massage Hartford's quad. "Great game, Harts," I say. "Feeling a little sore?"

My second-string QB doesn't even nod at me. *What's his deal?* Is he pissed that Evan will start next week?

As my phone vibrates in my pocket, I frown at the caller ID. Why is the Michigan volleyball coach calling me so early on a Sunday? I answer the call as I walk toward my office.

"Did you help OSU get Emma Watkins?" Jim Dawson demands.

I slow my stride. "What?"

"You did, didn't you?" he fumes. "Playing dumb about OSU volleyball winning a national championship, when the whole time you're banging their coach."

I suck in a breath. "What the hell are you talking about, Jim?"

"Still playing dumb?" When I don't answer, he says, "Read the news." *Click.*

Nausea roils in my gut as I close the door to my office and fire up ESPN on my phone's browser. RIVAL ROMANCE, reads one headline, and I stop breathing after I click on the link. There's a photo of Lauren yelling at me last night, her finger jabbing in my direction, and another of me mauling her with a kiss. The photos are dark and grainy, but our school colors and logos are obvious. I feel like I'm outside of my body as I scroll down to find a couple more photos of Evan and Emma talking in my car. Who the hell snapped these pics?

One happy Big Ten family? I read under the photos. *Star quarterback Evan Watkins plays for Michigan, and his twin, Emma, plays volleyball for Ohio State. What's behind their midnight rendezvous in Findlay, Ohio, the night after Evan's coach benched him? Does his sister have the same talent and temper? Are the twins close despite playing for the enemy?*

Their coaches don't seem to mind the rivalry. Jeremy Trent, quarterbacks' coach for the Wolverines, and Lauren Chase, head women's volleyball coach for the Buckeyes, pack a lot of heat into that kiss. Is this a one-night fling or a long-term fraternization? It will be interesting to see how Wolverine and Buckeye Nation respond to their coaches getting it on.

From a distance, I hear the ring of my landline phone. Numb, I stroll over to see *Detroit Free Press* on the caller ID. The local newspaper is probably the first of many to hound me for this story—at least they don't have my cell phone number. Just as that thought enters my mind, my cell rings. I'm about to decline the call when I notice it's from Tyler Watkins. I tense as I accept the call.

"What's going on with Evan, Coach?"

I swallow. "Mr. Watkins." The only reason I haven't heard

from him about yesterday's game before this is that he's been busy caring for his father. "How's your dad, sir?" My phone buzzes, and I pull it away from my ear to read texts from ESPN and NBC. So much for the media not having my cell number.

"We were at the ER all day—they thought Dad had internal injuries. Luckily, it's just a broken arm. But we had to miss our kids' games. I wake up this morning to watch clips of Evan *yelling* at you on the sideline. Then you bring him to meet up with Emmy? What the heck happened?"

I need to come up with a lie, quick. But incoming texts and calls muddle my mind.

My silence doesn't sit well with him, and his voice is insistent. "Why didn't Evan play?"

"Um..." Will my phone shut *up?* "We wanted to rest him for next week..."

"But he needs to play at least *some* snaps, right?"

A knock on my door rattles me further. "Mr. Watkins, this isn't the best time—"

"Are you in your office?"

I frown as the knocks increase in volume. "Yes?"

"I'm on my way to talk to you. I want Evan there, too. We're getting to the bottom of this."

"But sir, we have pract—"

Click.

I toss the vibrating phone onto my desk and run my fingers through my hair, still damp from my shower. What a shitstorm.

The door to my office swings open, and Harry Stevens sticks his head in. "Jeremy?" His gray, bushy eyebrows elevate.

"Hair, I'm sorry." I clutch my head as the annoying buzz of my phone fills the room.

He steps inside and closes the door behind him. "You're fucking a Buckeye?"

I suppose I should be offended, but an inappropriate laugh bubbles in my throat at his description of the situation. "Guess so." In addition to the cell phone cacophony, I can't think straight with the incessant ringing of my landline, so I take it off the hook. "Am I in trouble?"

He shakes his head. "Her workplace is suspect, but I'm glad you finally found someone. Lord knows I couldn't do this job without Joyce by my side."

Harry has been married for over thirty years.

"I don't care about this OSU coach business," he says, "but Froth might, once he finds out."

I wondered why my head coach hadn't come in to tear into me yet. "Froth already knows." Harry's lips part, and I add, "He caught me sneaking Lauren into my hotel room in Chicago."

"Whoops." Harry laughs. He points at the Band-Aid on my neck. "She give you a hickey?"

I snort as I shake my head. His amused attitude helps lighten the load on my shoulders. He's been around the block a time or twenty, and his steady gaze seems to convey that this will blow over just like any other scandal.

He dips his head toward my phone. "The vultures won't stop coming after you, huh?"

I grunt.

"What does your lady say about all of this?"

The pressure returns to my shoulders. "Haven't had a chance to talk to her. She's probably still sleeping—it was a late night." I heave a sigh as a grating sound bursts from my landline, warning me it's off the hook. "And Tyler Watkins is on his way here to get to the bottom of Evan not playing yesterday."

Once Harry places the landline back on the receiver, it starts ringing. He tosses his thumb over his shoulder. "Hide out in my office. Turn off your cell and use my landline if you want."

His kindness outweighs Froth's cruelty, times ten. "You're the best, Hair-Bear."

I close the door, settle myself behind his desk, and dial. Lauren's husky voice as she answers is the perfect mix of groggy and sexy. "Who is this?"

"It's Jer-Bear, sweet cheeks."

"Are you bothering me *again?*" she mumbles.

"It's not me this time; it's the national media. Our secret's out."

I hear a rustle like she's sitting up in bed. "Huh?" More

rustling. "Who's blowing up my phone with texts?"

I cringe. "Check out ESPN."

After a beat, she gasps. "What asswipe took these photos? Oh my God. Papafuckzzi piece of shit."

"I bet they followed Evan and me from campus. We refused to answer their questions after the game, and they didn't like that."

"Oh no." A new level of alarm has entered her voice. "What?"

"My text messages. There's one from an OSU football coach. An assistant—I don't know him. He can fuck off. But there's one from Rhonda, too." She inhales. "She wants to meet." She whimpers, "Jeremy."

If this asshole ESPN reporter gets Lauren fired, so help me...

Harry's door bursts open, and Froth stands in the doorway. The lines around his dark eyes tighten as he studies me.

"I have to call you back." I hang up and circle around the desk, bracing myself as I face my boss.

Froth's saccharine smile puts me more on edge. "Do you know who just busted my balls for the past thirty minutes, all because of you?"

I guess the athletic director's name.

"Oh, ho ho! That Oklahoma education's really working for you." He laces his arms across his chest. "If you're so smart, how can you fuck up this Evan situation so badly and make us look like retards on national TV? Then you get caught with that fucking Ohio coach?" His arms splay to the side. "Show some goddamn discretion, for fuck's sake. *You're* the reason I get accused of losing control of my program!"

I feel the effects of shit sliding downhill. The AD rips into Froth, who then rips into me. *Good times.* "Do you want me to apologize to the AD?"

"You don't talk to him—*I* talk to him!" he rasps. "He doesn't know about Evan's threat to transfer, and we're going to keep it that way."

"About that... Mr. Watkins is on his way to meet with Evan and me."

Froth's face flushes. "You're going behind my back, Trent? Trying to steal my job?"

"No! It wasn't my idea—Mr. Watkins insisted."

He looks me up and down. "I knew I shouldn't have let you suspend Evan. You did that to hurt the team."

"What?" My mouth drops open. "I suspended him to *help* him! To help the team as well."

Froth steps closer, and I smell coffee on his breath. "Don't say a word to the dad about the drug test. If Watkins transfers, you're done. You got it?"

I gulp. "Yes, sir."

Five minutes later, I'm back in my office waiting for my star player and his father. After I rip the phone cord out of the wall, my hand trembles as I sip lukewarm smoothie. This has been some morning. And it's about to get worse—when I have to choose between being honest or getting fired. In my gut, I know there's only one choice. I just hope whoever ends up coaching Evan can help him achieve his dreams. I also cross my fingers that Lauren will stay with me once I'm unemployed.

Mr. Watkins enters, wearing a Toledo High School polo shirt. As I rise to shake his hand, Harry brings Evan in. The boy's navy blue T-shirt and shorts make it obvious he's coming straight from warmup on the practice field.

"Sorry to take you both away from practice," Mr. Watkins says after Harry leaves.

"I'm glad you're here." *Liar.* I gesture toward the table and chairs to the side of my desk. "Evan, get the door, will you?"

"Yes, Coach."

After we sit, we stare at each other. "Interesting photos from last night," Mr. Watkins begins.

You think?

He turns to his son. "Why'd you need to talk to Emma in the middle of the night?"

Evan glances at me, then at his lap.

"There's a rumor that you were suspended for the game yesterday, Evan." His father waits for him to meet his gaze, which takes a while. "Is that true?"

Evan sits stock still as a bead of sweat trails down his temple. "Yes," I say. "I suspended him."

"Why?"

The father's question hangs in the air. Evan avoids looking my way, but I know he'll glower at me once I spill the beans. Here goes. "Because—"

"Because I had a positive drug test," Evan interrupts.

My eyes are almost as huge as his father's.

"For marijuana," he adds, still staring at his shorts.

Mr. Watkins wheels to face me. "Why didn't you tell me this, Coach?"

I wanted to.

Evan looks up at me, then at his father. "Because I threatened to transfer if he did."

Holy bomb drop. I can't believe he just admitted that.

As expected, the patriarch's face reddens, and his jaw clenches as he leans in toward his son. "Let me see if I got this straight. You use drugs, breaking team rules. Then, instead of taking responsibility for your behavior, like a man, you *blackmail* your coach into keeping your secret?" His lips curl down in disgust when Evan doesn't correct him. "I've never heard of such entitled, embarrassing behavior."

Evan flinches, but he doesn't break eye contact.

"We raised you better than that!"

The young quarterback wipes sweat off his forehead with the back of his hand. "I know."

A muscle ticks in Mr. Watkins' jaw. "Your mother and I wondered if you could handle this responsibility. Clearly, this is too much for you. I'm taking you home."

My breath quickens, and Evan's rapid blinks make him look as scared as I feel. "Please, Dad! Let me stay. I, I was stressed, but I'm, I'm handling it better now."

"Since when is stress an excuse to do drugs?" his father challenges.

"It's not," Evan mumbles. His chin trembles, and his hands squeeze into fists, but he loses his battle against crying as a tear leaks down his cheek. "Sorry," he sniffs. His thighs tense, looking like he wants to bolt from my office.

Most fathers would lay into their sons for showing such weakness—I know mine did the few times I cried as a child—but Mr. Watkins lowers his shoulders and pats his son's knee. "It's going to be okay. You're going to be okay. God's with you, no matter what." He lets Evan cry it out for a bit. "What's got you so stressed, son?"

I expect his answer to be along the lines of trying to fit in, wanting to be cool like the upperclassmen. Instead, I'm stunned when he says, "Coach Froth."

Mr. Watkins frowns at me before he cups Evan's shoulder. "Coach Froth?"

The poor boy's eyes spill over with tears. "He called me a fuh… a, uh, effing idiot." His chest jumps up and down as he swipes under his nose. "In front of the whole team."

"Is that true?" Concerned brown eyes meet mine.

"Yes," I admit. "He's said something like that to all of us."

Mr. Watkins squints. "But that's normal, right? Football coaches are tough. I remember mine lambasting me a time or two."

"I think it's beyond that." I chew the inside of cheek. "Coach Froth puts a lot of pressure on his quarterbacks. Intense pressure. He can be…" I search for the right word. "Cruel."

Leaning back in his chair, Mr. Watkins scowls. "Why didn't you tell us this during recruiting?"

My throat squeezes. He's right—I should've been honest about Froth's brutality. But all recruiting is a sales pitch, highlighting successes and omitting undesirable parts of the package. I'm starting to think there's more behind Evan's threat to transfer than keeping me quiet about his positive drug test.

"Dad." Evan takes a deep breath. "It wouldn't have mattered. You were set on me playing for your alma mater."

His father deflates, reminding me of the time his wife got on his case for pushing Evan too much.

"Besides, it's not Coach Trent's fault," Evan adds. "It's mine." His crying has stopped. "Emma made me promise not to get Coach Trent in trouble."

Mr. Watkins tilts his head as he sports a small smile. "Why's that?"

"Because it might distract Coach Chase, since they're *together*." He air-quotes that last bit. "And Emma doesn't want anything in the way of her team winning the national title."

Mr. Watkins's smile expands. "That sounds like my competitive girl. What else did Emma tell you?"

"She said we're only freshmen, but we're blessed to lead our teams. Our teams need us. And if I keep messing up, I won't take care of my team." He scratches the stubble on his cheek. "She said I'm good at taking care of people. Like when I helped her with her roommate situation."

His father nods. "Your mother mentioned something about that. How'd you help Emma?"

Evan shrugs. "Her roommate kept blowing her off, and I told Emma it was about the roommate's issues—her insecurity. How could anyone not like Emmy? And then the roommate had a meltdown, proving my point."

I think about Lauren's anguish from that night and feel grateful again for the girl being okay.

"That was good advice," Mr. Watkins says.

Evan nods. "But not as good as what Emma told me. She said God is challenging us because we're strong. She told me I'm Daniel, and Coach Froth is a lion in the den. If I keep the faith, he can't hurt me."

As I watch Mr. Watkins relax, I feel a new respect for Evan. Bringing the Bible into this discussion is brilliant. The fact that he's taking responsibility for his behavior will also win him favor with his father.

Mr. Watkins blows out a breath. "Your sister." He shakes his head. "How'd she get so wise?"

Evan smirks at him, and they say in unison, "Mom."

I let them share their moment before I add, "Emma also reminded you how much your dad sacrificed to make you the player you are."

"Right." He turns to his father. "No more smoking, I promise. I'm seeing a counselor and everything, and Coach Trent said I can play next week as long as I work hard. Let me stay, Dad. It's my calling."

Mr. Watkins drums his fingers on the table. "I must say, I'm so proud of you and Emmy. I can't wait to tell your mother how well our twins supported each other. That's a sign of great parenting."

Evan rolls his eyes.

"And great coaching," I add, earning a chuckle from the father and a gagging sound from the son. "Coach Chase drove Emma to meet us late at night after a long match, all to help Evan."

"Please thank her for me," Mr. Watkins says, "even if she is a Buckeye." He sighs, looking at his son. "Should you remain a Wolverine?"

Quiet settles over us as Evan's eyes plead with his father.

"Okay. You can stay." Before Evan jumps out of his chair, Mr. Watkins says, "As long as Coach Trent doesn't leak the playbook to the Buckeyes."

Evan shoots to his feet and whoops.

I groan at that lame joke. "This is going to be my life, isn't it? Nonstop harassment about my girlfriend."

"From that kiss you gave her, Coach, looks like she's worth it." Mr. Watkins winks at me, then he stands and accompanies his son out of my office.

Phew. It appears I've survived the rival romance revelation, assuming Froth calms down. And Evan owned up to his drug suspension, unraveling that knot. *Amazing.* Now all I have to do is hope Lauren's job is as safe as mine.

23

Rivaling, Part One
Lauren

After I enter my office, I toss my jacket onto the chair and rub my hands together to warm them. It's only the beginning of November, but it feels like winter has already arrived in Columbus. At least I don't have to stand out in the blustery wind to sneak a smoke anymore.

According to Jeremy, Emma found out about my smoking at some point, probably from another player. I hope my quitting makes it a non-issue for her and her parents. Since kicking that awful habit, my workouts have thrust into a higher gear, which is fortunate since I need an outlet for my unspent sexual energy.

Patrick pops into my office. "Have you seen Jim Dawson's latest email?"

I groan. The Michigan coach has had countless demands before our match with them in a few hours. "What's his bitchfest now?"

"He wants to be sure tonight's refs aren't from Ohio."

"Give me a fucking break. They're impartial Big Ten refs." I look out the office's interior window onto the court. "Has their team arrived yet?"

He shakes his head.

"Good. We can overflow the toilets in the visitor locker room before they get here."

"Great idea." His eyes narrow. "Or, I can stuff a dirty diaper into one of their lockers."

We share a grin. Patrick's wife went into labor two weeks early, and he's now the proud father of a baby boy. Today is Patrick's first return from paternity leave—no way he'll miss a chance to beat Michigan. We've played opponents with better national rankings, but we always get up for a match against the team up north.

On his way out, Patrick says, "I'll check with video to see if they have the camera angles all set for tonight."

I watch him leave, feeling grateful we both still have jobs. It's important to me that Patrick can take care of his family. After that shifty reporter outed Jeremy and me in September, Rhonda pressed me for details and scolded me for "making Ohio State look bad in the national media." But she didn't fire me, probably because we've played so well. I can't believe we've won twenty-four matches in a row. We didn't have that spotless of an in-season record the year we won the national championship.

Instead of bringing negative press to OSU, like Rhonda alleged, the ESPN story has drawn nothing but positive attention to my team's success. That same reporter wrote another article last week about the stellar records of OSU volleyball and Michigan football this season. We're both undefeated and ranked in the top five in the country. *The rival romance appears to help both coaches*, he wrote.

I have to agree. Though I've only seen Jeremy once since that September night—he came down for a quick trip on his bye week—we've worked hard to keep the fire burning via texts and video calls. Our regular seasons will end in a few weeks, but we both hope to continue playing after that, me in the NCAA tournament and him in a playoff among the top four teams in the country. Then we'll be able to spend more time together. I miss him so hard that I don't know how I'll make it till January.

When I hear a knock on my door, I look up from video of yesterday's practice. *Sanctified shit*. Andy Hunter, OSU's athletic director, stands in my doorway. He's never visited me before.

"Andy!" I bolt up from my chair. "Come in." My wild gaze sweeps across my office, taking in an open bag of Twizzlers spilling onto my desk, a pair of high-top Nike volleyball shoes tossed haphazardly on the floor, and a gas-station mega cup of soda sweating on my table. "Want something to drink?" I kneel and peer into my mini fridge. "I've got Mountain Dew, and, uh…"

Damn, I don't even have bottled water in here? "And Mountain Dew."

"None for me, thanks."

I straighten, cringing when he doesn't smile. What's he doing here?

"I know your match starts soon," he says. "But do you have time for a chat?"

"Of course!" I gesture toward a chair at my table.

As he crosses in front of me to take a seat, I notice how expensive his charcoal suit looks. It fits him perfectly. "Close the door."

My heart drops at that command. In an instant, I know why he's here. He'll finish what Rhonda started: terminating me. I thought my team's winning streak would cut me a break, but apparently years of underperforming and months of fraternizing with the enemy overrule that. My legs shake as I lower into a chair across from him. I shove my half-empty drink away from us and wince when it leaves a wet smear across the table.

Even without the trappings of his CEO corner office surrounding him, Andy still renders a commanding presence. A former college basketball player, he's six-foot-seven. His short, dark hair is neat, and his deep blue eyes assess me as he straightens his scarlet tie. I've enjoyed his tendency to crack jokes at staff meetings, but today his vibe is all business. The business of firing a coach.

He points at my computer screen, where practice video continues to play. "You've got yourself quite a freshman setter."

I look over at Emma executing sets from the near the baseline. Though she has to push the ball some distance, her accuracy is spot on. "Sorry." I pop off my chair, pause the video, and return to the table. "What do you want to discuss?" I hope the quiver of my voice is evident only to me.

"You play the team up north tonight."

I nod. *No shit, Captain Obvious.*

"How're the Buckeyes looking?"

I shrug. "My starting outside hitter twisted her ankle yesterday, but we should be okay." I recall the smug look Jim

Dawson gave me after they beat us last year. "No matter who's injured, we'll fight like hell to beat those punks."

A faint smile crosses his lips. "What does your boyfriend say about that?"

Grr. I wonder if he'd ask a male coach about his significant other's opinion. "He encourages it—he's just as competitive as I am. When his team plays OSU in a few weeks, they'll do everything they can to crush their rival."

"Everything they can?" Andy cocks his head. "Within the rules, of course."

I squint. *What is he suggesting?*

"Jeremy Trent," Andy continues after I don't respond. "He's a rule follower?"

"You could say that. He's a goody-two-shoes, actually. Have you ever heard of a vegan football coach?"

His head shakes.

"Well, now you have. He works out all the time, too."

After a beat, he leans in. "What I meant to ask...is Coach Trent a man of integrity?"

Again, I'm puzzled by his question. Does he think I'm sharing OSU football secrets with Michigan or something? "We keep our relationship purely personal. We don't talk shop with each other."

He frowns as he sits back, like I've frustrated him. After he shifts in his chair, he asks, "Where'd you two meet?"

"Outside the Watkins' house."

"Oh, right. He was recruiting Evan."

He knows Emma's twin by his first name? I guess Evan Watkins *is* rather famous.

"That must've been contentious," says Andy. "An Ohio State coach running into a Michigan coach at their recruits' house."

I remember Jeremy sliding his sunglasses down his nose to smirk at me with those beguiling green eyes. "For sure. He caught me—" I stop on a dime. What the hell am I thinking, telling my boss I was a smoker? I'm supposed to be a role model for my student-athletes. My big mouth is a thing to behold.

"He caught you?" he prompts.

Oh, what the fuck. They're going to fire me anyway. "Jeremy caught me smoking outside Emma's house. He threatened to narc on me to Emma's parents so she'd sign at Michigan instead of OSU."

Andy's eyebrows elevate. "Did he do it?"

"No. At first I couldn't understand why he kept my secret, but then I came to realize that's just who he is—he lifts up the people around him. He's got a huge heart. He was impressed that my team had won a national title, and he wanted me to have the chance to repeat."

He considers my response. "Your chances are looking great this year. You're doing a wonderful job with your team."

I exhale. "Thank you. By the way, I quit cigarettes. Jeremy helped me."

"Good to hear. Tough habit to stop." He crosses his long legs. "My mother was a smoker."

"Mine, too."

He gives a quick nod. "How *is* your mother?"

I angle my head to one side.

"Sorry, don't mean to pry. Rhonda told me your mother was diagnosed with cancer, but you don't have to talk about it if you don't want to."

"Oh." *How did Fuck-You Rhonda find out about that?* Athletic departments can be such gossip mills. Now that I think about it, I'm surprised it took a nosey reporter to break the story about Jeremy. You'd think one of my fellow coaches would have discovered the relationship first. My colleagues have given me all kinds of shit since September, including hanging T-shirts on my office walls when I least expect it. My favorite was the navy shirt with a big yellow M. Instead of the traditional *Go Blue* underneath the M, it read, *Go Blow.* I also liked the repeated MUCK FICHIGAN in rows across the front of another shirt.

"Mom's doing great," I answer. "Physically, I mean."

He smiles and nods conspiratorially.

I replay Andy's words in my head: his mother *was* a smoker. Did she die? How do I ask that? I should know more about my boss, but this is the first in-depth conversation we've ever had.

"Your mom...is she, uh, how is she...?"

His smile spreads as I stammer. "She's great as well. My parents just sold their house in Oklahoma and moved to a condo in Texas."

His response stirs a memory from Andy's bio. "You played at Oklahoma, right? Jeremy did, too."

"I know."

He does?

Andy smooths his hand down his tie. "I'm curious what happened with Evan Watkins earlier this season, when he didn't play in a game. You said you don't talk shop with Coach Trent, but do you have any insight about his suspension?"

I freeze. Jeremy specifically asked me not to tell anyone at Ohio State about the positive drug test. But even if he hadn't asked that, I know it's wrong to share insider secrets about my rival just because I'm dating one of their coaches.

When I don't reply, Andy says, "Whatever happened, Evan sure bounced back. He leads the nation in passing yards per game as a freshman... Impressive."

"What you asked me before, about Jeremy?" I look him in the eye. "All I can tell you is that his handling of the Evan situation proves his integrity. He's honest and trustworthy."

Andy watches me for a moment, then reaches over to shake my hand. "That's all I needed to hear. Thank you, Lauren. Crush your opponent tonight."

Once he leaves, I stare at my open doorway. I'm relieved he didn't fire me, but what the fuck was that about?

* * *

I can't believe we lost to Michigan. *Cockdamn doodle do.* I knew we were unlikely to last an entire season undefeated, but did we have to lose to *those* peckers? I didn't even look at Jim Dawson as I shook his hand after the fifth set, but I'm sure he wore an arrogant smile.

My players slump against their lockers, staring at the floor or the far wall, anywhere but at me. They probably expect me to lay into them after our first loss of the season, and to the team up north no less. But I can tell they're already being too hard on themselves. My outside hitter grips the crutches that rest against her elevated leg as she glowers at her injured ankle. She probably blames herself for the loss. To her left, Kaylee Stenstrom looks close to tears. She earned the start she craved, filling in for my injured hitter. She wasn't awful, but it's apparent she's not quite ready for Big Ten volleyball. I hope tonight's match will help her trust my coaching decisions better.

Emma's warbling voice cuts through the silence. "Sorry, guys."

"What're you sorry for?" Cherise asks. "You played awesome."

"I wanted to beat them *so bad!*" Emma huffs. She tugs at her sweaty uniform shirt.

You and me both, kid.

"You just don't want your twin to tease you for losing to his school," says Mariana.

Emma shakes her head. "He'd never do that, because he knows OSU's gonna to whip his butt in a few weeks."

I wonder how Jeremy will handle that if she's right. I read his text before I entered the locker room:

Tough loss, sweet cheeks. What does not kill you, makes you stronger. Call me.

"Oooh, I'm still so mad," Emma says, not letting go of tonight's match.

Energy vibrates off her, and she hops to her feet as if she can't stand to sit anymore. Her glare scans the room until it rests on a closed locker. When she cocks her arm back, about to punch the metal, I yell, "Not your hand!"

The last thing we need is our starting setter to break those golden fingers.

Emma lowers her arm but scrunches her nose, her gaze darting around like she still wants to hit something.

Cherise shoots up to grab her before she kicks the wall, hollering, "Not your foot, either!"

A broken toe on my setter might be even worse.

"Here." Cherise finds a wayward volleyball and hands it to Emma. "Throw it against the floor."

Emma's eyes light up as she accepts the ball. She lifts it over her head with both arms, then slams it to the floor so hard that it ricochets off the ceiling. "That felt good," she breathes.

I toss my tablet to the side and stride toward them. "Give me that fucking ball."

Emma grins as she hands it to me. I'm twice her age, but I'm determined to make it bounce even higher when I smash it down. Picturing Jim Dawson's face on the ball infuses me with vigor as I make it boomerang off the ceiling. After Cherise takes her turn at letting out her rage, I spin around to find that Dana has wheeled a ball basket into the locker room.

Every player, including my injured hitter who perches on her crutches, starts slamming balls to the floor. I duck as one careens off the ceiling toward my head. Amid the sound of bouncing balls is a giggle or two. Balls fly and zigzag around me, and soon boisterous laughter fills the locker room. I let out a contented sigh as I watch my team punish the balls as they shove each other, laughing and screaming. When I have to duck again, Cherise holds up her hand.

"You almost beheaded Coach!" she yells.

I wheel the basket closer as the players suspend their action. "That was cathartic, but Cherise is right—no more injuries."

Breathing hard, players grin as they toss the balls back into the basket.

"Let's do a quick debrief before you hit the showers," I say.

Their grins fade, and they take seats in front of their lockers.

I wait a beat. "Well, I, for one, am really glad we lost tonight."

My statement has the anticipated effect of shock and awe. Twenty sets of eyes zoom in on me.

"We've smashed ass this season," I continue. "That win against Wisconsin was especially sweet."

Mariana aims a satisfied smile at me. She was on fire that night.

"We've locked up an NCAA bid. And make no mistake—the NCAA tournament is our true focus. Regular-season wins are the appetizer for the postseason, but emerging as the best team in the country is the whole enchilada."

A thrill of excitement zings up my spine. This team has the special sauce to go far in the tournament. I can feel it. "But before tonight, we lacked something important. We weren't quite ready to go all the way. Do you know what we were missing?"

Heads shake.

"Adversity," I say. "No team waltzes down easy street and wins it all. The tournament will test us like nothing else, and we need some difficulty now to make us stronger for the future. Fichigan exposed some holes in our defense, and Patrick, Dana, and I will figure out how to patch those up. Tonight's loss was painful, but it'll fire us up to work like hell so we don't let it happen again."

A new resolve flares in the eyes of my players. Emma's foot shakes like she wants to sprint out to the court and start another five-set match.

"Use this energy at Monday's practice. Funnel your emotion into outstanding effort. I'll expect that from all of you."

Cherise nods as she watches the rest of the team respond to my words. I'm pleased by their eye contact.

"It's late—I'll let you get out of here." I scoop up my tablet. "I hope we get a chance to play those team-up-north tools in the tournament. I want to prove to my boyfriend, without any doubt, that *we're* the best university."

The sound of catcalls is my cue to get out of here. Mariana says something in Spanish, and from the blush on Emma's cheeks, I can tell it was lewd. Patrick and Dana exit the locker room, but before I go, I fist-bump my injured hitter's shoulder. "Take it easy on that ankle tonight."

"Yeah."

Her unenthusiastic answer doesn't sound convincing. "Injuries are the worst, huh?"

She looks down.

"We both know you suck at patience."

Her eyes slide up, and she smirks at me.

I lower my chin. "But I don't want you to rush this. Courtney said you'll be back soon. Okay?"

She breathes out through her teeth. "Okay, Coach."

I'm about to leave when I notice Kaylee watching us. I step over to her. "Hey. You okay?"

She nods.

I raise one eyebrow. "Really?"

"You don't have to worry about me."

"Text me if you need anything." When she rolls her eyes, I frown. "I mean it, Stenstrom."

Her mouth locks tight. Then she says in a small voice, "Sorry I lost the match for us."

I take her elbow and guide her toward one corner of the locker room. "That is complete pig poop. You're a big reason we almost beat them. Great job stepping up to fill in for an injured starter. I told you you'd get your chance."

"But I kept getting blocked!"

"Kaylee." I let out a sigh. "That was your first college match! Nobody kills it the first time. College ball's faster and more complex than club ball, but you'll get it. What'd you learn out there?"

"That I suck."

That response doesn't sound like the reported progress she's made in counseling. I scowl at her as I wait for a revised answer.

She exhales. "That I need to get better."

"Okay, let's hear specifics."

Her mouth pinches. "I was in the wrong coverage a few times. I need to learn the defensive formations cold."

I nod.

"And I need to mix up the attack more?"

"Excellent." She was too predictable with her hits tonight.

Cherise materializes at my side. She wears a sports bra after taking off her uniform shirt, exposing her toned shoulders and abdominal muscles. "Hey, KayKay. Want to get in some extra hits tomorrow? I could set you."

I still as I await Kaylee's reply. Sunday is an off day, and I'm not allowed to mandate practice. But student-athletes can volunteer to play.

"That'd be awesome." Tension drains from Kaylee's face.

I walk out of the locker room feeling buoyed despite our loss. *I love this team.* I pull out my phone. After Jeremy answers my call, I narrow my eyes and hiss, "Jim Dawson's the fucking reason God created the middle finger."

Rivaling, Part Two
Jeremy

"**Y**ou were right about the noise!" Evan yells, competing to be heard over the surge of vibrating sound engulfing us from above.

Fans resumed their raucous cheers the second a Michigan music major finished singing the national anthem. Too bad they couldn't get UM alumna Madonna to perform. Her level of celebrity would fit the magnitude of today's rivalry.

THE GAME has finally arrived the Saturday after Thanksgiving, and I'm grateful it's home at the Big House this year. A thundering sea of blue undulates from the stands, drowning out the corner pocket of ugly red Fuckeye fans. I was so excited I couldn't fall asleep till after one last night. Too bad I had to set the alarm for five to be ready for our noon kickoff. It's cold and dry—perfect weather for whooping ass.

"About to poop your pants?" I yell back.

Evan beams. "Good thing I've got adult diapers under my uniform!"

But he doesn't look nervous. The kid has shown poise beyond his years, putting up numbers far exceeding freshman efforts from the likes of Adrian Nichols or Drew Brees. He's a big reason we're ranked third in the country behind the other undefeated teams, Clemson and Ohio State. Froth won't allow more drug tests until the season's over, but I don't need one to know Evan's stayed away from marijuana like he promised.

Evan lifts his hand toward someone in the stands, and I follow his gaze to find his parents sitting on the thirty-yard line in the family section. Emma would be here as well, but she's in Indiana awaiting her match at Purdue tonight. I'm sure Lauren and the rest of the team will watch the game on TV from their hotel. Just about all residents of Ann Arbor and Columbus have cleared their calendar for the next few hours.

Motion a few rows up from Mr. and Mrs. Watkins draws my eye, and I see Taryn waving her arm side to side. I light up for a second, then tense as I notice the gray-haired man sitting next to her: *Dad*. I've talked to my father on the phone a few times this fall, and he's seemed different from the man I knew as a child. Not as hard. Not as cold. I have to admit that each conversation has chipped away at the icy wall between us. Still, when Taryn asked if Dad could be her plus one, I froze. Only when Mom insisted she didn't want to attend the game did I relent. There's still a layer of mistrust to thaw between Dad and me.

But my trust in Lauren has only continued to grow. She's helped me with my work problems, like Austin Hartford's hostility toward me after he discovered I was dating a Buckeye. I didn't know how to fix the issue with my backup QB, but Lauren recommended I have a frank discussion with him about his role on the team. The dreadful situation with Emma's roommate reinforced the importance of those tough conversations.

Following Lauren's advice, I empathized with Austin about the emotional struggle he must experience as the senior backup to a freshman phenom. I told him how important he is to all of us by mentoring Evan and being ready to lead the team in case of injury. To my surprise, Austin opened up to me right away. He reminded me of the time Froth eviscerated him in front of the entire team after we lost to OSU one year ago. He didn't understand how I could even think of dating an OSU coach. Most of my players have given me hell for being with a Buckeye, but the sense of betrayal is even deeper for Austin. So, once again, the source of the problem was Bill Froth. Since our discussion, Austin has returned to his typical gentle demeanor around me.

I'm lucky my girlfriend is so strong. Media coverage of our relationship has continued to dog us. I guess there's something appealing about a romance between hated rivals during a time of such intense political divisiveness in our country. I didn't have time to read every news story yesterday, but the exhilaration of the Michigan-OSU matchup has heightened reporters' prurient interest in us. One article asked, *After they marry, will their babies wear scarlet and gray, or maize and blue?* Ridiculous. Of course our babies will wear maize and blue.

The official's whistle brings me out of my ruminations. Our special teams unit is on the field, ready to kick the ball to our rival to start the game. On the kickoff return, I catch a Buckeye player shoving a Wolverine's back to prevent him from tackling the receiver. I holler, "Illegal block!" as an official's yellow penalty flag flies out of his pocket. "Good," I mutter. OSU's speedy receiver ran the ball all the way to their forty-yard line, but that penalty will set them back ten yards.

As the official announces the guilty player's number, the crowd roars. On the opposite sideline, Sean Malone throws his arms in the air. The OSU head coach is typically stoic, a calculating mastermind of the game, but he's ticked about this penalty on the opening kickoff. *What a whiner.* If he's already protesting such an obvious penalty, this will be a long game for him.

God, I want to beat Coach Malone and his team. The buzzing energy of over one-hundred thousand Michigan fans pours down from the stadium and thrills up my spine. We're taking down the nation's number-two team and qualifying for the playoff as one of the best four teams in the country today. I can feel it.

Too bad OSU scores a touchdown on their first drive. But I won't let those pompous jerks disrupt us—we'll just have to answer with a touchdown of our own. Before OSU's kickoff, I listen to our offensive coordinator review a few key points to the players huddled around him. Hair-Bear's relaxed delivery seems to spread a calm confidence through the players, but then he spews a fiery enthusiasm that jacks up the energy and determination of every single Wolverine. From the huddle, Evan looks up, meets my eye, and grins. Neither of us can freaking wait until he takes the field. I've taught him some devious plays for this game, and I'm eager to unveil them.

It takes only three minutes on the game-clock for us to drive down the field and even the score at seven. Somehow, the crowd succeeds at increasing its volume—I can't hear myself think.

Froth stomps his foot when Ohio State runs the ball into the end zone to go up 14-7. Froth's defense better step up, because Evan can't win this game on his own.

When we get the ball back, Evan completes a couple of short passes, followed by a good yardage gain when our running back breaks some tackles. But on the next first down, our running back gets tackled for a loss, followed by Evan having to throw the ball away on second down due to excellent coverage. We're facing third and long. Harry shrugs at me before he signals the next play to Evan, and I try to keep my face neutral as I realize it's one of our deception plays.

Evan receives the snap and pivots to the right to throw a backward pass to Talik. Evan sprints down the left side of the field while the defense rushes toward Talik. From behind the line of scrimmage, Talik cocks his arm back and launches the ball to a wide-open Evan. The receiver has become the quarterback, and the quarterback has become the receiver. After catching the ball, Evan glides into the end zone.

Damn, it's deafening. I grin as I watch Evan and Talik leap and butt each other's torsos mid-air. Other teams have used that play before, but no one has made it look so easy. After we kick an extra point, tying the game, members of the offense return to the bench near me. I nod at Evan. *This. This is why I demand so much from you every day.* This is what makes all the hard work worth it.

Talik usually ignores me, but today he meets my gaze after he removes his helmet. Maybe our extra time together, preparing plays like these, has brought us closer. During the commercial break, he saunters over to stand next to me. Excited chatter from my headset ceases when I remove it. I smell the sweat of Talik's pads and the oil of his braided hair. "Not bad, Talik."

He doesn't say a word.

"Evan know you're gunning for his job, throwing like that?"

That gets a smirk out of him. "That little boy will never give up the ball again, unless you design more tricked-out plays like that one."

Referring to a player of Evan's height as a little boy amuses me. I think about media chatter over Talik's rising star. He's got one more year of college eligibility left, but they're predicting he'll go first round in the draft due to his 1,300 receiving yards this season. "Evan's gonna miss you next year."

"Yeah?" Talik ponders my statement as he looks toward the assemblage of players and staff dotting our sideline. "There're some things I won't miss. Some *people* I won't miss."

I follow his gaze and notice Froth and his strength coach yelling at our starting kicker. Beefy Tony Masten's even more animated than Froth as they get in the shorter player's face. I wonder what the kicker did wrong on that PAT.

"Hey, Coach Trent?"

I look at Talik.

"You ever think about coaching in the pros?"

I twist my mouth to one side. "Nah. Money's even more important at that level. I want to make a difference in my players' lives." I huff out a breath, realizing that goal is a pipe dream considering the verbal abuse and corruption of big-time college sports. "At least I used to want that. Seems like a fantasy now."

We watch the kickoff result in a touchback, followed by our defense trotting out to the field. Harry waves Talik over so he can prepare the offense for the next series.

But before Talik leaves my side, he says, "It's not fantasy, Coach. It's reality."

I watch his retreating form as he jogs to the huddle. Warmth spreads across my chest. I was hoping Talik's stellar performance this season indicated he'd followed Evan's lead and stopped the weed, and his statement seems to confirm that. *This*, I think, sliding the headset back on. This is what makes the hard work all worth it.

***

Damn. OSU just scored again, putting them up by four. Deep in the fourth quarter, the back-and-forth lead changes have exhausted me. Evan settles in behind center for yet another offensive series. With only a little over three minutes left in the game, this will likely be our last.

Froth has taken over the play-calling from Harry—stolen,

more like it—and the rushing play he signals goes nowhere. As our running back returns to the line, his panted breaths are visible in the cold air. *Put the ball in Evan's hands*, I plead. But idiot Froth calls for another running play that the defense sniffs out in an instant. It's third and nine, and this time I can't stay silent. "End to the wind," I say into my microphone, begging for the trick play we developed with the tight end.

Froth jerks his head in my direction, and I hear his voice over the headset: "Too risky."

I shake my head. "Evan's got this."

After he glowers at me, Froth signals the play.

Our offensive line settles into their stance, with our tight end looking like a guard. When the ball snaps, the tight end darts forward, now an eligible receiver. Evan whizzes a short pass to him, and the tight end turns downfield to gobble up twenty yards before OSU's defense takes him down. Mirroring my reaction, the crowd seems to exhale before going apeshit.

Thank you, Coach Hanlon. I grin as I remember feeling like a hero when I ran for twenty-five yards on that play in college.

Cognizant of time ticking down with over fifty-yards to cover before winning the game, our offense hustles to the line. Froth calls a running play that once again gets stuffed. Hallelujah for him signaling a pass play next. But the Buckeyes double-team Talik, forcing Evan to scramble and search for an open receiver. I tense as I see a defensive lineman barreling toward him. Just as Evan spins away, the OSU linebacker tackles him from his blindside. Evan slams to the ground, and I cringe as the side of his helmet bounces on the turf. Silence consumes the stadium.

I'm out on the field, crouching by a motionless Evan, before our athletic trainer and team physician materialize at my side. Evan's eyes are open, and he moves to get up, but the physician tells him to stay down as he asks Evan some questions.

Instead of answering, Evan asks, "I didn't fumble, right?"

I'm concerned that he's not with it enough to realize he's still cradling the ball in his elbow. "Right," I tell him. I see red shoes nearby and look up to see the linebacker fidgeting as he stares at Evan.

"Hey. You okay, man?" the Buckeye asks.

Evan turns to blink at him and manages to sit up. He looks down at the ball, then back at the player. "Dude, that was some hit."

The linebacker's mouth spreads in a slow smile. "You tough, freshman."

"Okay, let's see if you can walk to the sideline," orders the trainer.

"I want to stay in!" says Evan.

Our team physician shakes his head. "You know you have to sit out at least one snap." That's another sign that Evan is woozy—he should know that basic rule. The trainer and physician pull him to his feet, and cheers swell from the crowd as Evan walks toward our sideline.

The trainer looks as worried as I feel. He angles his head toward my end of the bench, startling me into action. I hustle over to Austin Hartford, who's practicing throws with a backup receiver under Harry's supervision. TV coverage has gone to commercial, but we need to get Austin out there soon.

"You got this, Hartford." Harry's tone is soothing, but Austin's face beneath his helmet looks like our school colors mixed together: green.

After Austin steps backs and throws to the receiver on the sideline one last time, I cup his shoulder. "C'mon, Harts, time to get out there."

He tenses.

"Deep breaths. Just like the Western Michigan game." I pat his butt, and he jogs out to the huddle awaiting him.

I need deep breaths, too. Because we're behind by four points, a field goal won't help us. We have to score a touchdown. I look at the game clock—only 1:46 left—then to my right. Our team physician squats in front of Evan, who sits on the bench with his helmet off. There's no doubt Evan is capable of marching us down the field and winning this game. There's overwhelming doubt that Austin can do the same.

Harry sidles up to me. "Go check on Watkins. I got this."

I give him a grateful nod.

"I'm fine," Evan insists as I near him. He pushes up to stand. He doesn't wobble, but I notice him wince as he rises to his full height. Does his head hurt?

"Sit your butt back down," I demand. "Let Dr. Kasten examine you."

Evan scowls but obeys my command.

Play resumes, and I watch Austin endure a vicious sack by the same linebacker who injured Evan. Given the OSU player's posturing, I gather he isn't regretful anymore. Froth calls time out to stop the game clock.

Evan groans. "Let me out there!"

Froth pushes his way in as he rips off his headset. "We need our starting QB," he says. "He's ready to return, right?"

"Yes!" says Evan.

"No," counters Dr. Kasten.

Froth grips his skull. "We've got maybe three plays left! Get him in there."

"It's likely he has a concussion, Coach," Dr. Kasten explains.

Froth shakes his head. "You know that for sure?"

"Well, all indications point to—"

The physician's hesitation is all the opening he needs, and Froth beckons for Evan to get up. "Move it, Watkins."

I step in front of Froth to block his view of my QB. "Bill, you can't put a concussed player out there."

Froth shoves me aside and points at Evan. "Get out there and win the game, Watkins."

Evan glances at me before he grabs his helmet and pops to his feet. As he jogs to the offensive huddle, cheers swell in the stadium. Austin's slack jaw when he returns to the sideline indicates his confusion. The sick clench of my gut signals my horror. I have to get Evan out of there before another big hit rattles his brain, turning his gray matter scarlet.

"Stay ready," I tell Austin. "This ain't over."

"Okay, Coach."

I stalk toward my boss. "Take him out, Bill. Now."

He barks into his headset, ignoring me.

Harry's on the other side of Froth, also speaking into his

headset, and it takes me a second to realize they're arguing with each other. What the hell? They stand five feet away yet they refuse to look at each other and talk like normal human beings. I don't know if Harry's trying to convince Froth to remove Evan or change the offensive play he just called. Harry scowls, clearly as frustrated as I feel.

"Take Evan *out*," I shout, but Froth ignores me again.

The official's whistle yanks my attention to the field, and I hold still as Evan takes the snap. He hustles out of the pocket, hounded by the crafty Buckeye linebacker. I gasp as the defender lunges for Evan, who manages to launch the ball in the receiver's direction before the linebacker can touch him. AJ leaps for the ball, but the pass is so high that it angles up off his fingertips. My eyes widen as the OSU safety covering AJ lunges for the tipped ball. The crowd emits a collective sigh of relief when he falls just short of the interception.

Christ, that was close.

The OSU defender still lies prone on the field, and their trainers rush out to him. Our offense returns to the sideline for the injury time out. I waste no time grabbing Evan and escorting him to the bench.

"Wha?" he mutters.

"Evan." I crouch in front of him and wait for his unfocused eyes to settle onto me. "Do you trust me?"

After removing his helmet, he massages his temples. "Yeah."

"What did Adrian tell you to focus on, one at a time?"

He blinks. "One snap."

"Right." I glance behind me, happy to see that Froth and Harry have removed their headsets, now standing close, locked in a verbal battle. But soon Froth will notice his QB missing from the huddle. "I have a new focus for you today, okay? Are you listening?"

Evan nods.

"One brain." I pat his head. "You've only got one of those. And it's a damn ornery, punk-ass brain that drives me nuts sometimes, but still, it's a good brain. It's an NFL quarterback brain."

He smirks, but I can tell I have his attention.

"You gotta take care of that brain to reach your dreams, Evan. It's not the force of the hit that's important. It's rushing back and sustaining another quick head injury that causes long-term problems. You know it, right? You know you're done for the day, no matter how big this game feels. It's just a game. You're more important than one game."

He blows out a breath.

"You know it's over for you today."

I can feel him coming to my side. I've tapped into his niggling self-doubt, his uncertainty about his fitness to play when it's clear how fuzzy he feels. He starts to speak as Froth's shout next to me drowns him out.

"What the fuck are you doing, Trent? Get Watkins back on the field right now."

I rise, grateful I have a height advantage over my boss, and try to angle myself between Froth and Evan. "Dr. Kasten said he has a concussion. He's done, Coach."

Froth reaches around me to yank Evan's elbow. "Get out there!"

I turn to watch Evan's Adam's apple bob as he swallows. After he stands, he looks at me, then at his head coach. "I...can't see straight, sir. I won't be able to help the team. Sorry."

My eyes close for a second, full of Thanksgiving gratitude. The boy is growing up.

Froth glares at me. "Fucking bullshit." He leans toward me and sneers, "I better not find out you're throwing this game because of your girlfriend."

I glower at Rabid Frother and fight the twitching desire to slug him. The swell of crowd noise jolts us out of our stare-off.

Cheers rain down, and we turn to find that Austin just completed a long pass to the receiver near the OSU sideline. I'm grateful Harry's running the show while Froth and I argue. Talik, who caught the ball, hands it to the official and lopes back to the huddle. I look at the scoreboard to see we're on the OSU thirty-three-yard line with less than a minute left. Holy shit, we can still win this thing.

Froth must have come to the same conclusion, because he speed-walks toward the action, leaving us behind.

I clutch Evan's biceps. "You played one hell of a game. No regrets."

"But…" He pauses as he hears the official's whistle to start the next play. I'm not sure if his squint suggests resignation or a headache. He slumps and agrees, "No regrets."

My heart breaks for him. "Let's go root for Harts."

Evan nods and trails me down the sideline, closer to the OSU end zone. We watch Austin complete a short pass to Talik, but the defense tackles him before he gets a first down, forcing us to burn our last time out to stop the clock.

We're on the twenty-five-yard line with forty seconds left, leaving passes as our only option. After Austin listens to a few pointers from Harry and me, he jogs back onto the field. I wish I'd stuck some antacids in my jacket. The crowd's staccato buzz seems suspended between an orgasm and a panic attack.

Austin rushes out of the pocket, pursued by the aggressive defense, and his pass hits the turf far short of his receiver. I close my eyes—it's now third down. After Austin barely avoids another sack and manages to throw the ball away, a hush falls over the stadium. It's fourth down and our last chance to win the game.

Our center snaps the ball, and Austin scans his receivers. He's getting good pass protection this time, but nobody's open. Seconds tick down as he keeps moving his feet. The linebacker thunders toward my QB and lunges for him. Austin's in the defender's clutches as he releases the ball. I freeze as I watch it float toward the corner of the end zone, where Talik leaps and plucks the ball from the air. I inhale, my eyes alight with wonder, before a Buckeye slams into Talik. When they go down together, the ball dribbles out from under Talik's body.

I deflate in an instant. The OSU defender pops up, crosses his arms in front of him, and shoots his hands out to the sides. His body language conveys the bitter truth: incomplete pass. Incomplete dreams. Michigan loses again.

Instead of storming the field like they hoped, Michigan fans sit stock-still, stunned by the loss. The small number of Buckeye fans, however, go wild in their corner. OSU players high-five and hug each other. Feeling like I need to vomit, I shoot a longing look toward the locker room. But first I need to demonstrate good leadership.

Evan stares at the turf, looking crestfallen. I tap my shoe against his and say, "Hey." When he peers up at me, I try to lighten my dark expression. "I'm proud of you." I step toward him, and it just feels right to wrap him in a hug. After I let him go, I notice the tremble of his lower lip. To give him some cover, I hand him his helmet, and he doesn't hesitate before sliding it on. The last thing he needs is some ESPN asshat criticizing him for crying after a loss. If I weren't so pissed off, I'd want to cry as well.

Heading to the locker room, I run into the OSU quarterbacks' coach. I force myself to shake his hand. "Good game, Coach."

His smile seems smug, but he offers, "You got one hell of a QB there, Coach."

"Thanks," I say, but my silent retort is *Keep away from my QB, knuckledick*. Hearing Lauren's word in my head somehow lightens my mood as I keep walking. But I halt when I notice Austin and Talik talking to an OSU player.

Austin's a graduating senior, and Talik's entering the draft. This is their last home game as Wolverines, their last game against their rival. I wish it had ended differently for them, but I know they gave it their all.

"Hey, Talik and Austin!" I holler.

They turn to me.

"Awesome effort. Michigan won't be the same without you."

Talik nods, and Austin says, "Thanks, Coach."

"You already know Evan's gonna miss you. But I'll miss you both, too."

***

I'm back in my office when Lauren calls. "Hey, we're about to start warmup, but I had to talk to you. How *are* you? How's Evan?"

"A little woozy. We'll know more in the next couple of days."

She exhales. "That was scary. Emma and I were freaking

out."

"Yeah. He'll be okay, though. And he's got next year to avenge the loss. The seniors, not so much."

"I'm so sorry, Jeremy. I know how bad you wanted it."

I sigh. "Thanks." I collapse onto my chair. "I'm beat."

"I bet. You coached one hell of a game."

I frown. We still lost.

She continues, "After the game...did you tell Evan you were proud of him?"

My head cocks to one side. How does she know that? "Yes?"

"Thought so." A smile enters her voice. "I read your lips on the TV coverage. Between your showdown with Froth about whether to play Evan and the heartfelt hug you shared, the announcers were more interested in the sideline activity than the game on the field."

"Huh." I had no idea TV cameras were on us either time. "So, are you ready to derail the Boilermakers tonight?"

"Purdue's a good team. We better be ready."

A knock on my open door lifts my gaze, and I straighten in my chair the moment I see Harry. His ruddy complexion has turned pale. "The AD just left Froth's office," Harry tells me in a trembling voice. "He's sick of losing to OSU." His head shakes. "He fired Froth."

I don't move.

"You know what that means," adds Harry.

"Jeremy?" Lauren asks.

I close my eyes as sickness spreads in my belly. "I just got fired, Coach Chase. Guess I no longer work for your rival."

25

Repeating
Lauren

I stop pacing the Chicago hotel room carpet to check my phone again. It's almost midnight—Jeremy should be here by now. After Froth got the boot, Jeremy learned he and his fellow assistant coaches would have to stay through next week so they can coach the Wolverines in their bowl game. However, he decided to miss their next practice to support me and my team as we play for a national championship tomorrow night. *"What're they going to do if I miss practice?"* he'd said. *"Fire me?"*

I wince, remembering the bitter tone of his voice. I still can't believe Froth and his staff got canned after losing in the last seconds to the number-two-ranked team in the country. Michigan was undefeated before that, for fuck's sake. I guess that's more evidence of our intense rivalry. Their athletic director couldn't stand losing one more time to the Buckeyes.

And *I* can't stand the thought of losing tomorrow night. We've clawed our way through the tournament, barely squeaking by in our fifth match last night to qualify for the NCAA final against Stanford. My starting libero broke her thumb in the third match, but Tatum has filled in for her quite well. Too bad we didn't get to play Michigan in the tournament, but at least they lost in the second round.

A soft knock on my door elevates my shoulders as I give a happy gasp. I fling open the door to find my hunky coach with a duffel bag strap on his shoulder and a grin on his face.

"Ready to crush the Cardinal?" he asks.

"I'm ready to crush *you*." I wrap my arms around his neck and draw him down for a kiss. He tastes minty, in contrast to my

257

chocolate-peanut-butter breath.

"You taste so good," he breathes. He nudges us backward over the entry threshold as we keep kissing. When I reach for his belt buckle, he laughs. "Let's get inside first, sweet cheeks." After letting me go, he closes the door and sets his duffle onto the bed. "I don't think I was followed, but you can never be too sure."

He points at the bouquet of red carnations on the dresser. A gray bow encircles the vase. "Phew. I was kicking myself for running out of time to buy you flowers."

"Can you believe Rhonda sent those?"

His brows furrow. He peers closer at the round, brown blobs of candy on sticks mixed in with the flowers. "What're those?"

My mouth drops open. "You've never eaten a Buckeye?"

He swivels his head and looks at me with a sideways smirk.

"Oh." I redden. "Well, they're chocolate-and-peanut-butter bombs of love. I've been stress-eating them all night."

He plucks a stick out of the bouquet and takes a bite. His eyes close as he moans. "Amazing."

"I don't think they're vegan, you know."

He shrugs. "I'll make an exception."

I stare at him with my head angled to one side. He's never strayed from veganism in my presence before. And that's not all that's different about him. His depression beard has vanished, along with the morose attitude that accompanied his fuzzy facial hair during the past few weeks.

"You shaved?" I ask.

He rubs his jaw. "Like it?"

"Jer-Bear, I'll take you any way I can get you." We grin against each other's mouths as we meld together for another kiss. The nutty flavor of his mouth drives me nuts. I pull back to look up at him. "What's making you feel better? Got any interviews lined up?"

His big hand cradles the side of my head, and I lean into his touch. "Eh, I've got a few irons in the fire."

"Yeah?" What *is* that impish glint in his eye?

"We better get you to bed," he says. "You have a big day

tomorrow." His hand glides to the base of my neck, and his swirling fingers massage away my tension.

"Bed sounds good," I murmur.

Too soon, he yanks his hand away to unzip his bag. "But first, I have to give you your Christmas gift."

"What?" I huff. "It's only December nineteenth."

He withdraws a rectangular box wrapped in dark-red paper. "I can't wait."

"But I don't have your gift here." The truth is I haven't bought one for him yet since I've been consumed by NCAA volleyball.

"Duh, Chase—we're away from home." He thrusts the box into my hand. "Take it. Take it!"

After a beat, I accept the gift. "At least you chose the right color wrapping paper." His giddy energy feels contagious. As I unwrap the jewelry box, my heart skips a beat. Is this what I think it is? Are we ready for that? But the box is the wrong size, and it'd be weird to wrap up an engagement ring like this.

With trepidation, I open the box. Diamonds sparkling up at me take my breath away. It's the most beautiful bracelet I've ever seen. My eyes zoom up to meet his. "You got me a tennis bracelet?"

"A *volleyball* bracelet," he corrects. "Thought it'd bring you luck tomorrow." He lifts it out of the box. "May I?"

Dumbstruck, I nod. I feel the heft of the bracelet as he clasps it onto my left wrist. As I turn my hand, light catches the intricate crystal of the gemstones. "You can't afford this."

He chuckles. "You're worth it." He takes my left hand and scrunches the sleeve of my pajama top up to my elbow. Extending my bare arm, he lowers to kiss the sensitive skin of my wrist under my bracelet. Then, his lips brush along the inside of my arm, moving toward my elbow at a languid pace. I pulse my right hand into his hair and skim my fingers along his scalp to egg him on.

"Thank you for the good-luck bracelet," I whisper.

He straightens and gives me a smug smile, looking proud of himself.

I quirk one eyebrow. "You know what'd be even better?"

After he shakes his head, I nudge closer. "A good-luck fuck."

He laughs as he shakes his head. "Damn, I missed your dirty mouth."

***

I've never coached in front of such a large crowd before. We average three thousand fans for each home game, but there has to be four times that amount at the United Center tonight. It's fortunate that this year's final four takes place in Chicago—a doable driving distance for Ohio State fans. Patrick and Dana lead my team through the end of their warmup as I sneak glances into the arena seats.

I notice Jeremy first. I haven't seen him since this morning when he left for his mother's while I had practice, meetings, and meals with my team. He looks so handsome in his black collared shirt and dark jeans, and I decide I like him clean-shaven the best. Then I notice the red block O on his shirt, and my eyes expand. He still coaches for OSU's rival, but he wears Buckeye gear? Just at that moment, he looks up. His wink brings a smile to my face, steadying me for the battle ahead.

Motion from the other side of Jeremy draws my gaze to the waving Jenna and Tyler Watkins, also wearing scarlet and gray. When I see the big yellow M on Evan's navy shirt, I narrow my eyes, but then my smile returns. Emma will be so pleased her twin made it to the match. The team physician cleared him to practice once he healed from his concussion, and he should be preparing for the bowl game. But like Jeremy, Evan chose to be here instead.

Tyler Watkins raises his arms in a big, round O over his head—a signature Buckeye move. He nudges Evan to do the same, but Evan gives him a withering look and crosses his arms. He may be here to support his sister, but no way will Evan cheer for Ohio State. Tyler shrugs at me.

I hear an older male voice holler, "Go, Lauren!" I follow the sound to find my dad pumping his fist in the air a couple of sections over. Does he realize I'm not the one playing tonight? My mom, still healing from her hip-replacement surgery a few weeks ago, tugs his shirt to get him to sit back down. I have a feeling Dad had to sweet-talk Mom into attending the match, but it's kind of her to be here all the same.

I swivel back around to watch Emma set to our hitters. Feeling a tremble work its way up my legs and into my chest, I wish I could be the one to hit the ball straight down and expel these nervous jitters from my system. Coaching feels way more stressful than playing. I've prepared my team the best I can, but now I have to turn over the reins and let them run the show. I can only hope we put on a great one tonight.

***

"Time out!" I yell, and the official blows her whistle. Stanford won the first set, but we claimed the second. Now, in the third set, we're down 11-7, and I've got to slow my racing heart.

We make room for my six starters to sit as we gather around them. Emma's breathing hard, but her scowl looks feisty, not defeated. That sense of determination echoes in the hard-set jaws of my other five players. I let out a puff of air—this is just the mindset I've encouraged all season.

"We need to contain number two better," I tell them. Stanford's six-foot-six outside hitter has been killing us.

Mariana nods. "The beetch hits from the back row a lot."

I stifle a grin at her Colombian accent. "She does." I turn to my weak-side hitter. "Watch her torso. You're early on the block."

My player nods.

Patrick gives them a few pointers on defense. Somewhere in the crowd, his wife and baby watch us, and I hope their two month old's mini-headphones block the noise. I review our next offensive series, and Dana chimes in with a reminder about transitions. Too soon, the time out is over.

As my players stand to take the court, I grab my outside hitter's elbow. "How's the ankle?"

"Good, Coach."

Cherise takes Emma aside and tells her something before Emma returns to her position.

After Stanford serves the ball into the net, I settle back into my chair. It appears my called time out made her overthink the serve. *Side out, suckers*. We need them to make more unforced errors if we're going to have a chance.

Although Emma serves a screaming jump serve, Stanford's libero passes a usable ball to their setter. Their All-American hitter slams the ball, but Emma's there to make an incredible dig. One of my hitters has to set the ball to Mariana, whose dink dribbles to the floor before a Cardinal gets under it. Point, Buckeyes.

I lean across Dana to catch Cherise's eye. "What'd you tell Emma after the time out?"

Cherise grins. "To cheat up on the coverage. Their number two's got a vicious angle on her hits."

How did I miss that? Cherise's advice put Emma in the right position to make that dig. I reach out to pat her shoulder. "Nice coaching."

"Nice bracelet, Coach."

I steal my arm back and run my fingertips along the diamonds. Will they bring us luck tonight?

"Did your Wolverine boo get that for you?" Cherise asks.

My eyes taper. "Focus on the match, Evans."

She grins.

I peek up at Jeremy, ignoring my own advice about concentrating on the match. But his seat is empty. Searching around his section, I find him standing near the railing at the top of the stairs, talking to another tall man. I jolt when I recognize him: Andy Hunter. Why the hell is a Michigan football coach chumming it up with Ohio State's athletic director? I hear play on the court resume, and I tear my attention back to my team. The action of the close match absorbs me in a second.

An hour later, I can't believe it's match point. We're up 24-20 in the fourth set after coming from behind to win set three. One more point and we're national champions. But we can't let up now. We can't let Stanford stretch it to a fifth set.

"Angle the block!" I holler in my weak-side hitter's direction, straining to be heard over the burgeoning cheers filling the arena. All of the spectators are on their feet.

Tatum serves the ball, and Stanford's hit rolls up our blocker's hands—a tipped ball that sails out of bounds. Tatum sprints after it and dives with one outstretched hand, somehow punching the ball up behind her. The crowd *ooh*s at the save that definitely qualifies for the highlight reel on ESPN's *SportsCenter*. Then the spectators *aah* as Emma launches a gorgeous set from the baseline to my outside hitter. My hitter catches major air, levitating and smacking the ball so hard it ricochets off Stanford's block into the crowd, far out of bounds.

Oh my God. Coochiechanga amazeballs. We just fucking won!

Cherise screams as she bolts out of her chair, and the players on the bench join her by pouring onto the court. Leaping and embracing, they push into the starting six, and the pocket of players collapses to the court as they hug and celebrate.

Stupefied, I stare at Dana and Patrick for a second before we jump up and rush into a group hug.

"Yes!" Patrick yells after letting us go. He pumps his fist into the air.

I stand back and take a moment to observe the pandemonium around me. I was too shocked to remember much after our first national title four years ago, but I'm going to soak in all of the sunshine this time around. We've fought so hard for this moment! Mariana and Emma jump up and down as they hug. Tatum laughs while Kaylee pretends to launch through the air, reenacting Tatum's improbable save on the last play. The rollicking piano of "Ain't Life Grand" pumps from the speakers as an employee from OSU sports marketing shoves national-champion T-shirts into each player's grasp.

I swallow the lump lodged in my throat. I want to bottle up this feeling and drink it down the next time life gets hard. Faith, striving, and gratification swirl together in an elation elixir, and there's only one person I want to share a toast with in this moment. Looking up, I see Jeremy back in his row, hugging Evan. When he notices me watching him, he gives me a big thumbs up. Evan smirks before he lifts his long arms in a circle above his head. I touch my hand to my heart, flattered by two Wolverines celebrating a Buckeye win.

After we take a team photo with Cherise and Emma holding

the gigantic NCAA trophy between them, my players disperse to their family members waiting on the side of the court. Emma skips up to her family, and Evan lifts and twirls her as she squeals. Jenna hugs her next, and once she lets Emma go, she catches me spying on them. Jenna's eyes crinkle at the corners as she mouths, "Thank you."

I hold her gaze as I nod, but I should be the one thanking her. I'm honored she trusted me with her only daughter. No way we would've gone this far in the tournament without Emma's talents and hard work. It feels like the first time I can relax in months.

Getting engulfed in a bear hug quickens my breath. Jeremy lifts me off my feet and spins me around, echoing Evan's move with his twin. *Stupidly strong football players.* I grin as he sets me back on my feet and kisses me.

He stares down at me, his eyes alight with warmth and pride. "That was the best coaching performance I've seen."

My heart fills. The compliment means so much coming from such a gifted coach. "Thanks, Jer-Bear." I trace the Block O on his shirt with my finger as I inhale his subtle aftershave. "I can't believe you're wearing this."

He shrugs. "Wanted to support my girl."

"And what were you saying to Andy Hunter?"

He stiffens for a second, then the beginning of a grin peeks through. It seems to take effort for him to rearrange his face into a neutral expression. "Let's talk about that later."

It's clear he's hiding something, which amplifies my curiosity. "But—"

"Lauren!" my dad booms.

I turn to see my parents approaching. My dad's Ohio State jacket hides his small beer belly, and the intricate design of my mom's red and purple scarf completes her classy outfit. Dad tries to guide Mom by the elbow, but she shoos him away. She's walking quite well on her own, anyway.

"You look pretty," says Mom. "I love that bracelet." Before I have the chance to thank her or tell her about Jeremy's gift, she asks, "Why don't you throw away your butchy clothes and wear a nice outfit like that more often?"

I look down at my flowy scarlet blouse, dark-gray dress pants, and black pumps. *Because these shoes are fucking killing me, and I'm nervous my deodorant will fail and leave pit stains.* "Mom." I take Jeremy's left hand in mine. "You remember Jeremy."

She eyes him up and down. "Vegan Boy."

I giggle at the disdain evident in her pinched-together lips. His squeeze of my hand could indicate support of me or irritation with her, and I'm guessing the latter.

"What a match, honey," Dad says, leaning in to hug me. "I've got one question for you." He points at Jeremy. "Did this guy help you return to prominence?"

"Absolutely, Dad." I beam a smile up at Jeremy.

"Then I like him already." Dad pumps Jeremy's hand. "Good to meet you, Quarterback Whisperer."

Jeremy chuckles. "Thank you, sir."

"Go get the car," Mom snaps at Dad. "I'm not walking out in that cold."

Dad winks at me. "I'm so happy for you, Laur."

"Thanks, Dad."

After my parents leave, Jeremy shakes his head. "Your mom's never boring; that's for sure. And your dad seems like a cool guy."

I bump my hip into his. "That's just because he likes you."

My phone has buzzed nonstop in my pocket, and I remove it to read a few texts. "Sam and Alex are losing their shit." I purse my lips as I see a text from my athletic director. Before I open it, I look across the arena at Rhonda schmoozing with a man wearing a Stanford shirt—probably one of their administrators. She'll stop by to congratulate me later, I'm sure, and she'll make it sound like she's the reason we won.

"Andy Hunter texted me," I say to Jeremy.

His attempt at nonchalance doesn't fool me. *What's his deal?* I'm going to find out.

"Andy said, 'Have to get back to C-bus, but I want you to know I'm so thrilled you're part of the Buckeye family. Talk soon.'" I grin. "He'll have to cough up my bonus for winning the

NCAA title next time I see him."

"You deserve it." Jeremy's smile seems extra excited.

"Okay, Trent, you've been acting weird all night. Spill it, mister."

He drops his smile. "Later, okay? This is your night."

"Nope. I want to know what's going on." When he remains tight-lipped, I tilt my head. "This isn't my night; it's *our* night. I meant what I told my dad: you helped me get here. You lit a fire under my tired ass, infusing me with the energy I needed to push my team every day. I'm fucking grateful for you, you know?"

He folds my hands into his. "Back at you, Chase. You've helped me be a better coach. A…" Those green eyes drill into me. "A better man."

His words sink in with an *aw* factor that melts my insides.

"And I want to talk something through with you," he continues. "But not right now. I don't want to steal your thunder."

"How could anything you say trump winning the national championship?"

He nods. "Nothing could, you're right. This comes a distant second."

When I maintain my insistent stare up at him, his shoulders slump. "Okay, sweet cheeks. God, you're persistent." But his tone sounds more exhilarated than resigned. "I got a job offer."

"Yeah?" My voice perks up. "Where?"

He looks down at the OSU logo on his chest, and I gasp. "You'll be the OSU quarterbacks' coach?"

His grin splits wide as he shakes his head.

I scrunch my forehead. *Will he coach a different position?*

"Head coach," he says.

My jaw plunges as my heart stops. *No fucking way.* Ohio State head coach is one of the most coveted positions in all of college football. Jeremy has snagged it at age thirty-three? As a QB coach? From our rival, nonetheless? I lean to the side, peering around his solid frame to search for hidden cameras. Am I being punked?

Jeremy laughs, probably at the frozen incredulity on my face. "I didn't believe it, either. I'm too young for this position.

But once the news comes out, you'll understand." He squeezes my hands. "You'll have to keep this on the downlow. Andy's okay with me telling you—he knows you can keep a secret."

Unsure what I'm agreeing to keep private, I give him a slow nod.

He tugs me closer and lowers his voice. "The NCAA's investigating Buckeye football. Sean Malone and some of his staff have been making illegal payments to recruits."

My eyes open wide.

"I know. It's awful to hear. The news will break soon—maybe tomorrow."

"Holy fuckcakes." *Cheaters*. We're cheaters. The NCAA will embarrass us on a national stage, and we'll deserve it.

"Turns out Andy Hunter's friends with my Oklahoma coach, Chris Hanlon," he continues. "Andy's been searching for possible replacements ever since this NCAA investigation started, and Coach Hanlon talked me up, big time. The media coverage of Evan, and of you and me..." He smirks. "Well, it put me even more on Andy's radar. Guess we should thank that Michigan reporter who outed us."

I'm trying to comprehend these bombshells he keeps dropping.

"Never seen you speechless before," he laughs. "Listen, I won't be named head coach for at least a week—after news of the indictment sinks in, and after my bowl game." His expression sobers. "But Lauren, I won't take the job if you don't want me to."

I squint at him. He's joking, right? When he doesn't smile, I blink. "Okay, now I really am being punked."

"What? I'm serious, Lauren. We need to think this through. If you believe media coverage of us was hot before, it'll sizzle once the news gets out. This time people *will* ask for my autograph at bars and restaurants. We'll be famous—we'll have no privacy."

A burning sensation starts in my throat and works up into my nose. I blink faster as I take in some shaky breaths. *Don't cry, don't cry*, I order. But my stupid eyeballs won't listen.

"We're just starting our life together," he adds. "I don't want this to interfere with our future." A line creases his forehead. "Lauren? Why're you crying, sweetheart?"

I sniff as he rubs this thumb under my eye.

"I knew this would be too much," he says in a soft voice. "I'll tell Andy to find another coach."

"No!" My head shakes. "I'm not crying because I'm sad. I *want* you to take the job. There's nobody else I trust to take care of our athletes, to teach them how to be men. I don't care how young you are—they won't find a better head coach than you."

The crease on his forehead lightens a bit, but it's still there.

"You said *we*," I explain. "I'm crying because you said *we*. We have a future. We're starting our life together." I blink up at him. "I want that. I want there to be an us. You definitely want that, too?"

"God, yes." He cradles my face in his hands and delivers a kiss full of gentleness but also wanting and craving.

I smile up at him. "We'll live in the same town now, and that's all that matters. Who cares about all of the extras? The media can go fuck themselves."

"Well, one extra might be a good thing." His grin is devious. "Did I mention what my salary will be?"

My eyes narrow. "You arrogant football cockshlongs."

26

Joining
Jeremy

Camera flashes blind me as I look out at the myriad of media from behind the podium. We're in the football meeting room at the Woody Hayes Athletic Center for a press conference announcing me as head coach.

Buckeye Nation has endured the painful revelations of a cheating scandal involving their football staff over the past week, spoiling the holiday season for many fans. Now that it's December 30 and that shameful history has started to slide into the rearview mirror, the reporters look eager to start a new chapter.

"Coach! Coach!" they clamor. Thank goodness for the athletic communications staffer at my side to field their questions. I wish Lauren were here as well, but she wanted the spotlight to be on me, not our relationship.

"You go first, Rob," says the communications guy as he points at a gray-haired reporter in the front row. The cacophony of questions begins to simmer down.

The communications guy leans toward me and whispers, "Rob Hollis from the *Columbus Dispatch*."

I nod and try to remember Rob's face with his name. I'm sure I'll be buddy-buddy, or, if we lose, enemy-enemy, with all of these reporters soon.

"Coach," Rob begins. "You've formed a tight bond with Evan Watkins. Now that you're at Ohio State, what are the quarterback's plans—stay at Michigan or transfer to OSU?"

Wow, he's diving right in. It's nice he acknowledged my relationship with Evan, but probably only to butter me up so I'll share Evan's secrets. I answer by citing the NCAA transfer rule. "As you know, transferring means a mandatory year of sitting out. Evan's such a competitor; I doubt he'd want that."

"But what about a waiver, Coach?" Rob presses.

Damn, they're piranhas. In fact, Evan is seeking a mental-health transfer waiver as we speak, but these reporters shouldn't be privy to that information. The NCAA legislated that transfer athletes don't have to wait a year to play at their new university if they can prove their former school led to mental health symptoms. Between Froth's verbal abuse and Evan's marijuana problem, Mr. Watkins and I believe Evan will be granted the waiver.

I was surprised at first when Mr. Watkins approached me with the idea of Evan transferring, especially since Michigan is the man's alma mater. But Mr. Watkins soured on the university after learning how they'd turned a blind eye to Froth's cruelty for so long. He's also ticked about the whole coaching staff getting fired after such a successful season. We even won our bowl game a few days ago, despite all of the drama. At least our win will secure positions elsewhere for all the former Michigan assistant coaches.

With the Watkins family's emphasis on faith and morality, a football program that has just sustained a corruption charge might not have been high on their list for Evan's new school. However, Emma's stellar first year at OSU has helped them to grow fond of the scarlet and gray. And, Mrs. Watkins told me that where I go, Evan goes; she can't think of a better mentor for her son. After receiving such a meaningful compliment, I better not screw it up.

The *Dispatch* reporter waits for my answer. I could direct the reporter to ask Evan himself, but I don't want them to hound my young player, either. I shrug. "Nineteen year olds are hard to predict." Someone chortles at that truth. "Wherever Evan plays, I know he'll continue to break records throughout his college career."

"Next question," says the communications guy before he points at a female Fox Sports reporter.

"Coach Trent," the reporter begins, "how can you switch from Michigan to Ohio State? I mean, it's such a bitter, storied rivalry. What kind of mental shift does that require?"

Texts and calls from coaching friends and Michigan players have bombarded me with this very same question since the announcement a few hours earlier. I angle my head and ask, "Ohio State and Michigan are rivals?"

Quite a few laughs fill the room.

"To be honest," I say, "I used to freaking *hate* the Buckeyes."

More laughs.

"I was maize and blue through and through. No way could I picture myself as a Buckeye. But that all changed last May." As blue eyes and full lips flash through my mind, I remember the psychological research Taryn shared with me. "They say the best way to decrease tribalism is to get to know members of a different tribe. Learn their strengths and weaknesses, understand what makes them tick, find the commonalities between you and them." I look out at the reporters and see some of them nodding. Every sports fan belongs to a tribe, and every tribe has a team they hate. "I was so lucky to meet the person who challenged my beliefs about the Buckeyes. That person is Coach Lauren Chase."

I hesitate for a second. Though Lauren isn't here, she said I could talk about her today if it seemed right. *"Speak from your heart,"* she told me. *"Your fucking huge heart has gotten you where you are."*

So, I continue. "Imagine my surprise when I learned how fun, strong, and determined Coach Chase is. She already possessed the traits I worked to instill in my Wolverine players. You all know the Ohio State women's volleyball team just won the national championship, right? Coach Chase led her team to victory, and they'll continue to pursue excellence with her at the helm. She's already taught me so much about coaching. But more importantly, Coach Chase is a great person. She cares deeply about her players and staff.

"I had to reconcile my old belief, that Buckeyes were bad, with this amazing woman who happened to coach at Ohio State. I decided my old belief was wrong. And, since accepting this job,

271

I've met more remarkable Buckeyes, including Athletic Director Andy Hunter."

I look at Andy, who sits to the side of the room, then back at the reporters. "The improper actions of the former staff have appalled Mr. Hunter, along with every honest person in this department. He and I will work our butts off to restore the integrity of this hallowed program." We've already lost five scholarships for the next two years, and we have to forfeit our wins from last year. More penalties might be forthcoming. "It's a long road ahead, but I'm privileged to walk it with each and every one of you."

The room is quiet for a moment, and I sneak another glance at my new boss.

Andy's nod is slight, but it communicates his approval all the same.

Echoes of the desire I felt playing at Oklahoma fill my chest. Just like I did everything possible to win for Coach Hanlon, I want to please Andy and every Ohio State fan. I want to bring home another national championship for the Buckeyes, no matter how long it takes. One key hidden in my pocket is that Adrian Nichols plans to join my staff as QB coach after his season ends. He's been out for weeks with a recurring shoulder injury, and he and his wife have decided it's time to hang up the NFL cleats.

My wrist buzzes, startling me. I'm still growing accustomed to my new blinged-out Apple Watch, a Christmas gift from Lauren.

"A manly version of a diamond bracelet," she told me as she fitted it on my wrist. *"Now I can keep in touch with you no matter how busy you are."*

I smile when I read her text:

Jizzbomb answer, Jer-Bear.

"Coach!" hollers another reporter.
I turn to face him.

***

I shoot a quick text to Taryn from my watch before I unlock

Lauren's front door. Lauren didn't even hesitate when she gave me a copy of her key a few days ago. She's come a long way from her commitment phobia. I'll find out soon just how far she's come.

"Honey, I'm home!" I call.

I hear quick footsteps up the stairs, and I walk into the kitchen to meet her as she emerges from the basement. She's holding a folded cardboard box in one hand and a roll of packing tape in another.

"You don't have to do that," I say. "We can pay movers." We have an appointment with a realtor later today to view potential homes in Upper Arlington, a wealthy suburb near campus.

She scowls. "But I can't sit around doing nothing all day."

I grin at the fuzzy thread hanging off her head. "You have a cobweb in your hair." I reach to pull it away from her blond strands, wafting the scent of coconut in my direction.

"See?" She blinks at me. "It's scary-shit-on-a-stick down there. I have to start making headway now or we'll never be ready to move."

Her work ethic is one of many things I love about her. From outside the house, a dog barks, sending a thrill up my spine.

She squints as she listens. "That doesn't sound like my neighbor's dog. Wonder if he's having a play date." She turns to me and smiles. "We're getting a dog when we move into a bigger house, right?"

I suppress a grin by adopting a stern look. "As long as you don't name him Fucker."

"What the fuck else can we name him?" She pouts. "By the way, you rocked the press conference."

"Thanks. Good to have it over with."

"Were you nervous? I couldn't tell."

I shrug. "Wasn't the scariest thing I'm doing today."

Her head cocks to one side as she studies my face. "I'm kind of overwhelmed by those things you said."

"Was it okay? I know you didn't want the spotlight on you."

She swallows and slides her fingertips along the zipper of my OSU windbreaker. "They were the kindest words anyone's ever said about me."

I fold her hands into mine. "I meant every word." I bring her hands to my lips and kiss her knuckles. I wonder if she can feel my heart begin to thunder. My swift breaths bring on a lightheaded sensation—I've never been this nervous before a football game. "I'm ready to sign my letter of intent, make it official." *Thump, thump, thump.* "Are *you* ready, sweetheart?"

Her body stills. Those beautiful blue eyes stare up at me, so close that I can see her pupils dilate. Her lips part, and she gasps when I lower to one knee. Now I'm looking up at her, and I lock my eyes onto hers as I remove a small box from my pocket.

"Will you join my team, Coach Chase?"

As I open the box to reveal a shining diamond, she draws in a sharp breath. The sound mimics my own chest palpitations. *God, will she say yes?* Does she like the ring? Her best friend promised Lauren would love my first choice at the jewelry store—Sam better be right.

Lauren's gaze lifts from the ring to meet mine, and her eyes shine with mischief. "About fucking time, Coach Trent."

A laugh bursts from my lungs, and my shoulders sag with relief. Only this one accepts a marriage proposal with an F bomb. "I'll take that as a yes." I pluck the ring from the cushion inside the box and slide it onto her finger, loving the juxtaposition of her sparkly silver nail polish with the diamond's shine.

I rise and gather her into my arms. She feels so right snuggled into my body. Before our lips make contact, I pause. "I love you."

Her mouth slides into a smile. "Love you, too."

Her kiss is warm and insistent, calming my nerves and firing up my passion at the same time. I can never get enough of her soft, ready lips.

"Just remember—" She looks up at me with a brilliant grin. "—who said I love you first."

I shake my head. "Competitive, much?"

"You know it."

I want to ask her another big question. "Do you think—?" I take a breath. "Remember when you said you wanted to be a parent one day?" I wait for her to nod. "Do you think you still might want that? Maybe create little Buckeyes together?"

One of her eyebrows arches. "You know how old I am, right?"

"A very hot thirty-six," I answer.

"Which means…" When she hesitates, I hold my breath. "You better knock me up quick."

I chuckle as I shake my head.

She cradles the back of my neck, tugging me closer. "I have absolutely no doubt you'll be the best dad, Jer-Bear."

Despite the frisson of anxiety in my gut, my heart swells at her words. "How do you know?"

"I've watched you coach." She slides her hand down my collarbone and swirls circles on my chest. "You're such an effective teacher, mentor. Tough and compassionate."

I swallow. Raising children together seems way more important than winning football or volleyball games. I hope we get the chance.

"But don't even think about getting me up the duff till April," she adds. "No way do we want a newborn while we're both in season."

"Good point." I grin. "How 'bout we practice being parents in the meantime?"

She dips her chin, her eyes showing confusion.

I rush to her front door and open it to find Taryn waiting for me on the porch, just as we planned.

"She said yes?" whispers my sister. She shivers from the cold temperature.

My massive grin answers for me, and I reach out to souse the ears of the puppy wriggling in Taryn's arms. He barks with excitement.

"Here." Taryn hands me Mr. Wiggles. "I'll stop by later to congratulate you and puppy-sit while you're with the realtor."

I gather the puppy to my chest and smile at my supportive sister. "Thanks, Ryn." I close the door and turn to find Lauren standing in the living room, her mouth agape at the bundle in my arms.

"You got us a *puppy?*" She bounces on her feet.

I set the fuzzy Goldendoodle on his tiny paws. "Meet Brutus."

"Awww!" Her sing-song voice slides up an octave. "Little Brutie!" She giggles and crouches to pet him. "He's so damn cute." Looking up at me, she asks, "But didn't you want a pug?"

"I decided your idea was better. This way we can take Brutus on runs when he's older." *And, with any luck, he won't eat poop.*

From her kneeling position, she rolls and folds her legs to sit on the floor. "Come here, little Brutus baby," she coos. A softness seems to envelop her as she scoops him up and curls him under her chin. Her long, golden hair falls like a curtain over the squirming blond blob, and she grins as he licks her chin. Is it possible I'm falling even harder for this woman? Her effervescent spirit has brought such brightness to my life.

She pats the floor next to her. "Come play with your son, Coach."

I like the sound of that. I lower to sitting and drape my arm across her shoulders, folding her and our puppy into my side. As I smooth my hand down Brutus's mop of fur, I press a kiss into Lauren's hair.

A sigh of contentment travels through me as we stay like this for quite some time. We've joined together to become a family, and I'll fight like hell to protect us from any opponents, any difficulties in our future. I'll love this woman with everything I have to give.

We're together now. Rivals no more.

About the Author

Psychologist/author (psycho author) **Jennifer Lane** invites you to her world of sports romance and romantic suspense with a psychological twist!

Jen fell in love with sports at a young age and competed in swimming and volleyball in college. She went on to become the Honda Award Winner for Division III Athlete of the Year. She still gets high from the smell of chlorine and the satisfaction of smashing a beautiful volleyball set.

Jen's latest novel is *Rivals*, a romance between coaches from rival universities. Her *Blocked* trilogy also explores the transformation from hate to love. Particularly in this time of division, Jen's favorite theme is finding common ground.

A romantic suspense trilogy (*The Conduct Series*) and a psychological thriller (*Twin Sacrifice*) complete Jen's collection of stories. She calls Ohio home and shares writing space with her two trusted feline collaborators: Tuxedo and Tessa.

Whether writing or reading, Jen loves stories that make her laugh and cry. In her spare time, she likes to exercise and visit her amazing sisters in Chicago and Hilton Head.

Visit Jen at:
JenniferLaneBooks.com
Facebook.com/JenLaneBooks
Twitter.com/JenLaneBooks
Pinterest.com/JenLaneBooks
Instagram.com/JenLaneBooks

Jennifer Lane, Author
Sports Romance and Romantic Suspense With a Psychological Twist

Twin Sacrifice Psychological Thriller
Blocked New Adult Volleyball Romance
Aced (Blocked #2) New Adult Sports Romance
Spiked (Blocked #3) New Adult Sports Romance
Streamline New Adult Swimming Romance
Swim Recruit New Adult Novella (free!)
Behind the Catcher's Mask Young Adult Short Story
With Good Behavior (The Conduct Series #1)
Bad Behavior (The Conduct Series #2)
On Best Behavior (The Conduct Series #3)

Website: www.jenniferlanebooks.com
Amazon: www.amazon.com/Jennifer-Lane/e/B003WZV5YK
Twitter: JenLaneBooks www.twitter.com/JenLaneBooks
Facebook: Jennifer Lane, Author Jennifer Lane www.facebook.com/
JenLaneBooks
Goodreads: Jennifer Lane www.goodreads.com/author/
show/2798441.Jennifer_Lane
Pinterest: JenLaneBooks www.pinterest.com/jenlanebooks
Instagram: JenLaneBooks www.instagram.com/jenlanebooks

© Courtesy of Queen of The West Book Bash

Acknowledgements

My supportive writing team worked together for a big win! I'm grateful to...

Nicki Elson, critique partner. How rare to find an author who not only shares my passion for writing romance, but also a similar world view, enabling us to form a fast friendship. You had wonderful suggestions for Jeremy's characterization.

Jessica Royer Ocken, editor. *Rivals* is our tenth manuscript together! And you were speedier than wonder twins Emma and Evan Watkins in your edit of this one. Thank you for teaching me to become a better writer.

Gwynn Evans Harrison and **Kevin Kropf**, Kenyon College teammates/friends. I asked you to authenticate the volleyball and football aspects of the story, but you went beyond my expectations by suggesting important improvements to plot and characterization in chapters 16 and 24. Thank you, my friends! I look forward to our next euchre match. Gwynn, rein in your gloating tendencies. And Kevin, don't bet your parents' house this time.

Dan Irons, friend/cover designer. I knew you were a skilled graphic designer, and I appreciate Designs by Irons venturing into cover design to create this masterpiece.

L. Diane Wolfe, book formatter. I love your publishing company, and I'm happy to have you on board to polish the presentation of *Rivals*.

www.ingramcontent.com/pod-product-compliance
Lightning Source LLC
Chambersburg PA
CBHW060154070426
42447CB00033B/1315